ISLAMIC HISTORY

A NEW INTERPRETATION

2

A.D. 750–1055 (A.H. 132–448)

To my friend
Shaykh Aḥmad Zakī Yamānī
a modern wazīr whose statesmanship brings to life
many of the qualities of his great predecessors

ISLAMIC HISTORY

A NEW INTERPRETATION

2

A.D. 750–1055 (A.H. 132–448)

M. A. SHABAN

Reader in Arabic and Islamic Studies
University of Exeter

CAMBRIDGE UNIVERSITY PRESS

CAMBRIDGE

LONDON · NEW YORK · MELBOURNE

Published by the Syndics of the Cambridge University Press
The Pitt Building, Trumpington Street, Cambridge CB2 1RP
Bentley House, 200 Euston Road, London NW1 2DB
32 East 57th Street, New York, NY 10022, U.S.A.
296 Beaconsfield Parade, Middle Park, Melbourne 3206, Australia

First published 1976
First paperback edition 1978

Printed in Great Britain at the
University Press, Cambridge

Library of Congress Cataloguing in Publication Data

Shaban, M. A.

Islamic history A.D. 750–1055 (A.H. 132–448)

Bibliography: p. 212

Includes index.

1. Islamic Empire – History – 750–1258. I. Title.

DS38.6.S48 909'.09'7671 75-39390
ISBN 0 521 21198 0 hard covers
ISBN 0 521 29453 3 paperback

CONTENTS

MAPS

ACKNOWLEDGEMENTS

I am very grateful to my good friend and colleague Dr Richard Hitchcock who generously gave time and effort to read every chapter as I completed it. His sympathetic criticism and many useful suggestions were of significant help to the final draft of this book.

Once more I am greatly indebted to Professor C. F. Beckingham for reading the typescript with his usual thoroughness and for his scholarly advice and invaluable suggestions. Professor T. M. Johnstone took the great trouble of reading both the typescript and the proofs with meticulous care, correcting many mistakes and making many improvements for which I am most grateful. My thanks are also due to Mr Hugh Kennedy for undertaking the difficult task of compiling an accurate index for this difficult work.

My special thanks go to Lady Bruce Lockhart for typing the manuscript with skill and efficiency. She soon discovered that my spelling left a great deal to be desired and patiently corrected my unpredictable mistakes. I am also grateful to the editorial staff and the printers of the Cambridge University Press for the considerable patience they have shown and the great care they have taken in the production of this book.

Thanks are due to the Government of the United Arab Emirates, in particular to H.E. Aḥmad al-Suwaidī, H.E. Muḥammad Habrūsh, H.E. ʿAbdulmajīd al-Qaysī and H.E. Dr ʿIzz al-Dīn Ibrāhīm, who with a generous grant made it possible for the Exeter University Library to acquire most of the sources I needed for my research.

Finally, I must thank my wife and son for their understanding and tolerance of my idiosyncrasies during a period when I was working under great pressure to write this book.

PREFACE

This work is a continuation of my attempt to present a new interpretation of Islamic history. It deals with the three centuries between the rise of the ʻAbbāsids and the Saljūq invasion. This period witnessed the establishment of a new regime, its failure to live up to its revolutionary ideals and the gradual dissolution of a vast empire into lesser political entities. The ʻAbbāsids failed to establish a political structure supported by viable institutions to rule their domains. They also failed to take measures to accomplish the economic integration of their empire because they could not comprehend nor were they able to cope with the rapid expansion of trade. This problem was the more baffling to them for it demanded fundamental changes in the structure of the basically agricultural economy they had inherited to allow for an economic structure in which trade could be exploited to the advantage of all concerned. New taxation systems were required to divide the burden of taxes equitably between the prosperous inhabitants of the urban trade centres and the long-suffering agricultural communities. The entrenched vested interests in the cities took advantage of their political power to oppose such measures and the rural communities had no alternative but to revolt in the face of this continued injustice.

The impact of the vast increase in the volume of trade went far beyond the purely economic front, for it was not only internal trade that was involved but also an international trade of unprecedented dimensions. The wealth of the empire attracted trade in all sorts of goods, especially luxuries, from all parts of the world, and every region of the empire became interested in being an intermediary for importing such trade as well as for exporting the industrial output of the empire. Each region devised its economic policies and its attitude towards its neighbours within and outside the empire in accordance with its own interests. This economic cacophony was another major cause for the eventual political disintegration of the ʻAbbāsid regime because without a harmonizing influence from the centre, the competition of the regions for a bigger share in trade soon developed into uncontrollable inter-regional strife.

Lacking the political and economic organization to maintain its integrity the regime resorted to military power to control its domains. The recruitment of military forces to defend the empire against external enemies was in itself a continual problem for successive 'Abbāsid rulers. Now the need for and the use of the military to control the civilian population became the cause of further major crises for the 'Abbāsids. More men were needed to subdue more revolts and the military leaders came to occupy the centre of the political stage in the provinces as well as in the capital.

In some provinces military leaders were able to establish their own rule in place of 'Abbāsid misgovernment. But in the outer provinces neither the 'Abbāsids nor their military representatives were capable of maintaining their rule in the face of the aggressive opposition of the local populations under their own leaders. The Fāṭimids were the exception because they established themselves in Tunisia and then in Egypt, with the support of a Berber minority, to replace the crumbling rule of dynasties of military leaders in both provinces. However the revolutionary idealism of the Fāṭimids and their detailed planning failed to take into consideration the vital interests of the majority of their subjects whose support was indispensable for the survival of their regime in Egypt.

There has been a conspicuous lack of a comprehensive study of the history of the period under discussion. The existing studies deal only with limited aspects of this eventful era. Some writers have satisfied themselves with rehashing the stale conclusions reached in the nineteenth century. More earnest scholars, who have applied themselves to serious research on subjects such as the Ghaznavids, the Būyids, the Fāṭimids or the 'Abbāsid *wazīrs*, have laboured in vain. In most cases they have treated their subjects in isolation from other issues of the time and therefore have failed to examine and explain the interaction of these complex issues. Such studies have reached conclusions much the same as those of the proverbial four blind men who felt an elephant's leg, tail, ear and body respectively and concluded that it was like a log, a rope, a fan and something without beginning or end.

In this study an effort has been made to maintain a constant surveillance of the main events in the Islamic domains and to explain them in relation to each other, without being side-tracked by insignificant occurrences, in order to present a clear analysis of the history of the period as a whole. A deliberate attempt has also been made to keep to a minimum the infinite number of names of personages involved, for to have put down the names and the titles of all the Būyids, Ḥamdānids and 'Uqaylids would have served no purpose, and the close similarity of these names would only have confused the reader. As in my previous works considerable care has been taken to ascertain the exact meaning and to define the precise use of important terms used in the sources. The meaning of such terms varied from place to place and often enough changed over the centuries; and it is of vital importance to examine systematically these changes in order to obtain proper understanding of the source material.

Finally, I have left out, as much as possible, the discussion of developments in North Africa and Spain because from the beginning the ʿAbbāsids themselves did not concern themselves much with these regions. Furthermore, the history of North Africa and Muslim Spain warrant a separate study which I am now preparing in collaboration with Dr Richard Hitchcock. I hope it will not be long before its appearance.

Exeter
December, 1975

محمد عبد الحي محمد شعبان

I

THE FOUNDING OF THE 'ABBĀSID REGIME

Abū al-'Abbās served as the first 'Abbāsid *Amīr al-Mu'minīn* for a little over four years 749–54/132–6; a period that seems to have been only a prelude to the coming to power of his older and stronger brother Abū Ja'far. Indeed the figure of the latter loomed large behind that of the man who was supposed to be actually in power. Although other members of the 'Abbāsid family were engaged in various important functions, Abū Ja'far seems always to have been at the centre of things at the crucial moment. This is not to say that he was running the affairs of the empire in his brother's name, for the latter did not have this power. From the moment of his elevation to this high office the real authority remained in the hands of the military leaders of the Revolution. In fact, his selection as the new *Amīr al-Mu'minīn* and the imposition of this choice on the political leadership was the first manifestation of the usurpation of power by the military. Abū Salama, the *wazīr āl Muḥammad* and virtually the head of the provisional government, had not been challenged when he assumed the direction of affairs in Kūfa after the arrival of the revolutionary army there. Nevertheless, his vacillation and wavering for many weeks on the important question of installing a new *Amīr al-Mu'minīn* was a curious political mistake. It is true that he was endeavouring to find *al-riḍā min āl Muḥammad*, a member of the family of the Prophet acceptable to all, who would command the widest possible support throughout the empire. It is also true that the implementing of this important ideal of the Revolution was of vital importance if rule by consent was to be restored to the troubled empire. However, the military leaders, assured by their success, had no patience for the deliberations of the vastly experienced Abū Salama. Their political experience was limited to their pre-revolutionary struggle in Khurāsān, but now that they were suddenly thrown into the whirlwind of the politics of empire, they decided that the best course to ensure the continuous success of their revolution was to take matters into their own hands and hold on to their newly acquired power.

Of course they knew that the general Shī'ite opinion was in favour of an *Imām/Amīr al-Mu'minīn*, an all powerful leader who could bring justice to all. However, they also realized that by installing such a leader they would have to give up their own power. As they were not ready to accept this, they opted for an *Amīr al-Mu'minīn* who would not be an *Imām*. Overruling Abū Salama they made sure that the powers of the *wazīr* were not transferred to the *Amīr al-Mu'minīn*. The latter would be only a figurehead with minimum religious functions if any at all. The 'Abbāsids, the members of the House of the Prophet who had the weakest claims, were ready to accept the office on any terms. The military leaders did not find it difficult to secure the choice of Abū al-'Abbās, the weakest member of the family. As he was called 'Abdullah, which was the same as the name of his stronger brother Abū Ja'far, it was made abundantly clear that their choice was Ibn al-Ḥārithiyya – the son of the Ḥārithite woman; make no mistake! Other stronger members of the family had no alternative but to accept and respect this choice. Meanwhile, from the moment of his accession, when an uncle had to finish his inaugural speech for him, until his death, Abū al-'Abbās had the whole-hearted support of all the members of his family who were also not oblivious of their self-interest.

Although the new office of *wazīr* was a corner-stone in the structure of government as planned by the political leadership of the Revolution, the realities of the new situation made it redundant. Neither the military leaders nor the impotent *Amīr al-Mu'minīn* had any interest in continuing an institution that would have imposed limitations on their power. Moreover, Abū Salama, by his behaviour and his failure to achieve what he had set out to do, had made his position intolerable. It was an easy matter for Abū al-'Abbās, supported by his brother Abū Ja'far, to obtain the acquiescence of the military leaders and get rid of the hapless *wazīr*. However, while the decision to nominate Abū al-'Abbās was taken on the spot by Abū al-Jahm – the political commissar of the army and representative of Abū Muslim – in consultation with the other military leaders present in Kūfa, it is instructive to notice that the question of eliminating the *wazīr* had to be referred to Abū Muslim, the *Amīr āl Muḥammad*, in Khurāsān. The latter readily concurred and even sent his own men to carry out Abū Salama's execution. At the same time Abū Muslim decided, on his own, that Sulaymān b. Kathīr al-Khuzā'ī, the elder statesman of the Revolution in Merv, should also be eliminated. Among the original organizers of the Revolution it is clear that there was approval of Abū Salama's opposition to the 'Abbāsids. But from Abū Muslim's point of view such latent opposition to the newly established regime could only represent a serious threat to the whole enterprise and therefore had to be dealt with severely and decisively.

It should be noted that these developments took place in a relatively short period and were initiated by men who were closely involved in an all-consuming violent revolution. They still had to defeat their main adversary in order to establish their authority over the greater part of the empire. Abū Muslim, the organizer of the revolutionary army, had to stay behind in Khurāsān to safeguard the only secure base of this army with their homes and families. It is probably because of this factor that he was able to maintain his hold over the Khurāsāniyya in far away 'Irāq. It is not surprising that Abū al-Jahm, Abū Muslim's representative and political commissar of the army in Kūfa, took over the responsibilities of the *wazīr* without seeing the need of assuming the title. He thereby combined control of the army with control of the administration. Under the circumstances there was manifest co-ordination between the headquarters in Khurāsān and the military leadership in 'Irāq. The latter also had the complete co-operation of Abū al-'Abbās and all his brothers, uncles and cousins.[1]

Such harmony continued for only a few months until the major forces of the Marwānids were destroyed; cracks then began to appear in this united front. Some of the Khurāsāniyya became anxious to return to their homes.[2] They might have considered themselves on an extended expedition that had lasted over three years, but they could not have contemplated permanent settlement in 'Irāq. Their leaders did not seem to have had clear plans for them and even if they did, events were moving too fast for any such plans to take effect. The setting up of new camps at Hāshimiyya and then Anbār are not to be taken as attempts at establishing new capitals, but rather as temporary measures to house the army as circumstances required. Naturally Abū al-'Abbās would want some of the troops to stay in 'Irāq, at least for the time being, in order to bolster his regime, but he could not prevent those who wanted to return from doing so. Indeed he could have no serious objection to reducing

[1] For details of this phase see M. A. Shaban, *The 'Abbāsid Revolution*, Cambridge, 1970 pp. 138–68.

[2] al-Ṭabarī, Muḥ. b. Jarīr, *Tārīkhl al-Rusul wa al-Mulūk*, ed. M. J. de Goeje et al., Leiden 1879–1901, III, p. 75.

the size of an army that deprived him of any real power. In the event it was decided to raise the stipends of the Khurāsāniyya to eighty dirhams a month and to allow some of them to return home. This last measure resulted in two problems, however, one in 'Irāq and the other in Khurāsān.

In 'Irāq, and in Syria for that matter, there were many remnants of the defeated Marwānid forces. While some of them had taken advantage of the situation to settle down to a peaceful life, others like those of Jazīra, the hard core of Marwān's army, felt disgruntled and waited for a chance to turn the tide. Yet others were ready to throw in their lot with the new regime either out of conviction or because of the lack of a better alternative.[1] These last offered the insecure 'Abbāsids a golden opportunity of recruiting their own forces to balance the power of the Khurāsāniyya and to compensate for the loss of those who had returned home. Members of the 'Abbāsid family were appointed to lead newly formed contingents of these men and charged with mopping-up operations in various parts of the empire.[2] At least for the duration of the reign of Abū al-'Abbās this solution satisfied all parties concerned.

In Khurāsān, the problem was far more complicated and created serious trouble for Abū Muslim. It should not be assumed that, as the Revolution had sprung from Merv, all the population of Khurāsān and the East had rushed in to support it. Indeed there is no better indication that the situation there was precarious than the fact that Abū Muslim himself had to stay behind to tend it rather than lead the victorious army to reconquer the empire. Naturally he kept enough recruits at hand to support, if not to protect, his own position and very soon this proved to have been a wise decision. It should be remembered that although radical change had taken place in Merv, nothing much had happened to cause substantial change in the rest of Khurāsān and the East from the conditions that had obtained after the conquest. The treaties concluded between the Arab conquerors and the conquered populations of the various localities were still in force; and the taxes were allocated and collected accordingly. The Principalities of Ṭukhāristān were still intact and still governed by their princes or military lords albeit under Arab supervision. The city-states of Soghdiana kept their own socio-economic structures under their own princes. In short, the system

[1] *Ibid.*, pp. 52–7.

[2] Ibn A'tham al-Kūfī, *Kitāb al-Futūḥ*, Istanbul manuscript, Library of Ahmet III, no. 2956, vol. II, ff. 227B, 228B, 233B.

of protectorates created by the Arabs in the East was still in force.[1] Now, the sudden jolt of a revolution in their area caused them both anxiety and consternation, and even aroused the hopes that some of them had once entertained of regaining their long lost independence.

Fortunately for Abū Muslim the latter feeling was not widespread in these parts and minor uprisings, such as the one in Bukhārā, were easily subdued.[2] But as a leader, he was too vigorous and too revolutionary to leave things as they were in his own backyard. He embarked upon a grand plan designed to convert the population of the entire East to Islam. Nēzak the stubborn Hephthalite prince of Bādghīs was but one example of such converts. He became a close adviser to Abū Muslim and his followers were soon amongst the latter's forces.[3] The prince of Khuttal was not so co-operative; when he felt the pressure he called on the Chinese for help and when it did not materialize he went to China.[4] However, Abū Muslim must have shown a great deal of dexterity, and in his zeal perhaps tried to be all things to all men.[5] Nevertheless, during his short period of power he was able to set in motion a policy that irrevocably brought into the Islamic polity the mass of the indigenous population of the East and, as we shall see, their role was of paramount significance.

The trouble came from the Khurāsānian Arabs and particularly from those who had returned from 'Irāq. After their great victories in the west they seem to have had some delusions about their status at home. At first they agreed to join those who had remained behind with Abū Muslim to carry out his policy of the effective penetration of the eastern principalities and Soghdiana. But when they, like the others, were assigned to garrison duty in the various strongholds of the area their hopes of returning to civilian life were dashed and they immediately mutinied. Their concerted rebellion in Bukhārā, Tirmidh and Ṭāliqān was so serious that Abū Muslim himself had to lead the action against them. Although they seem to have had allies in Abū Muslim's camp, he was able to ride the storm and reaffirm his authority over his forces.[6]

When he saw that a relatively peaceful situation obtained in both east and west, Abū Muslim decided that it was time to see for himself what had happened in the heart of the empire. On the pretext of going on the pilgrimage he journeyed to 'Irāq with a suitable

[1] See M. A. Shaban, *Islamic History A.D. 600–750 (A.H. 132): A new Interpretation*, Cambridge, 1971, p. 172.
[2] Ṭabarī, III, p. 74.
[3] *Ibid.* pp. 100, 107.
[4] *Ibid.*, p. 74.
[5] *Ibid.*, pp. 74, 79, 119–20.
[6] *Ibid.*, pp. 81–2.

retinue. At Anbār he was cordially received by the *Amīr al-Mu'minīn* and Abū Ja'far himself accompanied him to Makka. On their way back after the pilgrimage they were informed of the death of Abū al-'Abbās and his will that the succession should pass to Abū Ja'far. It is significant that Abū Muslim, and all the members of the 'Abbāsid family, with one exception, accepted this nomination.[1] This one exception was 'Abdullah b. 'Alī, an uncle of Abū Ja'far. He was a leading member of the family who had distinguished himself in the fight against Marwān and in the subsequent campaigns in Jazīra and Syria. It was on his advice that the remnants of the Marwānid forces had been recruited into the 'Abbāsid armies. He commanded many of them together with a small contingent of the Khurāsāniyya. He was, moreover, capable of using these forces to bring into line the hard core of Marwān's army of Jazīra which had lingering hopes of resisting 'Abbāsid control.[2] Meanwhile, the Byzantines began to take advantage of the situation on their Arab borders and it became necessary for some action to be taken to discourage these attacks. 'Abdullah b. 'Alī and his forces were sent on a summer expedition for this purpose.[3] While on their way to the Byzantine borders the news of the succession of Abū Ja'far reached them and they turned back in revolt.

It is not enough to explain this revolt by attributing it to the ambitions of its leader because he would certainly have needed to convince the multitude of his followers that these ambitions were worth risking their lives for. And why should they object so strongly to the succession of Abū Ja'far? 'Abdullah's army was a good example of reconciliation between victor and vanquished, and hitherto had been serving the 'Abbāsid cause even against former comrades. Significantly their revolt was not against 'Abbāsid rule; it was against a particular 'Abbāsid in whose succession to power they must have seen a considerable threat to their own interests. Abū Ja'far was undoubtedly a man of strong opinions backed with powerful measures and he was bound to arouse strong objections. Apparently he had his plans for reconstructing the 'Abbāsid forces within a new structure of the whole empire. He visualized a strong central government supported by a cohesive army that would give it effective control over the provinces. While he had no objection

[1] *Ibid.*, pp. 88–9.

[2] *Ibid.*, pp. 41, 52–7; Ibn A'tham, vol. II, ff. 227B, 228B, 237A, B; al-Balādhurī, *Futūḥ al-Buldān*, ed. M. J. de Goeje, Leiden, 1866, p. 192.

[3] Ṭabarī, III, p. 91; Bal., *Futūḥ*, pp. 184, 189.

to recruiting men from Syria and Jazīra, he did not want to see them as a separate army operating from bases in their provinces. This would not only lead to a revival of Marwānid forces but would also enhance the autonomy of these provinces vis-a-vis the central government. In this formative stage of 'Abbāsid rule this could become a precedent that would endanger future 'Abbāsid policies. Obviously 'Abdullah was of a different opinion, and, being closely involved with the Syrians, his inclination would be to favour their interests. Furthermore, he probably believed that Syria with its long history of jealousy for its own autonomy, would resist Abū Ja'far's plans and thus threaten the security of the 'Abbāsids. Identifying the interest of his family with his own and that of his army, he led them in revolt.

Without any hesitation Abū Muslim, in full agreement with Abū Ja'far, swiftly marched at the head of all the available forces against the rebels. The Khurāsāniyya in the rebel army did not have any interest in supporting the rebellion; they quickly withdrew and joined Abū Muslim's forces. Although some of the Syrians also withdrew from 'Abdullah's army, it still constituted a formidable force. When the two armies met the ensuing conflict took four months before concluding in favour of Abū Muslim.[1]

At this point Abū Ja'far took a most unusual step, though one very much in character and one which assumed great significance. He sent his own representative to watch over the division of the booty taken from the vanquished army. Considering that this booty could not have been of any great value and that the share of the central government was no more than one fifth, Abū Ja'far's action could not conceivably have been taken simply for fiscal purposes. He was asserting his authority as *Amīr al-Mu'minīn* over Abū Muslim even at a moment when the latter had just won a great victory on his behalf. Abū Muslim completely understood the significance of this action. He expressed his objection in no uncertain terms, and instead of going back to 'Irāq which would have been his expected course of action, he headed towards Khurāsān declaring his dissent.[2] The dispute over the powers of the *Amīr al-Mu'minīn* came to a head at a moment of Abū Ja'far's own choosing. His future and that of the whole regime rested on the outcome and he

[1] Ibn A'tham, vol II, ff. 223B–239B; al-Azdī, Yazīd b. Muḥ., *Tārīkh al-Mawṣil*, ed. 'A. Ḥabība, Cairo, 1967, p. 178.

[2] Ṭabarī, III, pp. 98–150; Ibn A'tham, vol. II, ff. 238B–240A; Ya'qūbī, Aḥmad b. Abī Ya'qub, *Tārīkh*, Beirut, 1960, vol. II, p. 366.

was determined to win. He took all precautions, and used every means to persuade Abū Muslim to return to ʿIrāq. When he returned Abū Jaʿfar took the enormous but very much calculated risk of having him executed without delay. Interestingly, the Khurāsāniyya did not raise any objections. The authority of the *Amīr al-Mu'minīn* had acquired enough legitimacy to allow him to eliminate the *Amīr āl Muḥammad.* As a consequence of this action Abū Jaʿfar came into his own, and it was probably then that he decided to take the title al-Manṣūr, the one destined to win. This was not an empty boast nor was it a simple shot in the dark. Abū Jaʿfar certainly had a genius for long term planning which characterized most of his actions and this one was no exception. He decided on a title not only for himself but also, in due course, the title of al-Mahdī for his successor, with all its messianic connotations. It was no secret that the ʿAbbāsids had set themselves apart from the Shīʿites, but Abū Jaʿfar was aware that there was a great deal of sympathy for these dangerous rivals in all parts of the empire. However, given time an ʿAbbāsid–Shīʿite reconciliation was not necessarily impossible and it was certainly desirable. The Khurāsāniyya had rejected the notion of *Imām/Amīr al-Mu'minīn*, therefore he could not take the title *Imām*. The next best thing that might appeal to the Shīʿites was a title *Manṣūr/Amīr al-Mu'minīn* especially when it would be followed by a title *Mahdī/Amīr al-Mu'minīn* in the not too distant future. For almost a century, from the time of Mukhtār, the notion of a *mahdī* had been in circulation; prophecies of messianic expectations had been widely believed and there was no harm in exploiting them for the purpose of reconciliation.[1] There was resistance to this idea from some of the leaders of the Khurāsāniyya and indeed from ʿĪsā b. Mūsā, a most respectable member of the ʿAbbāsid family. But by the end of Manṣūr's long rule 754–75/136–58 this opposition was easily brushed aside at the crucial moment of the confirmation of Mahdī.[2]

Manṣūr's long-term planning was at its most striking in the period before the establishment of Baghdād. Practically every aspect of his policies was involved in this project. Yet, without the benefit of planning committees or consulting bodies, he single-handedly planned its construction, taking into consideration strategic, economic, administrative and demographic factors. In one year he was living in his palace on the site and the whole Round City was

[1] See Shaban, *Islamic History*, p. 95.

[2] Ṭabarī III pp. 331, 371, 344, 455; Yaʿqūbī, *Tārīkh*, vol. II, pp. 379–80.

finished in no more than four years at the low cost of 4,000,882 dirhams.[1] In his own lifetime it became a great metropolis.

The focal point of the new structure of government was Manṣūr himself. Although he gathered all secular powers in his own hands he had no delusions about the restricted functions of his office. He was not much different from an Umayyad ruler, and being a realist he laid no claim to religious authority to strengthen his position. However, by bestowing titles with religious connotations upon himself and his successor he was clearly indicating his thinking about the future. Meanwhile, he was vigorously pursuing plans for a highly centralized government projecting his authority from Baghdād. The base of his power was the Khurāsāniyya for whom living space was provided around the city. Inside the walls were the administrative departments, the heads of which were directly responsible to him. These departments were to co-ordinate the work of the various functionaries in the provinces.[2] To make sure that he was well informed about affairs in all corners of the empire and to ensure that the representatives of the central government were behaving properly, he appointed his own independent agents who reported directly to him every day, even on such mundane matters as food prices in their respective areas.[3] The official title of such an agent was *ṣāḥib barīd*, postmaster, but more important and to emphasize his direct relationship to the ruler he was also given the honorary status of *mawlā Amīr al-Mu'minīn*. This is not to be confused with *mawlā* meaning a freed slave, a client or a non-Arab member of the army related to a certain man or an Arab clan, as was the case under the Umayyads. Under the 'Abbāsids assimilation had certainly done away with this type of relationship as far as the army was concerned, and virtually deprived it of any meaningful or significant sense in the rest of society. As we shall see, the term *mawlā*, like many other similar terms, went through many different changes in various parts of the empire during the period of this study.[4] Knowing that *mawlā* could mean so many things and capitalizing on the special relationship that it used to denote, Manṣūr simply gave it a different twist to establish a new relationship between himself and members of his administration, and in this case

[1] Ṭabarī, III, p. 326.

[2] Jahshiyārī, Muḥ. b. 'Abdūs, *Kitāb al-Wuzarā'*, ed. M. al-Saqqā et al., Cairo, 1938, pp. 96–135; Azdī, *Mawṣil*, p. 215; Ya'qūbī, *Kitāb al-Buldān*, ed. M. J. de Goeje, Leiden, 1892, pp. 240, 243.

[3] Ṭabarī, III, pp. 414, 435; Ya'qūbī, *Tārīkh*, vol. II, p. 384.

[4] See below, p. 31.

it can only have meant confidant of the ruler. Ibn Khaldūn carefully explains this special relationship for us, calling it *iṣṭināʿ* i.e. "choosing another person for oneself for a special affair which this person is required to accomplish in a sufficient manner".[1]

In Manṣūr's administration, there were more than fifty persons given this title and all of them acquired very high posts – at least seventeen were postmasters in areas they had originally come from or about which they had special knowledge.[2] Some of them were Arabs and as might be expected many were non-Arabs.[3] Of the latter some were given or assumed Arab names. Probably their original names were ostentatiously un-Islamic or difficult to pronounce. There are examples of many *mawlās* and their descendants serving successive ʿAbbāsid rulers over a period exceeding a century and in the same capacities.[4] At least one of them was a prince from the eastern principalities, another was a brother-in-law of Manṣūr, and a third was his own step-son.[5] This last example recalls the English custom of kings raising their illegitimate sons to the higher echelons of the nobility. Indeed under Manṣūr's successors there were cases closer to the English custom, when brothers or relatives of favourite concubines were appointed to high offices and accordingly were given this honorary status.

Manṣūr's internal espionage network was so successful that he was reputed to have had a mirror in which he could distinguish between friend and foe.[6] Certainly, dismissed provincial governors knew only too well that they could not get away with any riches they might have extorted while in office. The special accounting department that Manṣūr established for this purpose was fully informed and was a good example of the strictness of his administra-

[1] Ibn Khaldūn, *al-Muqaddima*, Beirut, 1961, pp. 237–8, 326–7; also see E. W. Lane, Arabic-English Lexicon, reprinted Beirut, 1968 s.v. *ṣnʿ*, vol. IV, p. 1733.

[2] Ṭabarī, III, pp. 139, 140, 145, 151, 306, 319, 323, 367, 380, 392, 428, 454, 455, 456; Jahshiyārī, pp. 101, 124, 125, 129, 134; Bal., *Futūḥ*, pp. 185, 287, 293, 294, 310, 401; Azdī, *Mawṣil*, pp. 198, 296; Yaʿqūbī, *Buldān*, pp. 241, 242, 244, 245, 247, 249; Yaʿqūbī, *Tārīkh*, vol. II, pp. 384, 392; Ibn al-Athīr, ʿIzz al-Dīn, *al-Kāmil fī al-Tārīkh*, ed. C. J. Tornberg, Leiden, 1866–71, vol. VI, pp. 22, 50, 213, 467; Ṭayfūr, Aḥmad b. Abī Ṭāhir, *Kitāb Baghdād*, ed. H. Keller, Leipzig, 1908, p. 349; Yāqūt, *Muʿjam al-Buldān*, Beirut, 1957, vol. III, pp. 25, 26.

[3] Ṭabarī, III, p. 323; Yaʿqūbī, *Buldān*, p. 244.

[4] Ṭabarī, III, pp. 367, 428, 454, 529, 576, 582, 583, 979, 998, 1384, 1500, 1838; Ṭayfūr, pp. 7, 16, 19, 120, 121, 142; Jahshiyārī, pp. 124, 277; Bal., *Futūḥ*, pp. 293–4; Athīr, *Kāmil*, vol. VI, p. 200.

[5] Ibn al-Jawzī, ʿAbdulraḥmān, *al-Muntaẓam*, manuscript, biography of ʿAlī. b. Ṣāliḥ 229 A.H., cf. Miskawayh, *Tajārib al-Umam*, ed. H. F. Amedroz, Oxford 1920–1, vol. I, p. 16; Ṭabarī, III, p. 456; Ibn Ḥazm, *Jamharat Ansāb al-ʿArab*, ed. ʿA. Hārūn, Cairo, 1962, p. 21.

[6] Ṭabarī, III, p. 166.

tion.[1] One *mawlā*, whose descendants attained very high positions, namely Khālid b. Barmak, seems to have been the fiscal expert under Manṣūr. He accompanied the revolutionary army on its march and was in charge of all its financial matters.[2] Manṣūr made use of his expertise, appointing him head of the central department of revenues and then later governor of those provinces which had particularly difficult taxation problems.[3]

It goes without saying that Manṣūr did not want to revive the office of *wazīr*; instead he had a *kātib* who was more of an administrative assistant and strictly without any executive powers. The choice of a native 'Irāqī, Abū Ayyūb al-Mūriyānī, as a second occupant of this office may indicate Manṣūr's awareness of his own lack of knowledge about the intricate affairs of 'Irāq. However, it seems to have been an experiment which was abandoned after the death of Abū Ayyūb. Manṣūr did not appoint anybody to replace him and continued as always to exercise direct control over all departments of his government.[4]

On the whole Manṣūr sought to incorporate the administrations of the provinces into the central government over which he himself had full control, hoping, perhaps, that this in turn would eventually lead to the integration and unity of the whole empire.

The organization of the military forces was a more difficult problem because of the unexpectedly increasing demands on many internal and external fronts. Manṣūr would have been content to rely on the Khurāsāniyya alone to meet security requirements, for the revolt of 'Abdullah b. 'Alī had shaken his confidence in troops from Syria and Jazīra even under the leadership of members of his family. Although Abū Muslim had done his utmost to recruit new forces from the indigenous population of the East, the process of Islamization had not yet taken root enough to allow such an effort to be wholly successful. Apparently the more powerful Hephthalite and Soghdian princes stood aloof from the Revolution and saw no reason to become involved in an adventure that might drag them as far afield as North Africa. However Abū Muslim's political manoeuvring, persuasion and pressure had convinced some of the lesser princes and military lords that they should join the cause and rush to 'Irāq as fast as they could mobilize their followers. In Baghdād, living quarters were provided for small contingents from Balkh, Khuttal, Isfījāb, Ishtīkhan, Bukhārā, Fāryāb, Farghāna, Khwārizm,

[1] *Ibid.*, p. 415.
[2] Jahshiyārī, p. 87.
[3] *Ibid.*, pp. 89, 99, 136.
[4] *Ibid.*, pp. 96–135.

Gurgān and Bādghīs.[1] A combination of events forced Manṣūr to fall back on other sources of recruitment to meet lesser tasks, leaving the Khurāsāniyya free to cope with serious emergencies.

Egypt was easily brought into the 'Abbāsid domains and the Arabs of this province co-operated with the new regime. They helped suppress some minor Coptic uprisings and subsequently were entrusted with the security of the province.[2] Further west, North Africa had been in a turmoil for decades; and so was Spain.[3] Berber revolts and differences between the Arabs in these regions were still raging. Since it was obvious that it would require enormous military forces to bring these vast territories under control, the decision was soon taken to abandon Spain completely and leave the Arabs there to their own devices. In North Africa the Berbers were not only attempting to regain their independence but also were very bold on the Egyptian borders with Libya.[4] This dangerous situation was compounded by the possible threat of a Byzantine comeback. The security of Egypt demanded that the 'Abbāsids should hold as much as possible of the North African coast. The presence of a sizable Arab population in Tunisia decided the issue. It was hoped that should they prove to be as co-operative as the Arabs of Egypt, they could eventually uphold 'Abbāsid authority in their region on their own. But meanwhile the Khurāsāniyya were chosen for the difficult operation of pushing the Berbers back as far west as possible. After considerable difficulties and successive campaigns over more than ten years, 'Abbāsid rule was established only as far west as Qayrawān 772/155 and never beyond. Yet, the powerful thrust of the Berbers of north-west Africa made it necessary that a large contingent of Khurāsāniyya should be stationed there. This was done first on a rotational basis but eventually they were permanently settled there.[5]

The revolt of 'Abdullah b. 'Alī encouraged the Byzantines to resume their aggressive activities and in the following year 755/138, they overran the stronghold of Malaṭya and razed its fortifications. However it was possible to spare some of the Khurāsāniyya to restore the balance of power on this dangerous front. Malaṭya was

[1] Ya'qūbī, *Buldān*, pp. 248–9.

[2] Maqrīzī, *Khiṭaṭ*, Cairo, 1249 A.H., vol. II, p. 261.

[3] Shaban, *Islamic History*, pp. 149–52.

[4] Athīr, *Kāmil*, vol. v, pp. 237–40; Ibn 'Idhārī, *Al-Bayān al-Mughrib*, ed. G. S. Colin and E. Lévi-Provençal, Leiden 1948–51, vol. I, p. 63.

[5] Bal., *Futūḥ*, pp. 232–3; Ṭabarī, III, pp. 370–3; Ibn 'Idhārī, pp. 73–9; Azdī, *Mawṣil*, p. 91.

recaptured and its fortifications were rebuilt, but no Khurāsāniyya could be spared to man this important stronghold. Men from Syria and Jazīra were recruited and encouraged to settle there and in similar strongholds all along the borders. These men were granted land allotments in these areas in addition to the regular army stipend of eighty dirhams a month.[1]

In Khurāsān and the East, 'Abbāsid authority was severely shaken after the execution of Abū Muslim. The loss of his effective leadership deprived the 'Abbāsids of the stability previously afforded them in these vast regions. Even those who had been willing to support the new regime had their apprehensions about its intentions. The sudden turns of the regime appeared to have deviated from the purposes of the movement born in their midst. The disappearance of the men who played such an important part in organizing the Revolution could hardly have helped the situation. The successors of Abū Muslim, as governors of the East, could not restore the sagging confidence in the regime. The first of these governors carried out the instructions of the central government to the letter. This approach led to an outright mutiny of his forces and he was accidentally killed in the scuffle.[2] The following governor realized that because of the demands of the central government he was put in an impossible situation. Although he had been one of the most faithful sons of the Revolution and indeed closely associated with Manṣūr against even Abū Muslim, he nevertheless led an uprising against the central government. He succeeded only in dividing the population of Khurāsān against itself, creating more reasons for instability.[3]

Another symptom of unrest took the shape of a popular revolt amongst the indigenous population of western Khurāsān between Nīshāpūr and Rayy, led by a certain Sunbād. Although it was a minor affair in itself, it was potentially dangerous because it threatened to cut off the vital northern route between Khurāsān and the west. In the event it proved to be even more serious for it resulted in the opening of a new front, which the 'Abbāsids could hardly contain, in the mountainous region to the south of the Caspian Sea.[4] Most of this region was still independent under the rule of its own princes who stubbornly resisted Arab advances. Alarmed by the Sunbād uprising, the 'Abbāsids rushed a newly recruited army from the

1 Ṭabarī III, pp. 121–5, 135; Bal., *Futūḥ*, pp. 165–6, 187–190; Athīr, *Kāmil*, vol. V, pp. 370–2.
2 Ṭabarī, III, p. 134.
3 *Ibid.*, pp. 100–1, 134–5; Ibn A'tham, vol. II, ff. 233B, 237A.
4 Ṭabarī, III, pp. 119–20.

Fārs province which, interestingly enough, had both Arabs and Persians among its members. Although the uprising was soon subdued, this army, probably because of a dispute with the central government over its share of the booty, started a revolt of its own.[1] There was no alternative but to send out all the available Khurāsāniyya to deal with the situation, particularly as Sunbād was able to flee and take refuge with the Prince of Ṭabaristān. The army of Fārs was soon dispersed and Sunbād was never heard from again, but hosts of enemies were stirred up. The neighbouring Daylam felt threatened and joined their brethren of Ṭabaristān to pose a continual threat to the road to Khurāsān. As there were not enough Khurāsāniyya to station there permanently Manṣūr once again had to fall back on recruits from Syria and 'Irāq to form a big garrison at Rayy under the command of his own son and heir apparent.[2]

In 762/145 the inevitable Shī'ite revolt broke out simultaneously in Ḥijāz and the region of Baṣra. It had been no secret that the other members of the House of the Prophet, namely the descendants of 'Alī, were increasingly disappointed by the usurpation of what they considered their inherent rights, in addition to the apparent revisionism of the 'Abbāsids. It was only a matter of time before they would attempt to bring down 'Abbāsid rule. But as usual with most Shī'ite revolts, this one was poorly planned, and was more akin to political agitation than a serious attempt to launch a new order. It was as if its leaders were convinced that simply by declaring their intention to take over the whole Muslim community would fall in line behind them. They did not realize that although there was a great deal of sympathy for them, the community at large was not quite willing to go through another convulsion in so short a period. Only four thousand Khurāsāniyya under the militant anti-'Alawid command of 'Īsā b. Mūsā were enough to crush the revolt in both Madīna and Baṣra in a very short time. Two new names, Muḥammad the Pure Soul and his brother Ibrāhīm, were added to the register of 'Alawid Shī'ite martyrs.[3] It is difficult to see why this revolt is given such prominence in our sources; perhaps it was because it was the last revolt of its kind. Henceforth Shī'ite revolts took a completely different course, following new strategies and adapting themselves to new causes. The simple cause of legitimacy proved to be insufficient to win for the descendants of the Prophet what they believed to be their proper rights. It is significant that Ja'far al-Ṣādiq, a descendant of 'Alī through his son Ḥusayn, did not support the

[1] *Ibid.*, p. 122. [2] *Ibid.*, pp. 136–43. [3] *Ibid.*, pp. 174–257.

cause of his cousins although he was one of the most respected leaders of the 'Alawids at the time. Later he was to become the fountain of wisdom for the Ismā'īlī Shī'ites.[1]

The suppression of the Pure Soul's revolt was by no means the end of Manṣūr's troubles. Watching the Arab difficulties on the Byzantine front, the Khazars seized the opportunity to advance in the Caucasus. Suddenly the whole northern frontier from the Mediterranean to the Caspian was under attack and Manṣūr had to mobilize all possible forces to meet these formidable enemies. Surprisingly no call went to Khurāsān for new recruits; it must have been realized that there was no chance of help from this troubled region. As the Arabs and Persians of Fārs had just become disgruntled, the necessary forces had to come from 'Irāq, Syria and especially Jazīra, which was particularly threatened by the Khazar attack. Desperate as he was, Manṣūr required every man of Kūfa and Baṣra whose wealth amounted to ten thousand dirhams and more each to volunteer to fight the enemy. The frontier was finally stabilized and the threat averted, but garrisons had to be set up across the Caucasus and recruits were paid regular stipends to settle there.[2] An attempt was made to establish a big base at Rāfiqa near Raqqa but it was soon abandoned and the bulk of the 'Irāqī and Syrian recruits were stationed at Ruṣāfa, across the river from Baghdād, where living quarters were built for them. The only man who could be trusted to be in charge of these new forces was the heir apparent, and indeed they were called the army of Mahdī.[3]

The eastern regions continued to show signs of unrest. The Hephthalites of Harāt, Pūshang and Bādghīs who, under Nēzak, had joined Abū Muslim, decided that their co-operation was not only useless but probably also harmful to their interests. Led by a certain Ustād-Sīs and supported by their brethren from Sīstān they revolted, trying to re-establish their own control over their principalities. With some help from the central government but mainly with his own forces, the governor of Khurāsān was able to defeat the rebels and punish their supporters in the south.[4] An important result of this victory was the widespread conversion to Islam of the Hephthalites. One of their leaders was Muṣ'ab b.

[1] *Ibid.*, p. 254.

[2] *Ibid.*, pp. 318, 328, 353, 371; Ya'qūbī, *Tārīkh*, vol. II, p. 371; Ibn A'tham, vol. II, ff. 241B–2B.

[3] Ṭabarī, III, pp. 366–7, 372–3, 491.

[4] *Ibid.*, pp. 354–8.

Ruzayq of Pūshang whose descendants, the Ṭāhirids, were soon to play an important part in Islamic history.[1]

The last few years of Manṣūr's rule were comparatively peaceful, yet they were not particularly noted for important developments or great innovations in the government of the empire. He seems to have satisfied himself with setting up the machinery to rule his domains as he saw fit. Hishām's abilities as a ruler are reputed to have impressed Manṣūr and indeed his own rule can be best described as a re-establishment of Marwānid rule with minor modifications. His administrative and long term planning abilities were utilized to restore the *status quo* in favour of the 'Abbāsids without much thought being given to the underlying problems of society. In short, he was not a ruler who was profoundly concerned with reform and he does not seem to have realized that his empire was going through a period of fundamental change. As a leader of a supposedly revolutionary regime he introduced very little change and indeed was basically a conservative ruler.

Manṣūr inherited a fiscal policy based on an agricultural economy but it must be pointed out that as yet there was no universal taxation system for all the empire. Although in principle Muslims and non-Muslims paid appropriate taxes on the land under their possession, these taxes varied considerably from one province to the other, and there were many unjust anomalies.[2] Yet Manṣūr made no attempt to remedy this situation and was content to leave it unchanged.[3] This is the more disappointing in that he showed some signs of awareness of a major problem which was to bedevil the Islamic polity for generations if not centuries; the problem of the taxation of urban communities. Since in early Islam the great majority of tradesmen and artisans were non-Muslims the graded poll-tax was in effect a fair urban tax. The immense and rapid urbanization coupled with the increasing conversion of the subject peoples created many virtually tax-free zones. No system of taxation was introduced to replace the defunct poll-tax in cities and towns and subsequently all tradesmen and craftsmen were simply not paying any taxes. Indeed the textile industry, which was primarily a cottage industry, owed its fantastic development in every Islamic town to this tax loophole. In Baghdād Manṣūr was asked to help a man who had a

[1] See below, p. 43.

[2] Shaban, *Islamic History*, pp. 37–9, 48–9.

[3] Bal., *Futūḥ*, p. 272; A. K. S. Lambton, *Landlord and Peasant in Persia*, Oxford, 1953, pp. 32–3, wrongly ascribes to Manṣūr tax changes that were introduced by Mahdī, see below, pp. 23–4.

wife and three daughters to support; he refused exclaiming that such a man should have four busy spinners in his household.[1] This could well have been a remark passed by a Scottish laird in Shetland about the women knitters there. However two centuries had to pass before such workers were taxed because of the obvious difficulties involved.[2] On the other hand, tradesmen who needed shops for their businesses were easier targets for the tax collector. Emulating the later Umayyads who had built shops and rented them to the public for private investment, Manṣūr also had shops built in his city.[3] Tradesmen were charged a suitable rent, *ghalla*, according to the size of the shops they needed. Those who wished to build shops on state land were to pay a lesser rate and all payments were to go to the state treasury.[4] Unlike later 'Abbāsids Manṣūr did not have a private treasury and did not differentiate between his own revenue and that of the state.[5] These properties, *mustaghallāt*, were to be an ever expanding feature of every city. Of course this system of *mustaghallāt* was not enough to take care of the very complex problem of urban taxation, but it was a step in the right direction. But Manṣūr chose to overlook a more important tax loophole resulting from the rise of the cities and the huge volume of trade that passed through the hands of a relatively small number of rich merchants. According to Islam these wealthy people had to pay 2½% of their income, after certain adjustments, as *zakāt*. However since the time of 'Uthmān 644–56/23–35 the state had ceased to enforce the collection of this modest tax and it was left to every individual to dispose of it according to his conscience.[6] In effect this meant that while small businessmen had to pay some form of tax most of the wealth of the big merchants was not taxed.

As for international trade, from early Islamic times the rule had been that a tax should be paid at the port of entry, e.g. Baṣra, at the rate of 2½%, 5% or 10% according to the status of the merchant concerned, whether he was a Muslim or not. There were many exemptions and many ways of evading this tax altogether.[7] Manṣūr

1 Athīr, *Kāmil*, vol. VI, p. 19.
2 See below, p. 185.
3 Bal., *Futūḥ* pp. 117–18; Jahshiyārī, p. 47; Ya'qūbī, *Buldān*, p. 311.
4 Ṭabarī, III, pp. 323–4, 379; Bal., *Futūḥ*, p. 295; Ya'qūbī, *Buldān* pp. 241–2, 246; Yāqūt, *Buldān*, vol. IV, p. 484.
5 Ṭabarī, III, p. 590.
6 Qudāma b. Ja'far, *Kitāb al-Kharāj*, part seven, published as part of A. Ben Shemesh, *Taxation in Islam*, vol. II, Leiden 1965, p. 103; Ibn Sallām, *Kitāb al-Amwāl*, ed. M. H. al-Fiqī, Cairo, 1353 A.H., pp. 437, 573.
7 Bal., *Futūḥ*, p. 385; Ibn Sallām, *Amwāl*, pp. 421, 427, 532, 535, 528–9; Maqrīzī, *Khitat*, pp. 121, 122, 123.

seems to have taken some measures to tighten the control for the collection of this tax. We are told that he had walls built around Baṣra and that the expenses for this project were exacted from its residents to the tune of forty dirhams each.[1] As this measure did not have any military justification at the time it is possible to conclude that it was meant to control the volume of trade going into and out of Baṣra.

The Umayyads had appropriated for themselves a great deal of farm land all over the empire. Manṣūr simply confiscated it all and redistributed it among members of his family. The only difference between his action and that of the Umayyads was that he took into consideration female members of the family who were also given lands.[2] This seems to have established a tradition among the 'Abbasīds that their women were as much entitled to share in their wealth and exploit it as their men. While Manṣūr was very generous with his own family he was quite stringent with his employees. The highest salary he paid was 300 dirhams a month which was not much by the standards of the time.[3] This seems to have encouraged some to indulge in corrupt practices such as taking commission from favoured merchants or hoarding and speculating in food commodities; but these practices were not widespread, thanks to Manṣūr's alert spying system.[4]

Under Abū al-'Abbās new gold and silver coins had been minted. They had roughly 5% and then 10% less of the precious metals in them than those of the last Umayyads. To meet his increasing expenses Manṣūr issued yet cheaper money, stepping up this percentage to about 15.[5] These steps must have had some inflationary effect on the economy, but perhaps because of the gradual introduction of these coins, the effect went unnoticed and raised no problems. There was, however, some slight objection when Manṣūr, in order to withdraw the better coins from circulation, ordered his tax collectors to accept only Umayyad coins for taxes paid in cash.[6] The success of these limited economic measures is best shown in the fact that at his death Manṣūr left a healthy reserve in the treasury.[7]

Thanks to the Revolution, assimilation was a fact of life that could

[1] Ṭabarī, III, p. 374.

[2] Bal., *Futūḥ*, p. 294.

[3] Ṭabarī, III, pp. 434–5; Jahshiyārī, p. 126.

[4] Jahshiyārī, pp. 117, 118–19, 272.

[5] Maqrīzī, *al-Nuqūd al-Islāmiyya*, ed. M. S. A. Baḥr al-'Ulūm, Najaf, 1967, p. 17.

[6] Bal., *Futūḥ*, p. 469.

[7] Azdī, *Mawṣil*, p. 230; Mas'ūdī, *al-Tanbīh wa al-Ishrāf*, ed. M. J. de Goeje, Leiden, 1893, p. 342.

not be undone and it was left to take its course according to the circumstances of each province without much active interference on the part of the central government. In Khurāsān, where it struck roots, it was bound to gather momentum and no measures were taken to slow it down. On the other hand, in Egypt it was hardly effective; the Egyptians remained Copts and the Arabs continued their separate existence as they had done under the Umayyads. Naturally there were exceptions but it was to be some time before the two communities drew together. In the growing metropolis of Baghdād assimilation was not an issue. It was simply taken for granted as an accomplished fact, and the non-Arab converts were engaged in all walks of life on the same basis as the Muslim Arabs. It is worth pointing out that there is no justification for the belief of some modern scholars that the non-Arabs received preferential treatment at the hands of the new regime which, it is claimed, owed its victory to them. This is not true. It was a natural result of assimilation that more non-Arabs were brought into all government services and it is unnecessary to observe that they were the ever increasing majority over all the empire.

Finally, after a long, eventful reign and overcome by his worries and ulcers Manṣūr died, well over sixty years old.

2

TOWARDS A CIVIL WAR

If proof were needed that the foundations of the 'Abbāsid regime, as laid down by Manṣūr, were not as strong as they seemed, it was not long in coming. Hardly a generation after his death the empire was once more embroiled in a devastating civil war that explicitly pointed up the weaknesses of the regime. Over a period of thirty-five years three 'Abbāsid rulers followed the political orthodoxy of their founding-father without much deviation. Although some changes occurred, these were, on the whole, *ad hoc* measures which were attempted only as situations arose that threatened the central control. The general policy line was to enhance the power of the ruler and his central government, and that was thought to be enough to govern his vast empire. Changes in taxation were introduced to enrich the treasury without much regard to the interests of the tax-payers. Modifications in the administration were attempted for the sole purpose of tightening the grip of Baghdād over the provinces. The rulers persisted in assuming titles with religious connotations in the hope that this would give them some semblance of religious authority. They continued to use the Khurāsāniyya, their *force de frappe*, to counter the protestations of any dissident subjects. However, they failed to see that such a militia did not constitute a professional standing army or that it was no substitute for one. They could not comprehend that the use of this part-time military force to enforce the political will of the central government could only lead to serious complications. The lessons to be learnt from earlier precedents such as the dissolution of the Baṣran and Kūfan militia or the revolt of the Syrian army against its Marwānid masters were completely lost on these 'Abbāsid rulers.[1] In a fast growing metropolis like Baghdād, allowing the Khurāsāniyya to indulge in profit-making enterprises was the one sure way of losing them to civilian life altogether.

Assimilation was, in itself, an admirable achievement but it needed to be followed up by measures to consolidate it in order to integrate the peoples of the empire into one united community. In

[1] Shaban, *Islamic History*, pp. 111, 155.

a fast expanding economy and with a vastly increased volume of internal and international trade, consideration should have been given to the varying interests of all sections of the population and to those of the different provinces, in order that the economy could function under the most favourable circumstances. The relative calm within most of the empire allowed for a good measure of physical mobility for a considerable number of people as between one part and another, but this in turn caused population pressures to build up in areas of exceptional economic opportunities. The central government was either blissfully unaware of these problems or completely oblivious of its responsibilities.

Mahdī, the long-promised "divinely guided" ruler, finally came to power for a reign of about ten years 775–85/158–69. Everything had been prepared for his "coming", and provided that the quiet state of affairs that had prevailed in the last years of his father continued, an era of justice for all was conceivable. Indeed he inaugurated his rule with a grand gesture of reconciliation; he released from jail all his father's political prisoners.[1] Furthermore, as a "*mahdī*", and probably seeing himself above politics, he followed what can be described as a religious policy. He instituted a High Court, *maẓālim*, where he personally sat to hear the complaints of his subjects against his subordinates, in order that people could see that justice was being done.[2] He also sought to take advantage of his position as a ruler whose ideals were closer to Shī'ite ones than those of any of his predecessors, by pursuing a policy of reconciliation with, at least, the moderate Shī'ites. One of those released from Manṣūr's prisons was Ya'qūb b. Dāwūd, a man from Merv whose support of the Shī'ite cause needed no proof. His father and uncles had worked for the last Umayyad governor of Khurāsān and the East, and in this capacity the father had been of good use, as a spy, to Abū Muslim. Moreover, Ya'qūb and his brother had taken part in the revolt of the Pure Soul after which they had been imprisoned.[3] Appointing Ya'qūb to the unique position of "brother in God", Mahdī made use of his circumstances and contacts to put into effect the desired reconciliation.[4] To facilitate his task, Ya'qūb was given the right to appoint his own agents, *umanā'*, in all provinces, and these were granted a free hand and authority even over the governors in their respective areas.[5] This scheme to create what amounts to a

1 Ṭabarī, III, p. 461.
2 *Ibid.*, p. 408; Maqrīzī, *Khiṭaṭ*, II, p. 207.
3 Ṭabarī, III, pp. 506–7; Jahshiyārī, p. 155.
4 Ṭabarī, III, p. 464; Jahshiyārī, p. 155.
5 Ṭabarī, III, p. 486.

one-party system through a complicated network of political commissars did not bring about the desired results. First, the differences between the parties concerned were too deep for such a superficial attempt to succeed without real concessions on the part of Mahdī. Second, these political commissars with their extraordinary powers aroused the antagonism of the *mawālī* post-masters and the governors in the provinces. After five years of trying Ya'qūb was dismissed and returned to prison.[1]

Undaunted by this failure and probably as a reaction against it, Mahdī embarked on a purgative campaign against the so-called *zanādiqa*. Neither the origin of this term nor its derivation can be determined, but this very vagueness and the absence of any common cause among the people who were thus persecuted, lead us to believe that it was a nomenclature intended to cover all those who disagreed with Mahdī's religious policy. However, this campaign, couched as it were in religious guise, was bound to generate opposition on the same grounds even among members of his own family.[2]

In the administrative field Mahdī, not surprisingly, showed some ability, perhaps because of the training he had received from his father. Manṣūr had been presented with an illuminating report on the art of governing by Ibn al-Muqaffa', an official of his administration who had also worked for the Umayyads.[3] Trusting only in his own judgment Manṣūr does not seem to have made any effort to heed the advice contained in this report. In contrast, Mahdī seems to have studied it very carefully and indeed to have implemented some of its recommendations. Of course he was determined to retain full control of his government, and any advice that recommended measures to tighten this control would not be overlooked. In the event, a comptroller was installed in every government department and a chief-comptroller appointed to be in charge of all of them. Mahdī's chief administrative assistant–*wazīr* or *kātib*, the difference between the two was slight–had nothing to do with these new officials who kept their independence even from his "brother in God".[4]

There was another piece of advice in the report which was of great importance, especially in the light of later developments. This was the emphatic recommendation that the military forces should be strictly confined to their duties and under no circumstances should

[1] *Ibid.*, pp. 508, 517.
[2] *Ibid.*, pp. 499, 517–22, 534, 548–50, 588.
[3] M. Kurd 'Alī, ed. *Rasā'il al-Bulaghā'*, Cairo, 1946, pp. 117–34.
[4] Ṭabarī, III, p. 493; Jahshiyārī, pp. 146, 166.

they be involved in civilian matters, particularly the collection and administration of taxes. Mahdī understood the significance of this important piece of advice and, unlike his father who sometimes left both the department of revenues and that of the army under one head, he, Mahdī, always assigned to these departments separate heads and separate comptrollers in order to avoid any possible interference or involvement of the military in matters of taxation.[1] Furthermore, he was the first person who attempted to recruit men specially to serve in the police force which hitherto had been drawn from the army. To underline the importance of the duties of this new force, its members were recruited from the prestigious population of Madīna.[2] Unfortunately this policy was not long continued after Mahdī and, as we shall see, the result was disastrous.

The author of the report also recommended that tax anomalies in the empire should be eradicated, and that inflation should be taken into consideration in tax matters as well as in determining the stipends of the army.[3] Mahdī did not do anything to rectify the situation with regard to the tax anomalies, neither did he adjust the army stipends. But he did grasp the significance of inflation and realized that the existing system of taxation was causing the treasury a considerable loss of revenue. This system, as we know, was the same as that imposed by the Arabs at the time of the conquest, by which the conquerors took over in substance the systems they had found in the provinces. If the Arabs acquired any lands at the time, as in Syria and Jazīra, they were required to pay the Muslim tithe, i.e. one tenth of the produce. This arrangement kept the revenues on a level with inflation and presented no problem. The question was more complicated in the case of lands that had stayed in non-Muslim hands, as in the Sawād. Although many of the people there were eventually converted to Islam they continued to be required to pay the same taxes on the lands in their possession. This was a fixed rate in kind or cash assessed on the basis of area and kind of product.[4] This fixed rate, particularly in cash, was far behind the current prices of the relevant products, and that was where the treasury would stand to gain if a new system were to be introduced. His *kātib* suggested the sharing, *muqāsama*, system and it was soon implemented. The tax was assessed on the actual produce and the imposed rates varied from half to one third according to the method

[1] *Rasā'il*, pp. 122–3; Ṭabarī, III, p. 522.
[2] Ṭabarī, III, pp. 483, 548, 555, 762–3.
[3] *Rasā'il*, pp. 124–6.
[4] Shaban, *Islamic History*, pp. 48–9.

and expense involved in irrigation.[1] Another situation where a new system would benefit the treasury was where fruits and vegetables were concerned. Islam had originally conceived of levying taxes only on wheat, barley, dates and raisins, i.e. grapes; products that were familiar in Arabia.[2] Outside Arabia, in places such as Syria where olives were a major product, the Arabs did not realize at first that this was simply another taxable product. However, as early as ʿAbdulmalik, a tax had come to be levied on olives at the rate of 1 dīnār per 100 trees if these were within one day's distance of a market town, or 1 dīnār per 200 trees in remoter areas.[3] In the Sawād there were no olives, but there were many kinds of fruits and vegetables that presumably went untaxed for some time. We do not know when exactly this situation was rectified, or indeed whether it was at all rectified during the Umayyad period. But we know that in the neighbouring Fārs province Mahdī annulled a tax levied on certain fruit trees.[4] On the other hand we also know that he extended the *muqāsama* system to cover all agricultural products in the Sawād; the only concession to the producers was that their expenses should be deducted before the share of the treasury was set aside. Some adjustment was also made in consideration of distance from the markets.[5]

In Egypt, where the land tax was basically a fixed rate to be paid in cash, Mahdī instructed his governor to double the rate. This in itself gives us some idea of the rate of inflation during this period, and also about the increased level of taxation. A tax was also introduced on the cattle sold in the market places, but it seems probable that this was limited to cattle brought to big cities for slaughter.[6]

We do not have any information about changes in the land-tax in the other provinces but these were mostly areas that had had treaties of capitulation with the Arab conquerors, and accordingly had been paying an agreed sum. There was therefore no opportunity of introducing any increase in taxes there. It is reported that Mahdī ordered the imposition of a new tax on the markets and shops in Baghdād, but as we know that this practice was started under Manṣūr, it would seem that Mahdī only enforced the collection of

[1] Qudāma, Shemesh, p. 119; Bal., *Futūḥ*, p. 272.
[2] *Amwāl*, pp. 474–5.
[3] Abū Yūsuf, *Kitāb al-Kharāj*, Cairo, A.H. 1302, pp. 44–5.
[4] Jahshiyārī, p. 151; Hilāl al-Ṣābī, *Kitāb al-Wuzarā'*, ed. H. F. Amedroz, Leyden, 1904, p. 341.
[5] Qudāma, Shemesh, p. 118.
[6] Maqrīzī, *Khiṭaṭ*, vol. 1, p. 308; Shaban, *Islamic History*, pp. 38–9.

these "rents" and extended it to newly built shops outside the Round City.[1]

In accordance with the principle of engaging the army only in military activities, and as the internal situation was under control, Mahdī decided that his army would be best employed against the Byzantines. Beginning in 778/161, a series of increasingly aggressive summer expeditions alarmed the enemy and the situation soon deteriorated into an all-out war.[2] In 780/163 Mahdī himself went out with his army, including the Khurāsāniyya, and established a new base at Raqqa from which his son Rashīd led a successful expedition into Byzantine territory.[3] Returning to Baghdād Mahdī left his son to conduct the campaigns against the enemy and in addition put him in charge of all the western provinces of the empire.[4] This can only mean that the revenues of these provinces were assigned to the war effort on this important front. In 781/165 Rashīd put an army of 95,793 men – apart from volunteers – in the field. This force reached the sea coast opposite Constantinople and compelled the Byzantines to sue for peace. A three year truce was arranged, and the Byzantines agreed to pay a tribute of about 70,000 dinārs twice a year. Interestingly they also agreed to provide Rashīd's army with guides and promised to set up markets *en route* where provisions could be bought.[5] Indeed this was one of the most peculiar features of Byzantine–Muslim wars in ʿAbbāsid times; both armies in their advance into each other's territories actually bought their provisions from the enemy. One can only conclude that booty was not a primary objective in these wars, or that because of the strongholds on both sides of the frontiers, acquiring booty was so difficult that it was only attempted in exceptional circumstances.

In the East there were minor uprisings among the Soghdians in Bukhārā and Kish and also in the Hephthalite Principalities around Pūshang and Gūzgān. With a little help from the central government forces these areas were soon pacified.[6] Mahdī then turned to the stubborn Caspian provinces. In 783/167 a good part of the army stationed at Raqqa was dispatched to this region under the command of the heir apparent, Hādī. This expedition forced at least one of the

[1] Maqrīzī, *Khiṭaṭ*, vol. I, p. 103; Yaʿqūbī, *Tārīkh*, vol. II, p. 399; Yāqūt, *Buldān*, vol. IV, p. 448.
[2] Ṭabarī, III, pp. 485–6, 491, 493.
[3] *Ibid.*, pp. 494–9; Azdī, *Mawṣil*, p. 245–6.
[4] Ṭabarī, III, p. 500.
[5] *Ibid.*, pp. 503–5; Azdī, *Mawṣil*, p. 247.
[6] Ṭabarī, III, pp. 470, 484, 494, 517; Yaʿqūbī, *Tārīkh*, vol. II, p. 397.

princes of Ṭabaristān to declare his submission before Hādī had to turn back at the news of his father's death.[1]

As an important result of these campaigns, all the recruits that had come from Syria, Jazīra and 'Irāq during Manṣūr's reign were moved from Baghdād; some to the new base at Raqqa, and others to settle in the strongholds on the Byzantine borders. There must have been a great desire on the part of these men to settle there, for they volunteered to go even though they were given only stipends and no land allotments as had previously been the case.[2] This sudden and curious enthusiasm on the part of these men to accept transfer to these remote parts of the empire is contrary to their expected behaviour. Admittedly an incentive had been offered at the beginning, but the movement continued after that was reduced and even without it at all; and as early as Manṣūr we find people from the tribes of Azd, Ṭayy and Hamdān of Baṣra voluntarily moving to Ādherbayjān.[3] This uncontrolled immigration in areas that hitherto had hardly been noticed by the Arabs, eventually caused a serious revolt by the indigenous population under the leadership of Bābak.[4] Further west, within a few years, a major reorganization was to take place on the Arab–Byzantine borders.[5]

On the southern side of the empire another development was quietly taking place. The governor of Baṣra, a cousin of Mahdī, was, in addition, given charge of all the territories bordering the Persian Gulf.[6] This meant that all the possible inlets for the Indian Ocean trade were put under one authority in order to tighten government control over this trade. It is interesting to note that the reaction of the Arabs inhabiting the desert on the west coast of the Gulf, was to start attacking passing caravans.[7] This was only a portent of more serious trouble in this area.[8]

Mahdī was succeeded by his son Hādī whose rule lasted only for a little over a year 785–6/169–70, and was practically a continuation of his father's. A precedent was set at the time of this succession which was to become a rule at the succession of every new ruler. Hādī was away in Gurgān when his father died, and it seems that he was not very popular with some of the Khurāsāniyya in Baghdād, or, at least, it was feared that some might object to his succession. It was quickly arranged that all members of the army in Baghdād

[1] Ṭabarī, III, pp. 493, 517–18, 521–2, 551.
[2] Bal., *Futūḥ*, p. 166.
[3] Ya'qūbī, *Tārīkh*, vol. II, p. 371.
[4] See below, pp. 34, 56.
[5] See below, pp. 29–30.
[6] Ṭabarī, III, p. 501.
[7] Athīr, *Kāmil*, vol. VI, p. 51.
[8] See below, p. 116.

should receive two years' stipend as an immediate grant and their allegiance was thus secured.[1] Another innovation at the time was that Hādī separated what he considered as his private income from that of the treasury. This was the income from the extensive confiscated lands and properties of the Umayyads which he kept for himself, in addition to the "rents" of shops and other similar *mustaghallāt* that now included houses, public baths and grain mills.[2]

Two uprisings took place in the short reign of Hādī. A minor Shī'ite revolt in Madīna was very quickly suppressed and its leader killed. The only notable result was that one of his supporters, his cousin Idrīs, fled to North Africa where his son eventually established the Idrīsid dynasty.[3] The other uprising, in Armenia, was more serious. The continued influx of Arabs wishing to settle in the *thughūr*, border areas, met with resistance from the indigenous population in alliance with the Arabs who were already settled there. These disturbances encouraged the Khazars to resume their attacks and the general situation there remained unsettled.[4] Meanwhile, the government was trying to persuade some of the newcomers to move to other locations in order to relax the pressure on the more crowded areas.[5]

It was now the turn of the celebrated Hārūn al-Rashīd who succeeded his brother Hādī. In his reign 786–809/170–93 he followed the same basic policies as his brother, father and grandfather, but pressures were building up and strains began to show in the whole structure. An explosion was imminent. A great deal of myth surrounds this ruler, and modern scholars have preferred to leave the mystery unsolved. One late noted scholar, in an attempt to explode the myth, explained the whole thing in terms of the schizophrenia of Rashīd; fortunately this ingenious explanation was never published. However, we must hazard a logical explanation, for without it later developments can hardly be understood.

Like his father, Rashīd came to power full of good intentions. Gestures of reconciliation to the rival 'Alawids were freely offered and gratefully received. As if to announce the good news he went on a pilgrimage only a few months after his succession. He also made a point of visiting Madīna, and distributing a good deal of money among the inhabitants of the two holy cities.[6] Returning to Baghdād he began to plan his government in the light of prevailing

[1] Ṭabarī, III, pp. 545–6.
[2] *Ibid.*, p. 590.
[3] *Ibid.*, pp. 551–68.
[4] Ya'qūbi, *Tārīkh*, vol. II, pp. 426–8.
[5] Bal., *Futūḥ*, p. 190.
[6] Ṭabarī, III, pp. 604–5.

circumstances. The only troubled spots in the empire were the regions of Armenia and Ādherbayjān where internal conflict encouraged enemy interference. On the Byzantine borders the truce that had been concluded under Mahdī for three years had just come to an end and the enemy were beginning to prepare for a possible resumption of hostilities. Rashīd, having been deeply involved in the wars against the Byzantines during his father's time, and realizing the dangerous situation on his right flank, decided upon his priorities. He freed himself from all administrative responsibilities and took personal charge of the army. For the administration of the whole empire he fell back on his mentor and long-time associate Yaḥyā b. Khālid b. Barmak, a man whose loyalty, and that of his family, to the 'Abbāsids was absolutely beyond any shade of doubt. As he and his father before him had had long experience in the service of the 'Abbāsids in various capacities, particularly on the fiscal side, his ability was also proven. Rashīd appointed him as his *wazīr* with full executive powers and, for seventeen years, this man Yaḥyā and all his sons, served Rashīd faithfully in whatever assignment he entrusted to them.[1] Yet, as we shall see, when politics required their elimination, they were brutally sacrificed.

When hostilities were resumed against the Byzantines, Rashīd satisfied himself for the four years 786–9/169–74 with defensive action, in order to hold his territories.[2] Meanwhile, a major reorganization involving every aspect of the situation had been taking place on these borders. It was realized that the advanced strongholds in the *thughūr* that were established, fortified and maintained at great expense to the central treasury, were less than useless from a military point of view. They had been fast losing any military character that they might have had, or were intended to have had. The enthusiasm of the men to settle there had an ulterior motive which was far from that of fighting the enemy or defending their own frontiers. They had become engaged in a most lucrative trade with the Byzantines. Their proximity to the borders made these *thughūr* ideal outlets and trade centres for both Islamic and Byzantine products and any other merchandise that passed through their respective territories. Indeed the exceptional status of these frontier posts gave them almost complete immunity from taxes, a fact of benefit to all concerned except the central treasury in Baghdād.

1 *Ibid.*, pp. 545, 603, 606, 609, 631; Jahshiyārī, pp. 87–8, 177, 189–90, 204, 207, 210–11; Ya'qūbī, *Tārīkh*, p. 429.

2 Ṭabarī, III, pp. 521, 568, 605, 610.

Furthermore, instead of obstructing enemy advances, they were actually of considerable ḥelp to this very enemy. It will be recalled that the early recruits to man these strongholds had been granted land allotments as an incentive to settle there.[1] Although they were supposed to pay the stipulated Muslim tithes, they more often than not went tax-free. Naturally in their ample spare time they were able to cultivate these lands. One can imagine that in these tax-free and rather affluent localities prices would be low. Therefore any potential outside market for the accumulating surplus would be highly desirable. The Byzantines provided an obvious solution. After crossing Asia Minor and before entering Muslim lands, they could rely on these strongholds to supply them with badly needed provisions. It has been established that Muslim armies had to pay for their provisions while passing through Byzantine territories even after the conclusion of a rather successful campaign.[2] Under the circumstances the Byzantines would be expected to pay the asking-price for provisions, but that was not a difficult matter in view of the services rendered. This situation was obviously dangerous and made a complete mockery of the empire's system of defence against its primary enemy. Rashīd decided to dispense with all these advanced posts on the whole northern frontier, and instead, established a new line of defence to run along the southern slopes of the Taurus mountains roughly on a line between Tarsus and Aleppo. Even the term *thughūr* was dropped from current usage and *ʿawāṣim* was introduced instead. These were a chain of defensive positions established along this line with the main base at the town of Manbij, in charge of which he appointed a respectable ʿAbbāsid, ʿAbdulmalik b. Ṣāliḥ. Tarsus was refortified and a contingent of 3000 of the Khurāsāniyya was stationed there on a rotational basis. Another 2000 men disbanded from the *thughūr* of Antioch and Maṣṣīṣa, who had accepted to move to Tarsus, were given a rise of ten dinārs in their stipends in addition to land for their houses, but not agricultural land. These arrangements were made for Tarsus because of its exposed location.[3] However no similar arrangements were made for men stationed in other strongholds along the new defence line. Presumably the new organization convinced most of the men in the old *thughūr* that their situation there was not tolerable and that their

[1] See above, p. 13.

[2] See above, p. 25.

[3] Ṭabarī, III, p. 170; Azdī, *Mawṣil*, p. 262; Yāqūt, *Buldān*, vol. IV, p. 165; Bal., *Futūḥ*, pp. 169–70; Masʿūdī, *Murūj al-Dhahab*, ed. C. Barbier de Meynard and P. de Courteille, Paris, 1861–77, vol. VI, p. 437.

best course was to move voluntarily to the new *'awāṣim*. Of course, as was to be expected, some refused to return and were given further reason to complain when they were subsequently required to pay their taxes in full. Their discontent added a new dimension to the precarious situation in Armenia and Ādherbayjān.[1]

In 790/174 'Abdulmalik b. Ṣāliḥ, the commander-in-chief of the *'awāṣim*, had enough men to be able to resume and continue thereafter the customary summer expeditions from his base at Manbij.[2] Needless to say, the trade that used to pass through the *thughūr* soon found its way to the new *'awāṣim*, particularly to Aleppo, but the government now had a tighter control over it.

To keep an eye on the Byzantine front and at the same time to be close at hand if serious trouble broke out in Armenia and Ādherbayjān, Rashīd sought a central position in eastern Jazīra. Although thanks to the *One Thousand And One Nights* his name is eternally linked with Baghdād, it is a curious fact that he scarcely ever lived there. He had hardly come to power when he started looking for another suitable place. After three moves in ten years he finally settled in Raqqa which he made his headquarters.[3] Of course the Byzantine front had been on his mind, but he was also running away from a problem which was becoming increasingly difficult – the Khurāsāniyya in Baghdād. The first generation of these men had justifiably taken great pride in their achievements for which they were amply rewarded in every possible way. Their descendants had inherited their positions and gradually increased their influence as became clear at the succession of Hādī. They were now reverentially referred to as *abnā' al-dawla/da'wa*, the Sons of the Revolution, or simply the *abnā'*. Of course they continued to draw their stipends but they were also getting deeply involved in the commercial life of Baghdād, utilizing their prestige to increase their wealth.[4] As a military force they were hard to control and reluctant to forgo the soft life of the city for the hardships of campaigning. It is not difficult to imagine how frustrated a ruler would become in the face of such an overbearing force to whom he and his ancestors owed their very positions. Under the circumstances and until a substitute force was constituted, Rashīd preferred to stay away from his capital to avoid any possible friction with the *abnā'*.

[1] Ibn A'tham, vol. II, f. 249B.
[2] Ṭabarī, III, pp. 610, 612, 628, 629, 637, 645.
[3] *Ibid.*, pp. 606–7, 610, 645–6; Azdī, *Mawṣil*, p. 290.
[4] Ṭabarī, III, pp. 826, 827, 829.

'Abdulmalik b. Ṣāliḥ and his Syrian–'Irāqī forces were adequately holding the Byzantine front. In spite of some differences between the sitting population of Syria, particularly in Damascus, and some of the men who had recently returned from the *thughūr*, which caused some disturbance but which were soon ironed out, the situation was brought under control.[1] However, the precarious conditions in Armenia and Ādherbayjān demanded that some action should be taken; North Africa also was showing renewed signs of unrest. To complicate matters, an 'Alawid who had taken refuge with the Daylamites in the Caspian region began to agitate.[2] Military forces were needed to check all these threats but there were none available, unless new sources of recruitment were to be found. The faithful Barmakids were called upon to help, and Faḍl was dispatched to Khurāsān for this important task.

Although our sources represent this operation as a military expedition and Faḍl was probably accompanied by some Khurāsāniyya, it was really more of a political mission whereby Faḍl was expected to utilize his contacts and those of his associates in order to achieve his objective. They all knew the area very well, and they also knew that the Hephthalites who, even before their conversion, had co-operated with the Umayyads, were the best possible source of the badly needed recruits. Now that Islam had struck roots amongst them, it was probable that with some persuasion and incentive they might provide an ideal solution. The incentive Faḍl offered will be explained presently, but the persuasion came from some of the more co-operative princes of the Hephthalites themselves who were able to convince their peers of the value of such co-operation. Faḍl soon succeeded in his mission and new sources of recruitment were found not only among the Hephthalites, but also among the semi-settled Soghdian population of Ushrūsana. He called the new army the 'Abbāsiyya and grandly made them all *mawālī* of the 'Abbāsid ruler, thus giving a further new twist to the term *mawlā*. We are told that as many as 500,000 men were recruited, but actually only 20,000 of them went west with Faḍl.[3]

Their arrival seems to have coincided with Rashīd's move to Raqqa in 796/180, for there was a noticeable upsurge of activity on the borders. New strongholds were built and some men, apparently new arrivals, were stationed there.[4] Indeed in the following year

[1] *Ibid.*, pp. 624–5, 639; Athīr, vol. VI, pp. 86–91, Ibn Ḥazm, *Jamhara*, p. 252.
[2] Ṭabarī, III, pp. 612–13.
[3] *Ibid.*, pp. 631, 634; Ya'qūbī, *Buldān*, pp. 289–90.
[4] Bal., *Futūḥ*, p. 171.

Rashīd himself, as if to announce his newly acquired strength, led the summer expedition deep into Byzantine territory.[1] As new troops continued to arrive, Rashīd increased the pressure on the Byzantines all through the following decade. This effort culminated in a very big expedition in 805/190, again led by Rashīd, but as it had a limited success he was content to arrange for peace on favourable terms.[2] As a result of this peace, and probably also because of pressure from his Syrian–'Irāqī troops, Rashīd allowed the re-establishment of the discarded strongholds of the *thughūr* across the Taurus mountains.[3] Prisoners of war and gifts were exchanged between the rulers. An unusual period of peace started on these difficult borders and persisted even when a civil war broke out in the Islamic empire.

While Rashīd's attention had been so single-mindedly devoted to the Byzantine problem, the affairs of the empire had been left in the hands of the Barmakids. The father, Yaḥyā, held the home front while the sons, Faḍl and Ja'far, were sent to deal with any troublesome spots in the empire. Of course everything was done in the name of the ruler, but the Barmakids themselves should be held responsible for the success or failure of the policies they carried out. They seem to have enjoyed very good public relations, because our sources hardly voice any criticism of their actions even when these were manifestly wrong. Naturally their major responsibility was the fiscal administration of the empire which they and their appointees in the provinces effectively controlled.

If the success of their fiscal policy is to be measured by the wealth of the central treasury, then it was a huge success, but if it is measured by its results and effects on the peoples of the empire, then it was a dismal failure. It was certainly a strict conservative policy that never took reform into consideration. Although some minor adjustments were made as a result of complaints from some taxpayers their policy as a whole was characterized by a harsh efficiency which had eyes only for the interests of the treasury.

At an early stage of the Barmakid administration, it seems that some zealous tax-collector had suggested that the converts of the Sawād who, according to the new *muqāsama* system, were paying as much as half their produce in taxes, should also be subjected to the Muslim tithes. As this amounted to double taxation and was indeed a penalty for accepting Islam, it was quickly discarded.[4] When the

[1] Ṭabarī, III, p. 646.
[2] *Ibid.*, pp. 708–11.
[3] *Ibid.*, p. 712.
[4] *Ibid.*, p. 607.

farmers of the Fārs province complained that their tax rate was too high compared to the more fertile Shīrāz district of the same province, their rate was reduced to two-thirds of that of Shīrāz.[1]

If these measures seem lenient, the stringent methods of tax collecting that accompanied them more than compensated for any small loss the treasury might have suffered. Before the Barmakids' time, it had been tacitly accepted that in a bad year the collection of the full amount of taxes due should not be strictly enforced. Therefore the taxpayer would remain "in debt" to the treasury for a small portion of his tax, and in due course these arrears would be magnanimously dropped at a suitable occasion. But that did not do for Barmakid efficiency. Henceforth, not only had all taxes to be paid in full regardless of any mitigating circumstances, but also all arrears were vigorously claimed and special officials appointed for the task.[2] In some areas the taxpayers accepted the new rule with resignation, but in others they protested and the outcome was serious for the government.

In the region of Mawṣil the situation became most serious, for not only was the collection of arrears strictly enforced, but other efficiency measures were also introduced. Taxes on livestock, which had been in abeyance for all practical purposes, were demanded in full, in addition to long-forgotten arrears.[3] Furthermore, where there was some doubt as to whether a landowner should pay Muslim tithes or *muqāsama* rate, he was asked to pay a lump sum equivalent to the latter rate, which in effect meant that some of the Arabs there were losing their acknowledged tax privilege.[4] Consequently, it is not surprising that Khārijite type revolts broke out all over the region.[5] Attempts by the authorities to suppress these revolts by force only worsened the situation. Some of the Arabs of Mawṣil preferred to leave the region altogether and moved to neighbouring Ādherbayjān, thus spreading dissent further afield.[6]

In Ādherbayjān itself unrest was rampant as a result of the pressure of earlier Arab immigration and the demobilization of the *thughūr*. Men who had been encouraged to settle in these frontier areas and sometimes been given tax exemptions on their land allot-

[1] Iṣṭakhrī, *Kitāb al-Masālik wa al-Mamālik*, ed. M. J. de Goeje, Leiden, 1870, pp. 157–8; Maqdisī, *Aḥsan al-Taqāsīm* . . ., ed. M. J. de Goeje, Leiden 1877, p. 451.

[2] Ṭabarī, III, p. 649; Ya'qūbī, *Tārīkh*, p. 415; Azdī, *Mawṣil*, p. 314; Athīr, vol. VI, p. 105.

[3] Azdī, *Mawṣil*, p. 314.

[4] *Ibid.*, pp. 275–6.

[5] Ṭabarī, III, pp. 631, 645, 649, 688, 711.

[6] Azdī, *Mawṣil*, pp. 279–81, 287; Athīr, vol. VI, p. 105.

ments, suddenly lost this privilege and were asked to pay taxes. Predictably they objected and resorted to armed revolt.[1] The ensuing instability in these exposed regions simply invited Khazar attacks.[2] The indigenous population, who had patiently tolerated Arab encroachments on their territory and wealth, were certainly alarmed by a further influx of Arabs. Nor were they reassured by the presence of unruly elements in their midst who, instead of defending them against Khazar attacks, actually brought closer this dreaded danger. It is no wonder, therefore, that the so-called Khurramiyya revolt, which broke out a few years later led by Bābak, took root at this time in the region.[3] To cope with all this internal unrest and the external threats the central government had to find troops to contain the situation.

In Egypt efficiency measures were also responsible for unrest in a province that hitherto had not suffered from any. Late in the Umayyad period some Arabs from Mawṣil had been settled in the area adjacent to the desert on the east side of the Delta. Encouraged and subsidized by the government, they had reclaimed lands from the desert for agricultural purposes on which they had hardly paid any taxes.[4] Now, on instructions from the central government, these lands were surveyed and assessed for tax purposes. Furthermore, the measure used for surveying was a few inches shorter than the usual length, and the assessments were made to favour the treasury. As was to be expected, the result was armed revolt which could only be suppressed by fresh troops sent from Baghdād.[5] Another measure that antagonized Arabs and Copts alike was related to *aḥbās*, charitable and religious endowments: a purely Egyptian practice. The Copts used to set up these endowments for the benefit of the Church and the monasteries. As the management of such properties was left in the hands of the benefactors or their agents there was much leeway in the disposal of the income, in addition to the fact that they were also exempted from taxes. The Muslims found this tax loophole very convenient and had adopted the practice. Although the Umayyads had tolerated this action, the ʿAbbāsids found it alien to Islam and indeed Mahdī had tried to put an end to it. As these endowments had to be authorized by a judge, Mahdī had appointed a Ḥanafī judge to Egypt whose school of law did not permit the

[1] Ibn Aʿtham, vol. II, ff. 248B–249B.
[2] Ṭabarī, III, p. 648; Azdī, *Mawṣil*, p. 294.
[3] Ṭabarī, III, p. 732; Azdī, *Mawṣil*, p. 313.
[4] Shaban, *Islamic History*, p. 146.
[5] Maqrīzī, *Khiṭaṭ*, vol. I, pp. 80, 308; *idem*, vol. II, p. 163; Ṭabarī, III, pp. 626–7, 629.

principle of endowment. Since this move had met with objections, the Barmakids decided to allow the practice to continue, provided that such endowments were under the control of a judge who would see to it that the income was actually spent on charity. For this purpose a Mālikī judge, whose school of law allowed the principle, was appointed.[1]

Further west, in Barqa, Cyrenaica, where olives were an important product, a survey was made and a new assessment of taxes on a lump sum basis was put into effect. Also the collection of taxes on livestock was strictly enforced.[2] In North Africa the ʿAbbāsids had been having difficulties holding on to Tunisia. Differences between Berbers and Arabs and among the latter themselves were compounded by rivalries between the Arab–Berber military forces recruited in the area and the Khurāsāniyya brought in on a rotational basis to control the region. Finally it was decided that a large contingent of the new ʿAbbāsiyya troops would be settled there permanently under the command of Ibrāhīm b. al-Aghlab, who was also appointed governor of the region. Apparently a deal was struck with him which gave him virtual autonomy in exchange for an annual payment to the central treasury of 40,000 dinārs. This net profit to the treasury was in contrast to the previous arrangement whereby the treasury of Qayrawān had been receiving an annual subsidy of 100,000 dinārs from Egypt.[3]

The Barmakids' zeal in enriching the central treasury is, perhaps, understandable, but it is difficult to understand their equal zeal to enrich Rashīd himself and the close members of his family. They fervently used every means at their disposal, including corrupt practices, with complete disregard for the interests of all concerned, in order to achieve this unjustifiable objective. Shops, markets and other *mustaghallāt* in many towns; pasture land under public ownership; estates that belonged to rebels; lands that had been given in allotments in frontier areas; deserted properties which the owners had left because of the tax burden; properties whose owners died without heirs; even confiscated Umayyad estates that had been granted to members of the ʿAbbāsid family; all these properties were appropriated and added to Rashīd's private wealth.[4] The name

[1] Kindī, *Governors and Judges of Egypt*, ed. R. Guest, Gibb Memorial Series, vol. XIX, London, 1912, pp. 371, 372, 383, 387, 395.

[2] Yaʿqūbī, *Buldān*, pp. 344–5.

[3] Athīr, vol. VI, pp. 105–8; Yaʿqūbī, *Tārīkh*, vol. II, p. 411.

[4] Ṭabarī, III, pp. 607, 749; Azdī, *Mawṣil*, p. 287; Abū Yūsuf, *Kharaj*, pp. 200–1; Bal., *Futūḥ*, pp. 144, 151, 158, 179, 181.

of his son, who was a child then, was used in a tax-evasion device to secure tithe status for lands on which *maqāsama* was due. The owners of such lands formally sold their properties to this child but continued to cultivate them, paying the required tithe to the treasury in addition to a similar amount to the formal new owner. In these cases the efficient Barmakid machinery would certainly help to make the whole operation look legal. Needless to say, such lands eventually ended up as the private property of Rashīd's son, and the rightful owners lost them for ever.[1] Estates that had been ceded to Marwān II through the same device were now given to Rashīd's daughters, instead of being returned to their former owners. Zubayda, Rashīd's wife, had such vast interests in Egypt that an agent was appointed to look after them.[2] One has the feeling that the Barmakids did not exclude themselves or their associates altogether from this wealth-grabbing racket. Their life-style certainly betrays enormous wealth and the everlasting allegiance they inspired among their entourage, was due more to their celebrated "generosity" than to simple loyalty.[3]

In contrast with their stringent fiscal policies over almost all the empire, the Barmakids showed an unaccustomed leniency towards the East; it was the only region where they made real tax concessions. It will be remembered that Faḍl went to Khurāsān on a recruitment mission and, significantly, he was successful. Of course this was success at a price; he offered higher stipends to the new recruits and their leaders, and when this was not enough all tax arrears were forgiven, and the registers burnt.[4] It was even suggested that, if necessary, additional money would be provided from the central treasury for this region, i.e. that the revenues of the East should be spent there, and the central treasury should assume full responsibility for all the expenses of the new army.[5] It would seem, then, that the Barmakids in order to ensure the regular supply of troops from the East, made an agreement with the leaders of the area by which these leaders secured financial and political concessions. As we know that the Barmakids conceded autonomy to Ibrāhīm b. al-Aghlab in Tunisia, there is no reason that they should not have conceded the same to the indigenous leaders of the East, in return for their full co-operation. As we shall see, this very soon became formal policy under Ma'mūn.[6]

[1] Bal., *Futūḥ*, pp. 323, 371.
[2] Kindī, *Governors*, p. 392.
[3] Ṭabarī, III, pp. 673, 699–701.
[4] Jahshiyārī, p. 191.
[5] *Ibid.*, p. 228.
[6] See below, p. 50.

Meanwhile, this new eastern policy aroused tremendous opposition, particularly among the *abnā'* in Baghdād, an opposition that finally brought about the downfall of the Barmakids. The *abnā'* realized that the concessions accorded to the 'Abbāsiya in the East would eventually lead to concessions closer to home which would probably be at their expense. They felt that the new forces would ultimately ensure the erosion of their power in Baghdād and the loss of their privileged position in the regime. Furthermore their leaders, themselves from the East, had ideas as to how to deal with their old neighbours without having to concede as much as the Barmakids did. The successive indications of the failure of Barmakid policies encouraged their opponents, and Rashīd himself began to lose confidence in them. Six years before their final downfall Yaḥyā, the senior member of the family, resigned. Although he was to be in and out of office during this final period, his son Faḍl was dismissed from office and obliged to travel to Raqqa to ask Rashīd for forgiveness; he was forgiven but was not returned to office.[1] His younger brother Ja'far was the only one who remained in office until the very end. In other words, in the last six years of the Barmakids' power, the number of offices they held was reduced to a minimum, and other officials gradually took over their responsibilities. One of these was Faḍl b. al-Rabī', whose father was a *mawlā* of Manṣūr.[2] It was around this figure that the opposition to the Barmakids was built up, and in the light of his later behaviour, it is clear that he was mainly opposed to their eastern policy. 'Alī b. 'Īsā b. Māhān the leader of the *abnā'* in Baghdād was another figure who was also opposed to this policy.[3] Indeed, he was appointed as governor of the East especially to put into effect a policy completely opposite to that of the Barmakids. He tried to bring to heel the princes and chiefs of the region, and to reimpose the full authority of the central government on them. He also nullified any tax-concessions and advantageous fiscal arrangements they might have gained from the Barmakids. In contrast to the subsidy proposed by the latter, we are told that he sent to the central treasury as much as 10 million dirhams a year.[4] This new policy met with fierce resistance and provoked numerous uprisings in the region.[5] However, he persevered with his harsh measures until a major revolt, led by one

[1] Ṭabarī, III, pp. 646–7, 651, 667; Jahshiyārī, p. 227.
[2] Ṭabarī, III, p. 638; Jahshyārī, p. 269.
[3] See below, p. 43.
[4] Ṭabarī, III, pp. 649, 702, 716, 717, 727; Jahshiyārī, p. 228.
[5] Ṭabarī, III, pp. 637, 645, 650–1; Ya'qūbī, *Buldān*, pp. 304–5.

of his chief lieutenants, broke out in Samarqand. This leader was Rāfi' b. Layth who, interestingly enough, was a grandson of the last Umayyad governor of Khurāsān and the East. Although now a staunch supporter of the 'Abbāsids, he objected to the harsh treatment that was dealt out to his fellow countrymen of the East with whom he fully identified himself. He had the backing of other Arabs of the region with similar convictions, and in addition enjoyed the powerful support of the chiefs and princes of Soghdiana, Transoxania and the Principalities of Ṭukhāristān.[1] As this revolt spread and threatened to end in the secession of the whole East, Rashīd hurriedly changed course. In an obvious move to placate the rebels he sent back most of the recently recruited 'Abbāsiyya whose main task, significantly, was to arrest the unwanted governor 'Alī b. 'Īsā b. Māhān.[2] Of course they were also to try to persuade their fellow countrymen to revert to peace, and it was hoped that they would even fight against them if necessary. Any fighting that took place however was perfunctory and the revolt continued unchecked. Finally Rashīd himself had to go east to try to contain this serious revolt. As he did not have enough military forces, he planned to seek the help of the princes of Ṭabaristān and Gurgān.[3] However, this hope did not materialize and he died as soon as he had reached Khurāsān. His death brought the crisis to a new climax and the scene was fully set for the coming civil war.

In his last years, as he had been trying to strike a balance between the various pressures weighing upon him and at the same time find means of restoring stability to the empire, Rashīd had unwittingly helped the situation to deteriorate even faster. His overwhelming preoccupation with the Byzantine wars was totally misguided effort. There is very little evidence of any aggressive plans on the part of the Byzantines; they were merely reacting to his own grandiose plans, and in fact were very willing to reach peace on any reasonable terms. The problem was that his plans demanded more military forces than he could muster. The *abnā'* were not particularly keen to join in what they may have considered an unnecessary war. The Syrian–'Irāqī forces were in a demoralized state after their withdrawal from profitable positions on the frontiers. To support Rashīd's efforts the Barmakids promoted their eastern policy in order to recruit men from this vast region. However, the success of

[1] Ṭabarī, III, pp. 707–27; Ya'qūbī, *Tārīkh*, vol. II, pp. 425, 535–6.
[2] Ṭabarī, III, pp. 715–19; Ya'qūbī, *Tārīkh*, vol. II, p. 425.
[3] Ṭabarī, III, pp. 705, 733.

the scheme and the arrival of these men at the front antagonized both the *abnā'* and the Syrian–'Irāqī forces. Even the commander-in-chief 'Abdulmalik b. Ṣāliḥ showed enough opposition to force Rashīd to imprison him.[1]

The failure of the Barmakids' fiscal policies only added to the need for new troops to cope with new situations. From the point of view of everybody concerned the Barmakids were the culprits, the villains of the piece. Although they were rapidly losing power, that was not enough to placate their opponents who would not rest as long as any Barmakid continued in office, and who focused their rancour on the unfortunate Ja'far, the only one to remain in power until the end. A scapegoat was required and in this particular case Ja'far was the obvious target. When the moment of their downfall came, it is significant that only Ja'far was executed. Furthermore, and even more significantly, although he was executed near Kūfa, his body was sent to Baghdād where, on Rashīd's specific instructions, it was decapitated and cut in halves, one half hung on each of the main bridges and the head put up in the city centre. The mutilated corpse remained there for a year for everybody, particularly the *abnā'*, to see as a proof of their ruler's repentance.[2]

Just before carrying out this hideous act, Rashīd had been on the pilgrimage to Makka where he took advantage of this most celebrated occasion to announce his plans for the succession. These were not simply plans for nominating a successor. They included a major re-structuring of the government of the empire, which was to take effect immediately, during his lifetime. He seems to have been thinking of a compromise that would satisfy his critics, and at the same time keep the eastern policy alive albeit in a different form. For all practical purposes the empire was to be divided into two halves, the point of division being Rayy. While the western half would eventually come under the control of Amīn when the time came to succeed his father, the eastern half would go to Ma'mūn, the next in line for the succession. A most important stipulation was that the revenues and forces of each domain would normally be used only for the benefit of its respective regions. Ma'mūn would have complete autonomy and the final say on fiscal matters in his area. However, he was required to help his brother with military forces if the need arose. A most binding agreement was concluded, sworn and witnessed by hundreds of dignitaries, members

[1] *Ibid.*, pp. 688–94.
[2] *Ibid.*, pp. 675–80; Jahshiyārī, p. 234; Azdī, *Mawṣil*, p. 304.

of the 'Abbāsid family, *mawālī*, government officials and army generals. The only conspicuously missing witnesses were the Barmakids, although they were on the same pilgrimage.[1]

Like all agreements this one could not foresee every circumstance, and of course the parties concerned might put different interpretations on the same articles. Very soon it became clear that by dividing the empire, Rashīd had actually helped to set the opposing parties against one another, and had provided them with sufficient resources to become independent of each other. Furthermore, he was giving the East a legitimate ruler around whom its forces could rally. Indeed when Rashīd died, Rāfi' b. Layth saw no reason to carry on with his revolt, and wholeheartedly joined Ma'mūn's camp.[2] This polarization in the East was matched by a similar process in the western regions. 'Abdulmalik b. Ṣāliḥ was released from prison to help muster his Syrian–'Irāqī troops, and 'Alī b. 'Īsā b. Māhān began to mobilize his *abnā'* for the expected fight. The inevitable confrontation was to take place in a matter of a few months.

[1] Ṭabarī, III, pp. 655–65; Ya'qūbī, *Tārīkh*, vol. II, pp. 416–20.
[2] Ṭabarī, III, p. 777.

3

DISSOLUTION UNDER A NEW REGIME

In previous civil wars fighting had been limited to protagonists whose interests had been directly involved, and on the whole other sections of the population had chosen to remain out of the struggle, even when their sympathies had been with one party or the other. In this civil war, although the opponents were clearly identified, almost every section of the population in every region became involved and the prolonged struggle spread to all corners of the empire. The *abnā'* were fighting a determined battle to conserve their declining status in the 'Abbāsid regime, while the Easterners were struggling to consolidate the privileged new position created by their active participation in support of the wider interests of the empire. As Muslims and members of the army they took strong exception to being pushed aside by the *abnā'*, especially when these were not fulfilling their military responsibilities. The latter were determinedly opposed to any change which would give the Easterners a privileged place in the structure of the empire. Every group in the empire with vested interests that were threatened by change actively supported the *abnā'*, while every group that aspired to change sided with the Easterners. This situation created two opposing blocs, one reactionary, symbolised by the *abnā'*; the other progressive and represented by the Easterners. The problem was that while the reactionaries knew exactly what they wanted, the progressives had nothing in common beyond their desire to see the *abnā'* brought to their knees. Once this objective was achieved their apparently united front fell into disarray, and more and more new disorders ensued. At the same time the *abnā'* became divided among themselves as to how far they should accept their new situation. Amīn, Rashīd's successor, was the leader of the reactionary forces, while Ma'mūn was the hero of the progressives. Perhaps not surprisingly he had to contend with problems more serious and complicated than those that faced his less fortunate brother.

When Amīn came to power the treasury had more than ample reserves and he had no problem paying his army the customary bonus.[1] At the same time the Byzantine borders were as tranquil as they could be and there were no signs of disturbance there. Yet Amīn demanded from his brother financial or military help, and according to some reports both. It can only be concluded that this was a deliberate attempt on his part to invalidate the agreements arranged by Rashīd. It can also be gleaned that this was done under pressure from the *abnā'* and their allies in Baghdād, who had been encouraged by their success against the Barmakids and the death of Rashīd.[2] They now went all the way to restore the *status quo* and erase any possible traces of the eastern policy.

Predictably Ma'mūn objected, realizing that his brother's demands were only a pretext for the more serious intentions of Baghdād. Although Rāfi' b. Layth had declared his allegiance to him, his allies the princes of Soghdiana and the Principalities of Ṭukhāristān were undecided as to their course of action.[3] But Ma'mūn was fortunate enough to have in his service the two Sahl brothers, Faḍl and Ḥasan. Like many other senior officials in the empire, they were protégés of the Barmakids who, in their long tenure in office, had trained many such men. Naturally such men were not adherents of all the Barmakid policies, but as these two brothers had been chosen to serve Ma'mūn it was to be expected that they were strong supporters of the eastern policy.[4] It has been wrongly believed that they were originally from 'Irāq.[5] This mistake stems from the misunderstanding of a remark in a source that relates them to the district of Sīb where Faḍl was granted an estate by Ma'mūn. It also arises because Ḥasan eventually made his home in 'Irāq where he was practically exiled after his dismissal from office.[6] However another source clearly states that they came originally from the town of Sarakhs in Khurāsān.[7] This is confirmed by the fact that their cousins, of whom they had many in their service, were from Khurāsān.[8] The brothers Sahl and their cousins formed the nucleus of Ma'mūn's nascent administration in Merv. Faḍl, the head of this

1 Ṭabarī, III, pp. 764–5.
2 *Ibid.*, pp. 779, 784, 811–17; Jahshiyārī, p. 289; Ya'qūbī, *Buldān*, p. 305.
3 Ṭabarī, III, p. 815.
4 *Ibid.*, p. 730.
5 Dominique Sourdel, *Le Vizirat Abbaside*, Damascus, 1959, vol. I, p. 196.
6 Jahshiyārī, pp. 229–31, 306; Ya'qūbī, *Buldān*, p. 322.
7 Ibn Khallikān, *Wafayāt al-A'yān*, ed. Iḥsān 'Abbās, Beirut, 1972, vol. IV, p. 41.
8 Ṭabarī, III, pp. 975, 979, 985, 993, 996, 1000, 1011, 1026, 1027; Jahshiyārī, pp. 305, 318; Ya'qūbī, *Buldān*, pp. 307, 321, 406; Ya'qūbī, *Tārīkh*, vol. II, pp. 448, 452; Athīr, vol. VI, pp. 209, 215, 218, 220, 225, 246, 256; Ibn al-Abbār, *I'tāb al-Kuttāb*, ed. Ṣ. al-Ashtar, Damascus, 1961, p. 109.

administration, was significantly given the title *dhū al-riyāsatayn al-ḥarb wa al-tadbīr*, i.e. indicating that he was in charge of the army and of the fiscal administration.[1] In other words he was given full powers by Ma'mūn in order to muster badly needed support at this critical point. On the fiscal side the taxes of all the region were reduced by one quarter.[2] With this kind of incentive and the wide contacts of the Sahls and their cousins, the mobilization of the East became feasible. They did not, however, rely on the 'Abbāsiya leaders amongst whom Harthama b. A'yan of Balkh was the most prominent figure. Instead they cultivated their own new leaders directly from the Hephthalite chiefs such as Ṭāhir b. Ḥusayn of Pūshang, whose own men were as many as five thousand. His ancestors had supported and served the 'Abbāsid cause since the Revolution, and in the process had established useful connexions all over the region. Although his own father advised him against the venture he, probably after extracting more concessions from the Sahls, decided to accept the assignment and to lead the Eastern forces against the intransigence of Baghdād.[3]

Meanwhile 'Alī b. 'Īsā b. Māhān mobilized an army of 20,000 men from the *abnā'* and marched to Rayy where the two armies met. The result was a resounding defeat for the *abnā'*; 'Alī himself was killed and his army retreated in complete disarray to Baghdād.[4] In pursuit of his fleeing adversary Ṭāhir advanced to the city where he was met by unexpectedly fierce resistance. It took reinforcements from the East, fourteen months of siege and practically street to street fighting to capture a city that was largely destroyed. This obdurate resistance was partly due to the last ditch fight of the *abnā'*, but also to the population of Baghdād itself which took a major part in the fighting.[5]

Realizing Ṭāhir's difficulties Ma'mūn dispatched a strong contingent of the 'Abbāsiya under the command of their leader Harthama b. A'yan. As he had taken part in previous operations in the west under Rashīd, it was hoped that Harthama's presence in 'Irāq might attract some of the Syrian–'Irāqī forces to his side. The death of their leader 'Abdulmalik b. Ṣāliḥ at that time must have helped a little in this respect, in addition to the fact that some of them must

1 Jahshiyārī, pp. 305–6; Ṭabarī, III, p. 841.

2 Ṭabarī, III, p. 774; Azdī, *Mawṣil*, p. 318.

3 Ṭabarī, III, pp. 771, 925, 1063; Jahshiyārī, pp. 84, 290; Athīr, vol. VI, pp. 29, 104; Ya'qūbī, *Buldān*, p. 306; Ya'qūbī, *Tārīkh*, vol. II, p. 437; Ibn Ḥazm, *Jamhara*, p. 194; Ṭayfūr, pp. 113, 119, 129.

4 Ṭabarī, III, pp. 797–803, 820–30.

5 *Ibid.*, pp. 868–933.

also have seen the writing on the wall. When Harthama arrived at Baghdād, during the siege, a sizeable force of the Syrian–'Irāqī troops also reinforced Ṭāhir's side.[1] Ma'mūn's strategy was that after the fall of Baghdād Ṭāhir should proceed to capture the strong base at Raqqa, while Harthama should advance to the south to control the rest of 'Irāq. Meanwhile another army was sent under the command of Ḥasan b. Sahl who was to deputize for his brother Faḍl in Baghdād and help to re-establish civil authority there.[2] But these arrangements did not work out quite as had been planned. In the first place Ṭāhir and Harthama seem to have been uneasy partners even during the difficult period of the siege. Harthama seemed to have wanted some measure of reconciliation with the vanquished, while Ṭāhir and Ḥasan were definitely against such a policy. Indeed the unfortunate Amīn sensed this attitude on the part of Harthama, and tried to take advantage of it to save his own life when everything else was lost. In the event he did not succeed and was killed by one of Ṭāhir's close associates. When Ṭāhir marched to Raqqa, Harthama was recalled to Merv where he was imprisoned and died.[3] In the second place, when Ḥasan was proceeding to establish his own authority in Baghdād, he realized that the first step had to be the total demobilization of the *abnā'*.[4] This move created a sharp division among them; some were willing to accept it while others were determined to keep their positions. Nevertheless both sides were adamant in their opposition to Ḥasan and what he stood for, and once more fighting broke out between all parties.[5] This situation was not helped by the fact that quasi-Shī'ite uprisings started in the vicinity of Kūfa, Makka and Yaman. Although these movements were a portent of more serious trouble later, at this time they came to nothing, and after some time peace was restored in these areas.[6] However, in Baghdād chaos prevailed; the *abnā'* fought each other and at the same time they all fought the army of Ḥasan which in itself was not united. The Syrian–'Irāqī troops that remained with Ḥasan after Ṭāhir had left to go to Raqqa, began to waver as they saw no end to this interminable fighting.[7]

After the death of 'Alī b. 'Īsā b. Māhān, the leadership of the

[1] *Ibid.*, pp. 51, 68, 846.

[2] *Ibid.*, p. 975.

[3] *Ibid.*, pp. 903–30, 998; Ya'qūbī, *Buldān*, p. 306; Ya'qūbī, *Tārīkh*, vol. II, pp. 449–50; Azdī, *Mawṣil*, p. 341.

[4] Ṭabarī, III, pp. 998–9.

[5] *Ibid.*, pp. 999–1003.

[6] *Ibid.*, pp. 976–95, 1000–3, 1017, 1019–21, 1062–3, 1096, 1100.

[7] *Ibid.*, pp. 998–9, 1001–3; Ya'qūbī, *Tārīkh*, vol. II, p. 450; Azdī, *Mawṣil*, p. 341; Ṭayfūr, pp. 1, 142.

abnā' had fallen to Muḥammad b. Abī Khālid, who in turn was killed in the new fighting. His brothers and sons continued in this role but they changed sides so often that it is hard to keep track of their activities.[1] Finally, as a device to get rid of Ḥasan, a reluctant 'Abbāsid, Ibrāhīm b. Mahdī, was proclaimed the representative of Ma'mūn in Baghdād. Then, almost against his own will, it was decided that he should be set up as a rival *Amīr al-Mu'minīn* there.[2] Most important in this situation was the reappearance of the population of Baghdād as a strong force in the fighting. Some were on the side of the *abnā'* who objected to demobilization, others supported those who accepted this measure. The latter were particularly powerful on the east side of Baghdād where they seem to have had extensive commercial interests. Here, the merchants played a big part in arousing the population against the intrusion of Ḥasan, and were even willing to pay for the recruitment of the mass of the population as a kind of Home Guard to support the rival rule of Ibrāhīm.[3] Earlier, during the siege of Baghdād, Amīn, after exhausting his financial resources and in an attempt to raise forces from the same source, had had to find the means to pay them. Under the circumstances of the siege when food prices had rocketed and when cash had not been available, paying these recruits in kind had been the only possible way and indeed the best incentive.[4] This same method was used again to raise support for Ibrāhīm, and in fact these "volunteers" proved to be very effective in the type of urban guerilla warfare that took place in the city. These men were paid in kind in certain measures and this practice gave rise to a new vernacular term, *'ayyār*, which is a derivative of *'iyār*, i.e. measure. At the time this was a rather laudatory term but eventually with the deterioration of the uncontrolled activities of such men into brigandage, the term acquired a derogatory connotation and became equivalent to "thug" or "rogue".[5] A similar process happened with the term used to describe the men of the Syrian–'Irāqi forces, *zawāqīl*, which at first simply meant men who tied their turbans in a special way leaving the edges around their heads. When these men

1 Ṭabarī, III, pp. 843, 883, 935, 978, 998, 999, 1000, 1003, 1004, 1007, 1302; Ya'qūbī, *Tārīkh*, vol. II, pp. 439, 447; Jahshiyārī, pp. 196, 312; Athīr, vol. VI, pp. 225, 227.

2 Ṭabarī, III, pp. 1005–16, 1012–16, 1030–4, 1068.

3 *Ibid.*, pp. 1008–11, 1016, 1023, 1032–5.

4 *Ibid.*, pp. 872, 881, 882, 890, 896, 899, 900; Mas'ūdī, *Murūj*, vol. VI, pp. 452, 461, 463, 465.

5 Ṭabarī, III, pp. 881, 885–6, 894, 896, 899, 901–2, 907, 1008; Mas'ūdi, *Murūj*, vol. VI, p. 463; Athīr, vol. VI, p. 197.

did not come to the aid of the *abnā'*, the term *zawāqīl* also acquired a derogatory implication.[1]

The co-operation of the wealthy merchants with the *abnā'* to raise such a force, was a clear indication of the determination of these two groups to restore the *status quo* at any cost. Indeed the slogan of "commanding good and prohibiting evil" – which has always been used by reactionary groups in Islam to impose their own dogmatic viewpoints – betrays their true intentions.[2] The fact that this was the time of the rise in Baghdād of Ḥanbalism, the most conservative school in Sunnī Islam, emphatically underlines the nature of the prevailing atmosphere there. It is important to realize that the various schools of law in Islam, and for this matter the different sects, were not merely concerned with ritual and rites, but even more with taxes which were usually referred to by the Islamic term *zakāt*. In this respect the Ḥanbalites represented the extreme right wing that tried to perpetuate the inequitable taxation system which allowed the majority of the urban communities, particularly the wealthy merchants, to avoid paying any taxes. In clear contrast the Shī'ites, the traditional opposition party, began to comprehend the significance of the change in the economy and tried to adapt their movement to fulfil the aspirations of the tax-oppressed communities. Henceforth, Shī'ites became keen advocates of fair taxation and indeed where they succeeded in establishing their own regimes, there were always substantial and significant new fiscal arrangements.[3] In Baghdād, later developments show that while the small shop-keepers, who had to pay the treasury "rents" for their shops, turned to Shī'ism, the wealthy merchants continued to be avid Ḥanbalites.[4]

The unabated fighting in Baghdād finally forced Ḥasan b. Sahl to withdraw his army from the city, and Ma'mūn had to take some action to save the situation. He hurriedly announced the appointment of a respectable 'Alawid as his heir apparent, and for himself he took the title of *Imām*.[5] This was a desperate tactic to appeal to the Shī'ites in the empire, but it was too transparent to convince anybody of the sincerity of Ma'mūn's motives. In the event it only added to the highly charged atmosphere of Baghdād and even strengthened the determination of his opponents. Ma'mūn, who must have been

1 Ṭabarī, III, pp. 843, 844, 845, 847; Athīr, vol. VI, pp. 178, 179; Ibn Manẓūr, *Lisān al-'Arab*, Būlāq, 1891, s.v. *zql*.

2 Ṭabarī, III, p. 1009.

3 See below, pp. 130, 148, 166.

4 See below, p. 83.

5 Ṭabarī, III, pp. 779, 796, 1012–13, Ya'qūbī, *Tārīkh*, vol. II, p. 450.

one of the most supple politicians in Islamic history, made a complete about-turn in his proclaimed policies. In the meantime he took the most daring and risky step of his career; he decided to go to Baghdād himself. He proceeded from Merv with such extreme caution that it took him two years to reach Baghdād. Soon after he left Merv Faḍl b. Sahl was assassinated, almost certainly on Ma'mūn's orders.[1] Ḥasan b. Sahl, who was still in his camp to the south of Baghdād, was declared insane.[2] Most conveniently, the 'Alawid heir apparent died in circumstances which can only be described as suspicious.[3] Ṭāhir and his forces were ordered to leave their unfinished task in Raqqa and march on Baghdād; their arrival was to coincide with Ma'mūn's.[4]

Once he entered the city 819/204 everything there returned to normal, as if the events of the previous decade had not occurred. All symbols of his short-lived Shī'ite conversion were cast aside,[5] with one exception; Ma'mūn held on to the title of *Imām* which continued to be used by all the later 'Abbāsid rulers. Another addition to the lengthening list of his official titles was that of *khalīfa* which had long been in popular use, but was now given a twist to signify that the ruler was God's deputy on earth, instead of the simple earlier meaning of successor.[6] This was another attempt to consolidate the authority of the *Amīr al-Mu'minīn* by giving it greater semblance of a religious function.

It took some effort to bring the Syrian–'Irāqī forces of Raqqa and the opportunists of the *thughūr* under control, but soon the general situation in 'Irāq, Syria and Jazīra looked promising,[7] though troubles started in the other regions. The people of the East who had stood by Ma'mūn in his hour of need felt betrayed by his sudden reconciliation with Baghdād, and began to show signs of unrest.[8] Ṭāhir who had been given the responsibility of maintaining order in Syria, Jazīra, 'Irāq and Baghdād itself was the only obvious person to bring stability to his own region.[9] Accordingly a new arrangement was introduced, one that in fact amounted to the establishment of a new regime for the empire. The fact that Ṭāhir's

[1] Ṭabarī, III, p. 1027.
[2] Athīr, vol. VI, p. 252; Ṭabarī, III, pp. 1030, 1081–5.
[3] Ṭabarī, III, p. 1030.
[4] *Ibid.*, p. 1037.
[5] *Ibid.*, p. 1038.
[6] *Ibid.*, pp. 1097, 1112, 1117.
[7] *Ibid.*, pp. 1045–62, 1067–73; Ṭayfūr, pp. 138–9; Ya'qūbī, *Tārīkh*, vol. II, pp. 435, 455; Bal., *Futūḥ*, p. 185.
[8] Ya'qūbī, *Tārīkh*, vol. II, p. 450; Ṭabarī, III, p. 1043.
[9] Ṭabarī, III, p. 1039; Ya'qūbī, *Tārīkh*, vol. II, pp. 455–6; Ṭayfūr, p. 23.

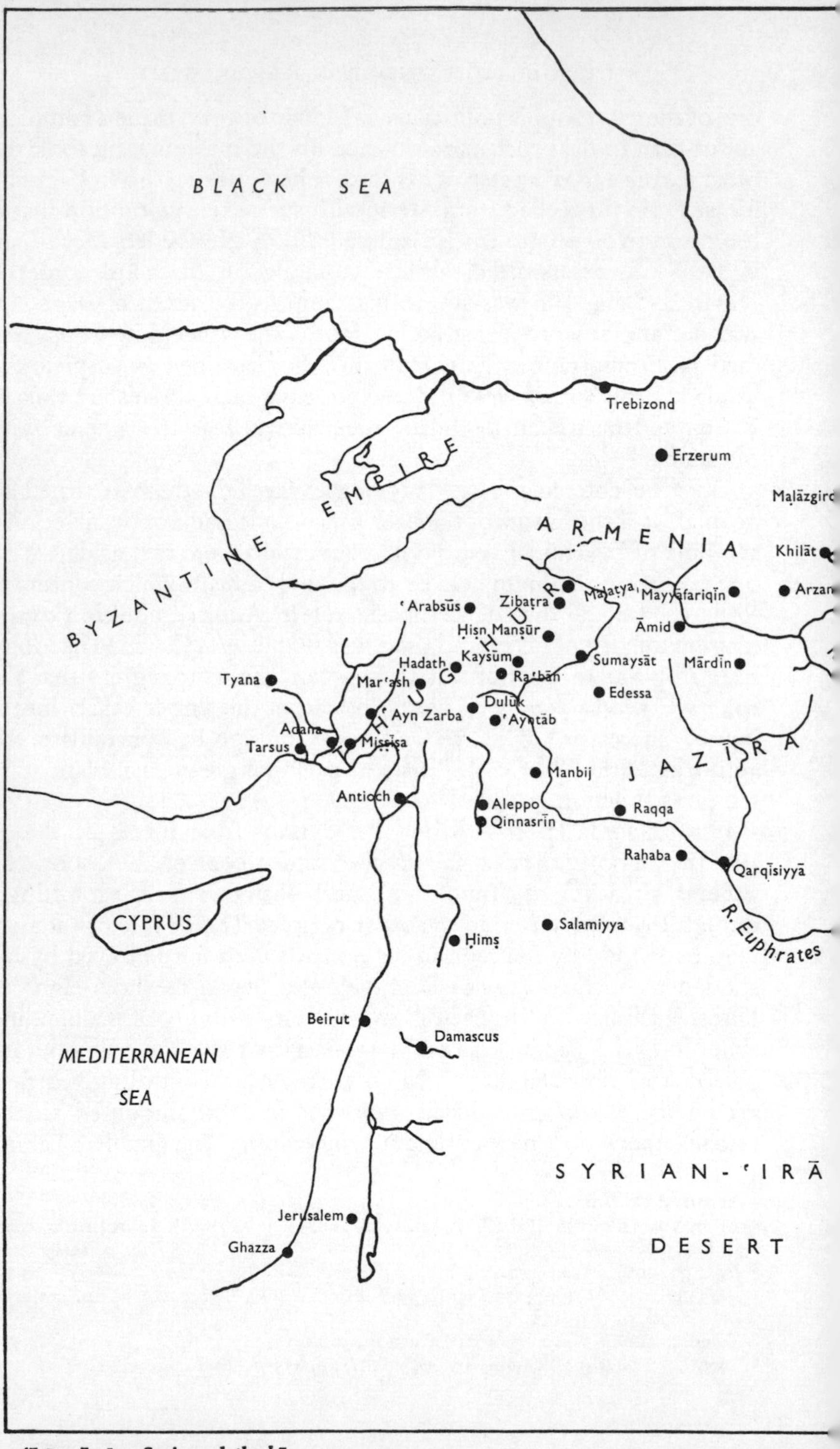

1 'Irāq, Jazīra, Syria and *thughūr*

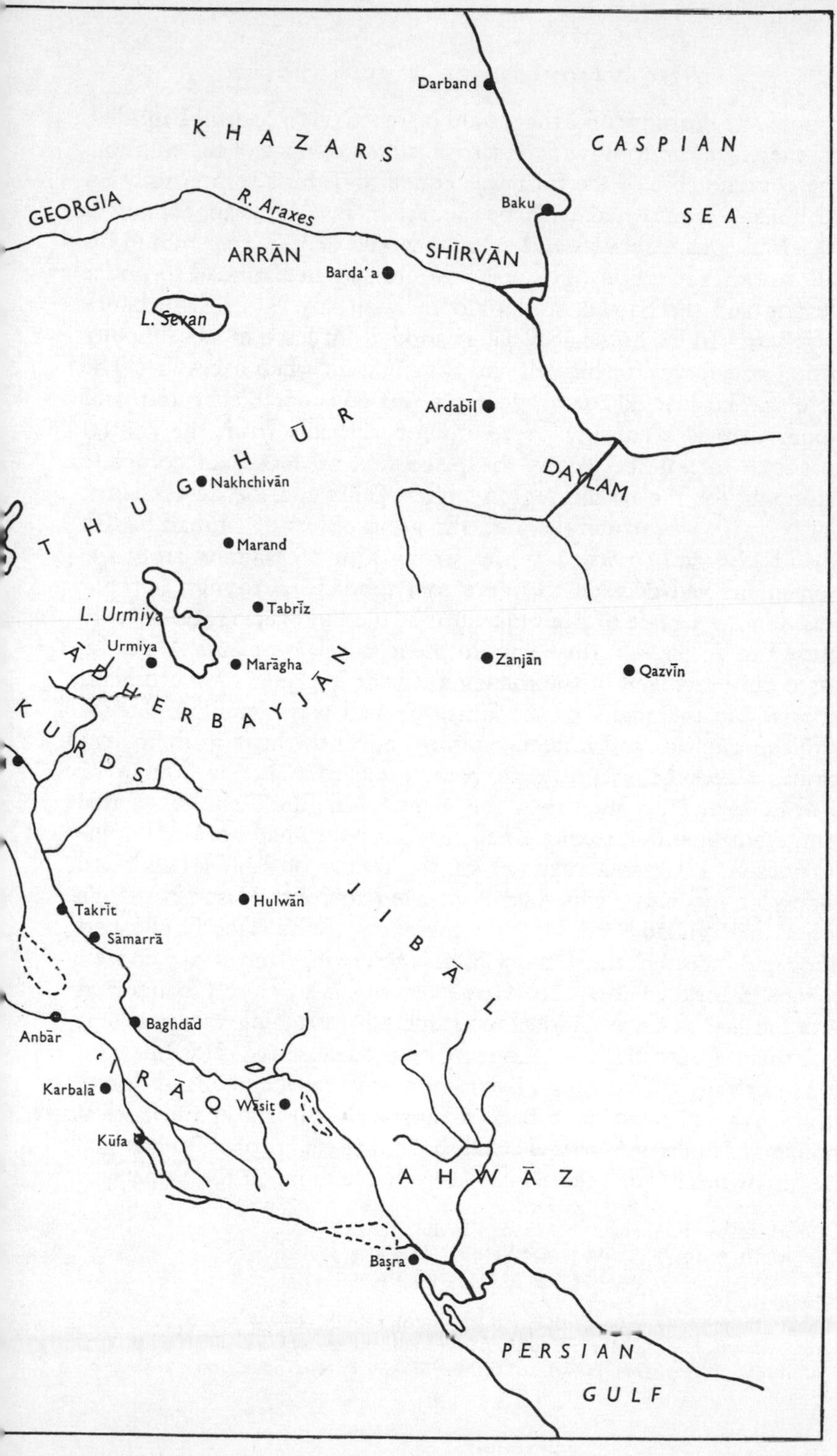

Darband
KHAZARS
CASPIAN
SEA
GEORGIA
R. Araxes
Baku
ARRĀN
SHĪRVĀN
Barda'a
L. Sevan
THUGHŪR
Ardabīl
DAYLAM
Nakhchivān
Marand
L. Urmiya
Tabrīz
Urmiya
Marāgha
Zanjān
Qazvīn
ĀDHERBAYJĀN
KURDS
Hulwān
Takrīt
Sāmarrā
JIBĀL
Baghdād
Anbār
'IRĀQ
Karbalā
Wāsiṭ
Kūfa
AHWĀZ
Baṣra
PERSIAN
GULF

troops were the only force that could be relied on to control Baghdād, and therefore had to stay there, provided the essence of the solution. The governorship of the East was added to Ṭāhir's responsibilities. He himself would make his headquarters in Khurāsān, while his numerous sons, nephews and cousins would deputize for him in his various other functions. His army would stay in Baghdād to police the city and the Sawād, and to cope with any other disturbance elsewhere.[1] In his home area Ṭāhir should not have much difficulty raising new forces for himself and for Ma'mūn when necessary. The price that he exacted for his services was considerable. In terms of money, it was a subsidy of 10 million dirhams from the central treasury.[2] In political terms the price was no less than complete autonomy for the whole region under Ṭāhir and his descendants. This bargain was struck through the good offices of Aḥmad b. Abī Khālid who had emerged as the strong arm of Ma'mūn from the moment he had decided to move to Baghdād.[3] Although he continued in the service of Ma'mūn until he died in 826/211, he actually refused to accept a formal appointment as *wazīr* or *kātib*.[4] Yet he was deeply involved in the management of Ma'mūn's government, especially in the affairs of the East. He had considerable influence with the Ṭāhirids and influence almost equal to theirs in their own region, where he was able to recruit the redoubtable Afshīn of Ushrūsana and his men into the army.[5] Ma'mūn's choice of this man, Aḥmad, at that particular turn of his policy had not been without reason. He was a member of the family of Abū Khālid, the leaders of the *abnā'*, who had continued to resist Ḥasan b. Sahl's policy in Baghdād.[6] While other members of the same family had taken and indeed changed sides in this struggle, Aḥmad had chosen to remain loyal to Ma'mūn. However, being so closely connected with the *abnā'*, he was an ideal instrument for reaching an agreement with them. Accordingly by choosing him as a close associate, Ma'mūn was practically announcing his willingness to reconcile this obdurate group. Aḥmad must have been a most valuable aid at the critical moment of Ma'mūn's arrival at Baghdād, and had probably arranged for his own family's reconciliation with Ma'mūn, in the same way

1 Ṭabarī, III, pp. 1039, 1043, 1044, 1102; Ṭayfūr, p. 232.
2 Ṭabarī, III, p. 1043; Ṭayfūr, p. 32; Ya'qūbī, *Buldān*, p. 308.
3 Ṭayfūr, pp. 5, 31–3; Jahshiyārī, p. 318; Ṭabarī, III, 1038.
4 Ṭayfūr, p. 216.
5 Ṭabarī, III, pp. 1044, 1064–6; Bal., *Futūḥ*, p. 430; Ya'qūbī, *Tārīkh*, vol. II, p. 457.
6 Azdī, *Mawṣil*, p. 341, 384; Ya'qūbī, *Tārīkh*, vol. II, pp. 439, 447; Ṭayfūr, p. 142; Jahshiyārī, pp. 302, 312; Ṭabarī, III, pp. 843, 883, 978, 1001, 1002, 1003, 1032.

as he was to arrange for the setting up of Ṭāhir in the East. Originally Aḥmad's family came from the district of Merv al-Rūd, and it is likely that, like the Ṭāhirids, they were of Hephthalite origin. The father Abū Khālid, whose personal name was Yazīd, became a high official in the administration of Hādī and Mahdī. It should be noted that his service was, at least in part, associated with army activities in the eastern regions.[1] Again this would indicate where his usefulness lay and would suggest that he did not sever his connection with the army. Indeed the emergence of his sons as leaders of the *abnā'* is a proof that they had their interests at heart.

Perhaps it is worth pausing, at this point, to consider another, different view of Aḥmad b. Abī Khālid, in order that the reader may get some idea of the problems involved in interpreting the source material. In his most exhaustive study of one aspect of this period, Sourdel has certainly collected all the available data. But it has to be said that some of his footnotes are superfluous, and that his understanding of the source material is often wrong.[2] It is not enough to lump together all the information collected from the sources without attempting a critical evaluation of it. In this case Sourdel, relying on a badly edited text as a source, accepts a copyist's mistake as a fact and thus asserts that Aḥmad was of Syrian origin.[3] This simple error makes him miss the point altogether, misleading us in the process. The author of this particular text was most hostile towards Aḥmad, and has nothing good to say about him. Furthermore, he accuses him of every possible vice including gluttony, homosexuality, ugliness, bad manners and even bad taste in food.[4] Carried away by this rabid hostility he also tries to cast doubt on his lineage. In this respect the editor reads the sentence concerned as, "wa kāna *shāmiyyan, mawlan li-Banī 'Āmir b. Lu'ayy*".[5] The reading *shāmiyyan*, i.e. Syrian, is a mistake of the editor or a copyist. Ibn Khallikān draws our attention to this common mistake of copyists, and points out that this word should read *sāmiyyan*, i.e. from the clan of Sāma.[6] The construction of the sentence also confirms that the reading and the meaning should be, "he was of the clan of Sāma as a client of the Banū 'Āmir b. Lu'ayy". The only Banū 'Āmir b. Lu'ayy we know was a branch of Quraysh, but our prejudiced author would not want to credit Aḥmad with such a distinguished relationship. Therefore he deliberately relates

[1] Ṭabarī, III, pp. 21, 369, 455, 520; Athīr, vol. VI, p. 51; Jahshiyārī, pp. 183–6; Ya'qūbī, *Buldān*, p. 247.
[2] Sourdel, *Vizirat*, p. 218, e.g. footnote 3, especially the reference to Jāḥiẓ.
[3] *Ibid.*, p. 219.
[4] Ṭayfūr, pp. 220–8.
[5] *Ibid.*, p. 216.
[6] Ibn Khallikān, vol. III, p. 357.

him to the clan of Sāma whose claims that they belonged to Quraysh through their ancestor Lu'ayy were disputable.[1] In other words this author was indirectly accusing Aḥmad of a false claim to a good ancestral line.

Aḥmad's arrangements for Ṭāhir and the East proved to be successful and the stability of the region was assured. Ṭāhir stayed in his position for two years until his death. Although there are reports that he had dropped Ma'mūn's name from the Friday sermon, such reports should not be taken seriously for two reasons.[2] Firstly Ṭāhir, who had been strongly opposed to Ma'mūn's Shī'ite gestures, may have had some objections or apprehensions about the continued assumption of the title *Imām*, which would have had to be mentioned in the sermon. Secondly, Ma'mūn himself did not pay any attention to these reports and dutifully on the advice of Aḥmad confirmed the appointment of Ṭāhir's son to succeed his father in the same position and with the same arrangements.[3]

Ma'mūn, then, turned to other pressing problems, the first of which was to bring into line the Syrian–'Irāqī troops who, in spite of the capture of their base at Raqqa, were now taking refuge in the strongholds of the *thughūr*. It took the Ṭāhirid forces of Baghdād almost five years to restore the Government's authority in these areas and destroy Kaysūm, the stronghold of their most prominent leader Naṣr b. Shabath of whose clan 'Uqayl we will hear again.[4] Once this was done the same forces were dispatched to Egypt, where for the first time revolts had seriously shaken the government's control. Since the last years of Rashīd's reign the Arabs of the Delta had stopped paying the newly imposed taxes. Amīn had been able to spare only a force of 1000 men from the *abnā'* to help contain the rebellion, but the civil war had put an end to all such efforts.[5] To complicate the situation the army in Egypt had become divided against itself and had carried on its own parallel civil war in the province. After his victory Ma'mūn had made all sorts of attempts to pacify the country, including dividing it between the rival parties there, but to no avail. Finally the Ṭāhirid army was able to impose law and order.[6] However, as nothing was done to reduce the objectionable taxes, the revolt started again almost immediately

[1] Ibn Ḥazm, *Jambara*, pp. 12, 13, 166–72, 173.
[2] Ṭabarī, III, p. 1064; Ṭayfūr, pp. 117, 130–1.
[3] Ṭabarī, III, pp. 1065–6; Ṭayfūr, pp. 3, 131, 132, 134.
[4] Ṭabarī, III, pp. 1067–72; Athīr, vol. VI, p. 198; Azdī, *Mawṣil*, p. 366.
[5] Maqrīzī, *Khiṭaṭ*, vol. I, pp. 80, 310.
[6] *Ibid.*, pp. 172–3, 178–80, 310; Ṭabarī, III, pp. 1086–94.

after the army's departure for Baghdād. This time it was even more serious because the indigenous population gradually joined the Arabs in their resistance and the whole country became enveloped in the struggle.[1] It took some time before the wrath of the central government was turned against this unexpected resumption of the revolt, because Ma'mūn was busy with plans for reorganizing his armies.

Perhaps the most important decision was to integrate all his military forces in a homogeneous army which would be composed of divisions to be deployed in accordance with the expected fields of action. There would be three divisions and each would include contingents from the *abnā'*, the Syrian–'Irāqī troops and the new troops from the East. The outcome of this plausible arrangement would be a standing army balanced enough to facilitate its control, and at the same time effective enough to diminish the likelihood of any particular group being able to establish its special interests in the areas of operation. The ultimate control of the army remained in Ma'mūn's hands, but of the three divisions one was under the command of the Ṭāhirid military governor of Baghdād; its function was to maintain law and order in that city, the Sawād and the nearby districts of southern 'Irāq and the Fārs province. In addition it would be held in reserve for any emergencies that might arise anywhere in the western regions of the empire. The other two divisions were to be under the command of Ma'mūn's son 'Abbās and his brother, Mu'taṣim, the heir apparent. The former was put in charge of Jazīra, the *thughūr* and the *'awāṣim*, i.e. he was given the main responsibility for the Byzantine borders and held in reserve for any trouble in Ādherbayjān. The latter was in charge of Egypt and Syria which would also mean that he was available for help on the Byzantine front.[2] For his administration Ma'mūn employed men most of whom had been trained under the Barmakids. It is significant that their appointments were merely as heads of departments directly responsible to him. In other words he meant to keep, as much as possible, the control of the army and the administration in his own hands without the mediation of an overall factotum like Faḍl b. Sahl.

In the midst of all these arrangements Ma'mūn made another about-turn. We remember that he had taken the title of *Imām*, to appeal to the Shī'ites, and though it had not had much effect he had continued to assume it. Now he proposed to take this function

[1] See below, p. 60.

[2] Ṭabarī, III, p. 1100.

seriously and guide the whole community to what he considered the right path; and if in the process he could effect a compromise between the opposing blocs in the empire, so much the better. The weakness of his previous attempt to reconcile the Shī'ites had been its lack of any substantial new ideological proposition at a time when every school of law, movement or sect was in the process of formulating its answers, not only to theological questions but also to the pressing social and political problems of the time. The Ḥanbalites had been steadily consolidating their position as the champions of orthodox Islam, and their notion of the paramount nature of revelation was being articulated to support their traditionalist interpretation of Islam. In contrast, the Mu'tazilites, hitherto a relatively obscure intellectual group, whose main concern had been with speculative theology, were putting forward strong arguments reconciling reason and revelation. This approach which clearly would allow religious dogma to develop in accordance with the needs of the times, had won them the sympathies of the Shī'ites. As in the case of their predecessors, the Qadarites of the late Umayyad period, the Mu'tazilites upheld tenets which were not void of implications for the political issues of the time.[1]

Ma'mūn seized on this system of ideas to effect the desired compromise and reconcile Shī'ite and orthodox ideologies. At first he encouraged and took part in elaborate discussions with the intellectual elite about the fundamental principles of Islam and their relation to all the contemporary issues, but always with a constant focus on the political significance of these questions. Finally, his decision was for the official adoption of the Mu'tazilite dogma. However the only tenet which was particularly emphasized was the Mu'tazilite insistence that the Qur'ān, the Word of God, was created and therefore could not be as eternal as God and was certainly less divine.[2] In other words the authority of revelation was not as paramount as the conservative Ḥanbalites were claiming, and in accordance with the Mu'tazilites, reason should be given its proper place in order to allow religious thinking to develop without undue hindrance. The logical political conclusion of this argument was that change was possible without a divinely guided ruler. This in itself shows that Ma'mūn was aware of the considerable change that had been taking place in the empire, and conscious of the strong resistance to it. One can only conclude that he was not only a

[1] Shaban, *Islamic History*, pp. 156–7.

[2] Ṭabarī, III, pp. 1040, 1098, 1099, 1105; Athīr, vol. VI, p. 288.

shrewd politician but also a progressive ruler. For almost a decade he continued to persuade his stubborn opponents of the feasibility of this politically imposed theological compromise, but to no avail. At last, and only months before his death in 833/218, while he was actually on the battlefield against the Byzantines, he tried to enforce religious conformity. He introduced what became known as the "inquisition", *miḥna*, which required that all dignitaries, especially those of Baghdād, must declare in public their adherence to the belief that the Qur'ān was created. Significantly, Aḥmad b. Ḥanbal was one of the very few who stubbornly refused to make such a declaration even in the face of torture.[1] Although this inquisition continued for fifteen years, under Ma'mūn's successors, it only helped the Ḥanbalites to sustain and strengthen their position and even finally enabled them to force the authorities to abandon this policy once and for all.[2] On the other hand the Shī'ites were content to see their opponents turning against each other and were not greatly interested in the whole controversy. However, after the repeal of Mu'tazilism and the official re-instatement of orthodoxy, the Ḥanbalites and the Shī'ites of Baghdād turned vehemently against each other.

The progressive attitude of Ma'mūn also shows to some extent in his fiscal policies. As mentioned before he had reduced the tax burden in the East by a quarter. Although it can be argued that this had been done in special circumstances, other measures confirm this was in accordance with his general policy. The taxes of Rayy were reduced by 2 million dirhams to 10 millions, and in the Sawād the *muqāsama* system was adjusted in favour of the taxpayer; the treasury's share was to be two fifths instead of half the produce.[3] Nevertheless when the district of Qumm demanded the same treatment as Rayy, this was not accepted, presumably because its taxes were thought to be reasonably assessed.[4] In Baghdād a new standard measure for grain was introduced to protect the consumer from being cheated by greedy merchants.[5] The effects of inflation on people of fixed incomes were recognized, and for the first time since the Umayyads, the salaries of government employees were increased.[6]

These liberal measures did not prevent problems arising simul-

[1] Ṭabarī, III, pp. 1112–31; Ṭayfūr, pp. 338–43.
[2] See below, p. 73.
[3] Ṭabarī, III, pp. 1030, 1039; Bal., *Futūḥ*, p. 320. Azdī, *Mawṣil*, p. 204.
[4] Ṭabarī, III, p. 1092; Azdī, *Mawṣil*, p. 368.
[5] Ṭabarī, III, pp. 1039, 1066; Athīr, vol. VI, p. 254; Ṭayfūr, p. 22.
[6] Ṭabarī, III, pp. 434–5; Jahshiyārī, p. 126.

taneously in three areas, the Byzantine front, Egypt and Ādherbayjān. The Byzantines, who had not taken advantage of the civil war and the subsequent disturbances, began to feel the impact of the recent efforts of Baghdād to control the *thughūr*. The Byzantine emperor started negotiations with Ma'mūn for the purpose of allowing trade to be resumed between their respective domains.[1] Ma'mūn's response was not favourable and a tense situation began to develop on this front. This tension was aggravated by conditions in Ādherbayjān where unrest had been fast turning into open revolt. The rebels were now making overtures to seek the help of the Byzantines, and were certainly continuing to trade with them. This was the formidable revolt of the Khurramiyya led by Bābak.

Any attempt to explain this revolt in religious terms is pointless, since the term Khurramiyya does not signify any specific relationship to any particular religion; the Persian word *khurram* meaning only "happy". It may have possibly been a component of a slogan of this revolt which was seized upon and used as a derogatory term by their opponents. It can also be noted that it was used to describe movements between which there could not possibly have been any relationship; very much as the term Khārijite had been used in earlier times.[2] The nature of this revolt can be explained by the socio-economic conditions of the region. Reference has already been made to the considerable influx of Arabs into this region and the pressure this immigration had put on its resources.[3] Although there are extensive fertile plains in this region, there are also many ranges of mountains that contain a wealth of mineral resources. Significantly the Arabs who had settled in the plains of Ādherbayjān were on good terms with the rebels. On the other hand the Arabs of the mountain ranges were most eager to fight the rebels, and were indeed at the very root of the problem.[4] These Arabs were in conflict even with their own cousins in the neighbouring region of Mawṣil.[5] The cause of this conflict was made crystal clear to Ma'mūn when he received a delegation from the region. They presented him with no less than forty samples of minerals from the area and plainly stated that these were the cause of all the fighting in Ādherbayjān.[6] Ma'mūn did not need this vivid reminder of the long and

[1] Bal., *Futūḥ*, p. 192; Ṭayfūr, p. 284.

[2] Mas'ūdī, *Murūj*, vol. VI, pp. 186–8; Miskawayh, vol. II, pp. 278, 299; Ṣābī, *Wuzarā'*, p. 343.

[3] See above, p. 26.

[4] Azdī, *Mawṣil*, pp. 356, 358, 364, 379–81, 383; Ṭabarī, III, pp. 1071–2, 1096; Ya'qūbī, *Tārīkh*, vol. II, pp. 445, 473.

[5] Azdī, *Mawṣil*, pp. 359, 366–77.

[6] *Ibid.*, p. 354.

complicated conflict. The central government, on its part, had long been active in trying to lay its hands on a share of this wealth. Since Manṣūr's time attempts had been made to tax the salt mines and the well-known oil deposits of this region.[1]

It is a fact that crude oil was a well-known and widely used commodity in those days and even earlier. Surface seepages have for long been a source of oil and bitumen and in certain areas of Persia gas-flares were used by the Zoroastrians. In the eighth century such deposits existed and the oil was referred to as *nafṭ*. Geographers, historians and jurists were absolutely clear about the distinction between *nafṭ*, crude oil, and *qār* or *qīr*, tar or pitch.[2] Abū Ḥanīfa, the famous theologian who died in 767/150 defined *nafṭ* as the fluid of a mountain that trickled to the bottom of a well, and was used as fuel for lighting a fire.[3] Another jurist described it as a mineral that appeared by itself, *ẓāhir*, in contrast to ore and gold that needed to be mined.[4] It seems, then, that the commonest way of obtaining crude oil was to dig a well in areas where seepage had appeared and simply skim off the substance which floated on top of the water. Marco Polo was not exaggerating when he described what he saw centuries later in Baku.[5] It is interesting to notice that we have references in our sources to the existence of *nafṭ* in many areas where great oil deposits are known to exist today. Such areas are Iran, 'Irāq, Arabia, Central Asia, Egypt and Ādherbayjān.[6] This *nafṭ* was not all of the same quality and its degree of purity differed from one place to another; the determining criterion was the colour, which varied from almost transparent to green and black. The best quality crude oil known at the time was that of the troubled region of Ādherbayjān.[7]

While pitch, tar and similar bitumen products were used, among other things, for caulking ships and curing camel skin disease, crude oil was used for purposes which required a more combustible sub-

[1] Bal., *Futūḥ*, p. 210.

[2] Abū Yūsuf, *Kharāj*, p. 61; Yaḥyā b. Ādam, *Kharāj*, ed. A. M. Shākir, Cairo, A.H. 1347, p. 32; Ibn Ḥawqal, *Ṣūrat al-Arḍ*, ed. J. H. Kramers, Leiden, 1938–39, pp. 256, 299, 488, 515; Iṣṭakhrī, pp. 75, 92, 313; Maqdisī, pp. 331, 332, 402.

[3] *Lisān*, *s.v. nfṭ*.

[4] Māwardī, *al-Aḥkām al-Sulṭāniyya*, ed. R. Enger, Bonn, 1853, pp. 341–2.

[5] Col. Henry Yule, *The Book of Sir Marco Polo the Venetian*, London, 1875, vol. v, pp. 48–51.

[6] Maqdisī, p. 402; Iṣṭakhrī, pp. 75, 92, 155; Ḥawqal, pp. 190, 254, 256, 300; Mas'ūdī, *Murūj*, vol. II, p. 25; Mas'ūdī, *Tanbīh wa al-Ishrāf*, ed. M. J. de Goeje, Leiden, 1894, pp. 60, 61; Maqrīzī, *Khiṭaṭ*, vol. 1, p. 28; Yāqūt, *Buldān*, vol. 1, p. 328; Hamdullah Mustawfī, *Nuzhat al-Qulūb*, ed. G. LeStrange, London, 1915, pp. 41, 207.

[7] Yāqūt, *Buldān*, vol. 1, p. 328; Mas'ūdī, *Tanbīh*, p. 60; Iṣṭakhrī, p. 190.

stance. The earliest example of such a use recorded in our sources was in 737/119 but thereafter references begin to occur more frequently in our sources, testifying to its use for many purposes and notably in warfare.[1] In 752/134, and significantly in 'Umān on the east Arabian coast, it was used for shooting flaming arrows at the enemy;[2] in 777/160 by a naval expedition against the Indians;[3] in 811/197 in the siege of Baghdād;[4] and in 837/222 in the fight against Bābak.[5] With this increasing use new weapons were soon developed similar to flame-throwers and what is popularly known today as a Molotov cocktail.[6] It was also widely used not much later in naval warfare in the Persian Gulf and southern 'Irāq.[7] Peaceful purposes included its use for lighting the two great mosques in Makka and Madīna until it was replaced by candles in 860/246.[8] Neither the Arabs nor the Byzantines were blind to the value of this important commodity.

As suggested before, the question of taxation added a new dimension to the issue of the minerals of Ādherbayjān. It must be realized that Islam had not originally contemplated any tax on minerals. Although silver mines had existed close enough to Madīna they had not been of particular importance, and the question of taxation had passed almost unnoticed. On the other hand, it had been decided that treasure trove should be treated as booty and therefore one fifth should go to the treasury. In legal terms the word *rikāẓ* had been used to denote treasure trove.[9] After the conquests and their aftermath it was realized that there were many kinds of mineral resources in the provinces that ought to come under some form of taxation. Jurists of the various schools of law became engaged

1 Ash'arī al-Qummī, *Kitāb al-Maqālāt wa al-Firaq*, ed, M. J. Mashkūr, Teheran, 1963, p. 33.

2 Athīr, vol. v, p. 347; also Ṭabarī, III, p. 78.

3 Ṭabarī, III, p. 476.

4 *Ibid.*, p. 869; Azdī, *Mawṣil*, p. 330.

5 Ṭabarī, III, pp. 1202, 1211, 1215.

6 Athīr, vol. VII, p. 362, vol. VIII, pp. 129, 205; Miskawayh, vol. I, pp. 282, 311; Thābit al-Ṣābī, *Tārīkh Akhbār al-Qarāmiṭa*, ed. Z. Bakkār, Damascus, 1970, pp. 19, 27, 59, 73.

7 Ṭabarī, III, pp. 1636, 1869, 1959, 2043, 2050, 2060, 2067; Athīr, vol. VII, pp. 264, 266–7, 270; Miskawayh, vol. II, p. 46; Maqdisī, p. 12; Abū Bakr al-Ṣūlī, *Akhbār al-Rāḍī* . . ., ed. J. H. Dunne, London, 1935, p. 244.

8 Ṭabarī, III, p. 1471. For other uses see: Ṭabarī, III, pp. 1236, 1415, 1511, 1578, 1581 1693, 1731, 2219; Athīr, vol. VI, p. 188, vol. VII, pp. 44, 98, 124, 186, vol. VIII, p. 222, vol. IX, p. 423; Miskawayh, vol. II, p. 80; Maqrīzī, *Khiṭaṭ*, vol. II, p. 196; Ṣābī, *Wuzarā'*, p. 19; Jahshiyārī, p. 300; Abbār, p. 101; Hilāl al-Ṣābī, *Rusūm Dār al-Khilāfa*, ed. Mīkhā'īl 'Awād, Baghdād, 1964, p. 10; Ibn al-Qalānisī, *Dhayl Tārīkh Dimashq*, ed. H. F. Amedroz, London, 1908, pp. 20, 40, 47.

9 Ibn Ḥanbal, *Musnad*, ed. al-Sā'ātī, Cairo, A.H. 1357, vol. IX, pp. 24–6.

in lengthy discussions about the definition of the term *rikāz*, and whether it should be extended to cover only some or all mineral substances; and if so, how should these be taxed.[1] Being more practical, the treasury decided that all minerals must be taxed to the tune of one fifth of the net produce. Of course, this process was put into effect gradually when and wherever possible. As early as Manṣūr, Ādherbayjān, where taxes had first been introduced on salt and crude oil, had become a major target for the execution of the plans of the central treasury.[2] With a variety of as many as forty mineral substances and the increasing aggressiveness and efficiency of the tax-collecting apparatus, the indigenous population of the region had had good reason for their apprehensiveness towards and mistrust of the central government. When the Arab immigrants forcibly appropriated some of their mines themselves,[3] the people of this unfortunate region had no alternative but to resort to armed resistance to protect their rights. The Byzantines, who were eager to have continued access to these minerals from a source so near at hand, were understandably willing to support this rebellion.[4] With this support and under the vigorous leadership of Bābak the rebels were able to defeat the successive expeditions Ma'mūn sent against them. Faced with this situation Ma'mūn decided to go to the Byzantine front and take command of it himself, in spite of the fact that he had delegated this responsibility to his son and brother. In fact the latter had his hands full in Egypt.

As mentioned before, the continued unrest among the Arabs of Egypt and their division into factions supporting the opposite sides in the civil war had created problems for Ma'mūn which had been temporarily brought under control by swift military action.[5] However, Ma'mūn's new governor had done nothing to alleviate the effects of excessive taxation, and on the contrary had introduced stringent measures for tax collection.[6] It seems that Islam had begun

1 Ibn Sallām, *Amwāl*, pp. 337–42.

2 Bal., *Futūḥ*, p. 210; Qudāma, Shemesh, *Kharāj*, p. 104; Ibn Khurdādhbeh, *Kitāb al-Masālik wa al-Mamālik*, ed. M. J. de Goeje, Leiden, 1889, pp. 34, 38; Abū Yūsuf, *Kharāj*, p. 61.

3 Azdī, *Mawṣil*, p. 358.

4 Fortunately I received the day I wrote this passage an offprint of an article by my good friend M. Rekaya, "Mise au point sur Théophobe et l'alliance de Bābek avec Théophile", *Byzantion*, T. XLIV, Bruxelles, 1974, pp. 43–67, which contains all the relevant references, although its author does not agree with the point of view expressed here.

5 See above, p. 53.

6 Maqrīzī, *Khiṭaṭ*, vol. 1, pp. 80, 311.

to strike roots among the Copts but no consequential adjustments had been made to allow for the new status of the converts. Furthermore, as a result of conversion, new ties and common interests had been established between Arabs and Copts. Under the circumstances, for the first time an Arab–Coptic revolt broke out and spread all over the country.[1] Mu'taṣim tried to cope with the situation, but when it became clear that he was unsuccessful, Ma'mūn had to leave the Byzantine front and come to Egypt with an army that included the renowned Afshīn and his men. With such a force the revolt was soon suppressed and Ma'mūn wisely proceeded to revise the land-tax system that had been in operation for almost two centuries. He realized that the doubling of the tax rate to two dinārs under Mahdī had not been unfair in the light of inflation. After all a judge's salary in Egypt had risen from 10 dinārs a month in 749/131 to 30 dinārs in 772/155, to 163 dinārs in 813/198 and to 200 dinārs in 827/212.[2] But Ma'mūn also realized that, because of the increased land holdings of the Arabs and the gradual conversion of the Copts to Islam, the Church, which had provided the basic machinery for the assessment and collection of taxes, had lost its usefulness for this purpose. Therefore, a new system, the *qabāla*, was introduced, by which one member of a local tax community contracted to undertake to pay to the treasury a fixed sum, and was then given the responsibility of collecting the tax himself. He would also undertake to make all necessary repairs to the irrigation system, and the expenses would be deducted from his payment to the treasury on an agreed basis. In return he was promised that unusual circumstances would be taken into consideration in case of arrears. To ensure the propriety of the process, it was conducted in the main mosque in the capital, Fusṭāṭ, where the fixed sum for each locality was announced, but not auctioned; and the person accepting would enter into a contract for four years.[3] Ma'mūn also put Copts in charge of some districts where they would have Muslims as their deputies.[4] This step was probably meant to fill the gap created by the absence of Church officials, and at the same time to ensure the acceptance of these appointees among all their subjects. Finally, while in Egypt he took a seemingly unimportant action that had ramifications later. He tried to normalize relations with the Nubians to the south who sent

[1] *Ibid.*, pp. 172–4, vol. II, p. 261; Ya'qūbī, *Tārīkh*, vol. II, p. 466; Kindī, *Wulāt*, pp. 394–400, 423–4.
[2] Maqrīzī, *Khiṭaṭ*, vol. I, p. 99; Kindī, *Wulāt*, pp. 354, 369, 421, 435.
[3] Maqrīzī, *Khiṭaṭ*, vol. I, p. 82.
[4] Sa'īd b. al-Baṭrīq, *Naẓm al-jawāhir*, ed. L. Cheikho, Paris, 1909, pp. 58–9.

a delegation to complain to him about Muslim encroachments on their territories.[1] From this point on Egypt's relations with the south and indeed with the rest of Africa were to become an important issue.

Having finished with Egypt Ma'mūn wasted no time in returning to the Byzantine front and starting action there in earnest. His attacks were two pronged and his general aim was to establish new *'awāṣim* across the Taurus mountains, the centre of which would be at the cross-roads of Ṭawāna, Tyana, where he actually settled a strong contingent.[2] It is most important to note that the Byzantines then asked again for peace, negotiating for the specific purpose of establishing points of communication and allowing trade to flow freely between the two empires.[3] Ma'mūn, however, refused and as if to emphasize his determination to win on his own terms began to conscript new troops from Egypt, Syria, 'Irāq and even Baghdād itself.[4] This last measure can only indicate that he was not getting enough of the hoped-for recruits from the East, in spite of his arduous efforts in this respect. No new development took place before his death shortly afterwards in Tarsus in 833/218 and it was left to his brother and successor Mu'taṣim to continue with these policies.

As soon as Mu'taṣim was proclaimed the new ruler in Tarsus and practically on the battlefield, an attempt was made to replace him by 'Abbās, Ma'mūn's son. We do not know the principal instigators of this attempt, but as 'Abbās himself supported his uncle it was doomed to failure.[5] Ma'mūn's appointment of his brother as his heir is a clear indication of his constant attempts to reach a compromise. During the civil war Mu'taṣim had opposed his brother, yet the latter, who had an adult son, had preferred to overlook the lapse and appoint the person better suited to the circumstances. It can be argued that it had been Rashīd's will that his sons should succeed each other, but it has to be admitted that the civil war had changed all that. It is a fact that both Mu'taṣim and 'Abbās had close ties with the army but the former's association with Afshīn indicates that he had closer ties with the new arrivals from the East. It must have been well known that he had certain plans for the army for he proceeded to put them into effect as soon as he came to power. He ordered the new stronghold at Tyana to be dismantled and the men

1 Maqrīzī, *Khiṭaṭ*, vol. I, p. 198.
2 Ṭabarī, III, pp. 1102–11.
3 *Ibid.*, p. 1110.
4 *Ibid.*, p. 1112.
5 *Ibid.*, p. 1164; Ya'qūbī, *Tārīkh*, vol. II, p. 471.

settled there to be withdrawn before he and his army returned to Baghdād.[1] When the Byzantines took this as a sign of weakness and attacked the other strongholds across the Taurus range, he marched back and inflicted a severe defeat upon them.[2] He then sent his army under the command of Afshīn to fight Bābak.

Before returning to Baghdād and again on the battlefield, Mu'taṣim discovered yet another conspiracy to replace him by 'Abbās. This time it is clear that it was led by a combination of Ṭāhirid men and the *abnā'*. It seems that the latter had not given up hope of regaining their power, and had encouraged certain suspicions on the part of the Ṭāhirids of Baghdād about the new plans for the army. However, the conspiracy was discovered in time and the leaders, including 'Abbās, were severely punished.[3] Having firmly established his authority, Mu'taṣim pushed ahead with his plans for the army which were embodied in building the new city of Sāmarrā about sixty miles to the north of Baghdād. It has to be remembered that his father had found Baghdād unsuitable, and had therefore moved his headquarters to Raqqa. During the civil war a good part of the city had been destroyed and Mu'taṣim decided that if he had to rebuild anywhere, it was better to build anew altogether away from the demands of population of the city. Although by moving the central government departments to Sāmarrā he meant it to be his capital, it was significantly known by the public as the 'Askar, the army camp.[4] Indeed, this was the true purpose of building the new city. There is every indication that Mu'taṣim built Sāmarrā as a clear announcement of his willingness to accept new recruits from anywhere. This open invitation was accompanied by a massive campaign to persuade more of the massive population of the East and the various peoples of the Caucasus regions, mainly the Armenians and the Khazars, to join the Muslim armies.[5] Ma'mūn's efforts in this respect had been more successful than Rashīd's; with a little more perseverance especially when Islam had begun to strike roots among these peoples, Mu'taṣim was determined to give these sustained efforts the best possible chance for ultimate success. The new city, and indeed the new opportunities that these peoples saw in the wealthiest and most powerful empire of the time, soon persuaded

[1] Ṭabarī, III, p. 1164.
[2] *Ibid.*, pp. 1234–62.
[3] *Ibid.*, pp. 1249–50, 1256–67.
[4] Ya'qūbī, *Buldān*, p. 264.
[5] Ḥawqal, pp. 467–8; Mas'ūdī, *Murūj*, vol. VII, p. 118; Iṣṭakhrī, pp. 291–2; Athīr, vol. VI, p. 319; Bal., *Futūḥ*, p. 203; Ṭabarī, III, p. 1194.

many to enrol in its service. Reports that Mu'taṣim had to move his new troops from Baghdād because they were posing a threat to the population there should not be taken seriously, because the same reports tell us that it was the people of Baghdād that were harassing these troops who, because of their small numbers, were not able to defend themselves.[1]

These new troops were the so-called "Turks". It must be said without hesitation that this is a most misleading misnomer which has led some scholars to harp *ad nauseam* on an utterly unfounded interpretation of the following era, during which they unreasonably ascribe all events to Turkish domination. In fact the great majority of these troops were not Turks. It has been frequently pointed out that Arabic sources use the term Turk in a very loose manner. The Hephthalites are referred to as Turks, so are the peoples of Gurgān, Khwārizm and Sīstān.[2] Indeed, with the exception of the Soghdians, Arabic sources refer to all peoples not subjects of the Sāsānian empire as Turks. In Sāmarrā separate quarters were provided for new recruits from every locality. The group from Farghāna were called after their district, and the name continued in usage because it was easy enough to pronounce. But such groups as the Ishtākhanjiyya, the Isbījābiyya and groups from similar small localities who were in small numbers at first, were lumped together under the general term Turks, because of the obvious difficulty the Arabs had in pronouncing such foreign names.[3] The Khazars who also came from small localities which could not even be identified, as they were mostly nomads, were perhaps the only group that deserved to be called Turks on grounds of racial affinity. However, other groups from Transcaucasia were classed together with the Khazars under this general description.[4]

The mistake is compounded by another which is even more astounding, and it is high time that it was utterly refuted; this is the generally accepted belief that these troops were slaves. All studies of this subject simply assume that the empire was run, ruled, policed and defended by slaves; and that this practice spread to all regions and continued for centuries. This is not only a gross misunderstanding of human nature, but it also goes against the over-

[1] Ṭabarī, III, pp. 1179–81; Azdī, *Mawṣil*, p. 416.
[2] Shaban, *The 'Abbāsid Revolution*, pp. 6–7; Mas'ūdī, *Murūj*, vol. II, p. 195, vol. III, p. 254, vol. VI, p. 422; Khurdādhbeh, p. 178; Ṭabarī, III, pp. 798, 891; Ibn Khallikān, vol. VI, p. 403.
[3] Ya'qūbī, *Buldān*, p. 264; Mas'ūdī, *Murūj*, vol. VII, p. 122.
[4] Ya'qūbī, *Buldān*, pp. 258–62.

whelming evidence to the contrary in our sources. This misconception was quite obviously inspired by studies in Ottoman History which were projected backwards to explain earlier developments. If the Ottomans had had "slaves" forming the "ruling institution", then it was assumed without any foundation that similar institutions were almost inherent in Islamic society. Fortunately, modern scholarship in the field of Ottoman history has come forward to challenge these erroneous conclusions that have survived far too long.[1]

In this case, it cannot be over-emphasized that Mu'taṣim was following the practice, started under his father, Rashīd, and continued under Ma'mūn on a wider scale, of persuading the chiefs and princes of the East to enrol in the army of the central government. Under Rashīd all the 'Abbāsiyya had been made *mawālī* of the ruler.[2] Under Ma'mūn only the leaders had been made his *mawālī*; thus Ṭāhir, originally a *mawlā*, or client of the Arab clan of Khuzā'a, had been created *mawlā Amīr al-Mu'minīn*, and had retained control over his own men.[3] Mu'taṣim threw the door wide open for men to come in groups under their own chiefs, or individually if they so desired. In most cases they came in groups, and we find many instances where their chiefs were native princes from the East. Afshīn, who was a prince of the region of Ushrūsana in Soghdiana, was certainly the prime example of such princes, but mention is also made of others from the same area, such as Kaydar, Dīvdād, Bukhārā-khudā, Būzbāreh, Sül-tegin, Marzbān b. Türkesh, 'Ujayf b. 'Anbasa, Khāqān Artūg, Bānījūr, Shīr-i-Bāmyān, and 'Amr of Farghāna with his retinue of princes.[4] Following an ancient institution in the East their followers formed corps that were called *chākars*, a Persian word meaning servants.[5] These *chākars* performed for their leaders the same military service that the knights of the Middle Ages in Europe performed for their kings. This whole institution was now trans-

[1] M. I. Kunt, "Ethnic-regional solidarity in the 17th century Ottoman Establishment", *International Journal of Middle East Studies*, vol. v, no. 3, June 1974, pp. 233–9; see also the introductory note by the editor S. J. Shaw, pp. 231–2.

[2] See above, p. 31.

[3] Khaṭīb, *Tārīkh Baghdād*, Cairo, 1931, vol. IX, p. 353; Ibn Khallikān, vol. II, p. 309, vol. III, p. 88.

[4] Ṭabarī, III, pp. 1042, 1169, 1194, 1197, 1203, 1212, 1222, 1225, 1228, 1239, 1241, 1246, 1301, 1312, 1313, 1335, 1373, 1474, 1605, 1616, 1657, 2022–3; Bal., *Futūḥ*, p. 431; Ya'qūbī, *Tārīkh*, vol. II, pp. 474, 475, 477; Ya'qūbī, *Buldān*, pp. 260, 290, 293–4; Ḥawqal, p. 499; Khurdādhbeh, pp. 40, 180; Iṣṭakhrī, pp. 291, 323; Maqrīzī, *Khiṭaṭ* vol. II, p. 251.

[5] Marvazī, *On China, The Turks and India*, Arabic Text, ed. V. Minorsky, London, 1942, p. 18.

planted from the East into the heart of the empire. The *chākars* continued in the service of their own leaders, who in turn were created *mawālī* of the ruler.[1] Other men who came individually and proved their abilities were made *chākars* of the ruler himself. The term used for this position was *ghulām* (pl. *ghilmān*) which is the exact equivalent in Arabic of the Persian term *chākar*. This latter term was Arabicized as *shākiriyya*. It is to be noted that the *shākiriyya* in Baghdād could only have been those of the Ṭāhirid forces who performed the task of policing the city itself and the Sawād.

Any *ghulām* of the ruler who proved his military ability could be promoted to the rank of *qā'id*, commander, and if he had special administrative talents he could be made *waṣīf* and then *khādim*.[2] These last terms should not be confused with the same words meaning kinds of domestic servants. They must be understood to denote certain ranks of employees of the ruler through whom he was afforded a degree of control over the machinery of government. In fact these were not much different from the *mawālī* of Manṣūr, and the new titles were due to the fact that the term *mawlā* had taken another twist to cover leaders who rendered military support to the ruler.

The highest rank a *mawlā* or a *khādim* or indeed anyone subordinate to the ruler could attain was *'abd* (pl. *'abīd*), slave, of *Amīr al-Mu'minīn*. As early as Abū Muslim a new phrase had been coined to describe loyal subjects, *'abīd al-sam' wa al-ṭā'a*, i.e. (those like) slaves who hearken and obey.[3] As this phrase had continued in usage it is possible to conclude that in the atmosphere of the time and considering the other titles discussed, the title of *'abd* was meant to denote a subject whose loyalty was beyond any doubt.[4] There are very many examples of men who could not have possibly have been slaves taking pride in describing themselves as, or being addressed with, this new title.[5] In fact Ṣābī, a high official of later 'Abbāsid administration, who was in a position to know the rules of protocol, tells us that *khādim* and *'abd* were the highest ranks to which anybody could aspire.[6]

1 Ṭabarī, III, pp. 8, 928, 1373, 1427, 1605; Athīr, vol. VII, p. 32; Ibn A'tham, vol. II, f. 271A.
2 Jahshiyārī, pp. 258, 276; Ibn Manẓūr, *Lisān*, s.v. *wld*; Ibn Khaldūn, *Muqaddima*, p. 684.
3 Ibn A'tham, vol. II, f. 235B.
4 Abū Shujā', *Dhayl* . . ., ed. H. F. Amedroz, Cairo, 1916, p. 216.
5 Ṭabarī, III, pp. 397, 572, 574, 700, 1096, 1158, 1223, 1260, 1311, 1316, 1327; Athīr, vol. VI, p. 375.
6 Ṣābī, *Rusūm*, p. 107.

Although we are in a relatively good position to know individual names and the original places from which the princes of the East had come, we unfortunately have no information about the recruited Khazars. We are faced only with new names of army commanders of whose origins we know nothing. Yet the existence of Khazars in the army leads us to believe that men such as Bughā, Yermesh, Waṣīf and Ītākh were in fact their leaders.[1] It is possible that such men were chiefs of nomadic groups vaguely identified as Khazars or Turks, without attachment to any specific place. The fact that Bughā was Mu'taṣim's brother-in-law indicates that he must have been a man of considerable standing among his own people.[2] Reports that Ītākh and Ashnās had been bought as slaves and then freed only to attain very high positions are almost certainly fictitious, and were probably put forward by their opponents.[3] It is highly improbable that the prince of Bāmyān would easily agree to be in the service of Ītākh if the latter had indeed once been a slave.[4]

Other reports that Mu'taṣim commissioned the buying of Turkish slaves from central Asia, and that as many as 4000 had been bought to form the nucleus of his army even during Ma'mūn's lifetime, are surely greatly exaggerated since the Arabic sources are least reliable when it comes to figures.[5] Moreover slaves, particularly Turkish slaves, men or women, were not cheap to say the least.[6] It seems that these isolated reports have confused the issue and in the process confused scholars as well. Mu'taṣim, in his efforts to take every possible precaution against the absorption of the new recruits and their involvement with local interests, had prohibited intermarriage between the civil and the military communities. As a result of this he had to buy female slaves and marry them to members of his army; and to encourage the practice, he even allowed for such wives in the stipends of their husbands.[7] In short, the myth that Turkish slaves were the mainstay of the army at that time has no foundation whatever.

Mu'taṣim was a man of considerable military ability, and he certainly knew that slaves would not make good fighters. His sound judgment in these matters is revealed by his choice of Afshīn and his men from the mountainous region of Ushrūsana (*Kūhbāniyya*,

1 Ṭabarī, III, p. 1383; Ya'qūbī, *Buldān*, p. 262.
2 Athīr, vol. VII, p. 62.
3 Ṭabarī, III, pp. 1017, 1383.
4 *Ibid.*, pp. 1335, 1373.
5 Ya'qūbī, *Buldān*, p. 255; Mas'ūdī, *Murūj*, vol. VII, p. 118.
6 Ḥawqal, pp. 435, 465.
7 Ya'qūbī, *Buldān*, pp. 258–9.

mountaineers) to combat Bābak and his followers who were defending a similar terrain.[1] Although these rebels had been defying the central government for two decades, Afshīn was soon able to crush their revolt. Returning triumphantly to Sāmarrā, he seems to have entertained some ambitions of getting the same price for his support as the Ṭāhirids, i.e. complete autonomy in his region in Soghdiana and possibly some control over neighbouring princes.[2] Mu'taṣim could not afford to pay this price because the Sāmānids, protégés of the Ṭāhirids, were already in charge of the whole region and were on very good terms with their patrons.[3] This delicate balance in the East which had been so recently established, would have been completely destroyed if Afshīn had been allowed to tamper with it. Expecting great rewards for his services, he found himself instead in prison where he died soon after. However, his men continued in the service of Mu'taṣim, and even his son was soon to be found among the commanders of the army.[4]

In Ṭabaristān where Islam had spread since the time of Mahdī there was an unexpected upheaval. Māzyār, the prince, who had prided himself on being a *mawlā* of Ma'mūn and had been very co-operative with his government, began to show signs of disagreement, particularly with the Ṭāhirids.[5] Being a member of one of the ancient ruling families, he apparently objected to being subordinated to the *parvenu* Ṭāhirids.[6] Furthermore he seems to have experienced some difficulties in controlling his subjects. The merchants of the prosperous ports on the Caspian, relying on their good connections in the Ṭāhirid domains, began to defy the authority of his tax-collectors.[7] In addition Ma'mūn had established a garrison at Chālūs, a move that must have undermined the authority of Māzyār in his territory.[8] It also seems that members of this garrison had taken advantage of their position to acquire lands that had been public property.[9] When Māzyār's patience was exhausted, he simply arrested all members of the garrison who were mainly Arabs and *abnā'*.[10] He also ordered the walls of the defiant ports to be razed.[11]

1 Ṭabarī, III, pp. 1188, 1190, 1196, 1199, 1203, 1205, 1219.
2 *Ibid.*, pp. 1303–18.
3 Athīr, vol. VI, p. 362, vol. VII, p. 192; Ḥawqal, p. 467; Maqrīzī, *Khiṭaṭ*, vol. I, p. 173.
4 Ṭabarī, III, p. 1664.
5 Ya'qūbī, *Tārīkh*, vol. II, p. 477; Mas'ūdī, *Murūj*, vol. VII, p. 137.
6 Ṭabarī, III, p. 1268.
7 *Ibid.*, pp. 1271, 1272, 1278, 1298–9.
8 Ibn Rustah, *al-A'lāq al-Nafīsa*, ed. M. J. de Goeje, Leiden, 1892, p. 151.
9 Ṭabarī, III, pp. 1269, 1270, 1277.
10 *Ibid.*, pp. 1273–4, 1278.
11 *Ibid.*, p. 1275.

Both Mu'taṣim and the Ṭāhirids moved fast, and Māzyār was quickly arrested and replaced by a more pliable member of the same family.[1]

In contrast to Ma'mūn, Mu'taṣim was not a political animal. In the internal policies of the empire he followed his brother's steps; some tax anomalies were adjusted, and support for the Mu'tazilites continued unabated.[2] In the building of Sāmarrā plans were made for shops and such *mustaghallāt* that netted as much as 10 million dirhams a year.[3] In the administration there was no doubt who was in charge of the army but in the fiscal field he introduced a new element. Hitherto this responsibility had always been given to men with long experience in government service, but Mu'taṣim in his straightforward military manner decided that it should be left to financiers. It is probable that he also thought that such an important section of the population should be represented in government. In the light of the participation of the merchants of Baghdād in the civil war and especially when the capital had been moved to Sāmarrā, such representation was a gesture towards these men whose economic powers could not be ignored. One of the wealthiest merchants of Baghdād, Muḥammad b. 'Abdulmalik al-Zayyāt, was chosen as a *kātib/wazīr*, a position that he held for 12 years throughout the reigns of Mu'taṣim and his son.[4] It was during this period that many of the rich 'Irāqī families of non-Arab origin began to move into various departments, not only of the central government, but also those of the provinces. Although many of them were big landowners, their interests were certainly intertwined with those of the big merchants in the capital and the provincial towns. Very soon and for a long time they were to dominate and practically monopolize the key positions in government, handing them down from father to son for generations.[5]

However, the most influential figure in Mu'taṣim's reign was the chief judge of Sāmarrā, Aḥmad b. Abī Duwād. He was undeniably an Arab, and of course a Mu'tazilite, but these facts do not explain his power at that time. He seems to have been behind all Mu'taṣim's decisions, even in fiscal matters, to the extent that he was able to persuade him to pay two million dirhams from his own treasury for clearing and dredging a river in Farghāna in Central Asia.[6] Of

[1] *Ibid.*, pp. 1275–303.

[2] *Ibid.*, p. 1272; Bal., *Futūḥ*, pp. 143–4.

[3] Ya'qūbī, *Buldān*, pp. 257–64.

[4] Ṭabarī, III, pp. 1183–4.

[5] *Ibid.*, p. 1331.

[6] *Ibid.*, pp. 1253, 1326; Ya'qūbī, *Tārīkh*, vol. II, p. 478; Mas'ūdī, *Murūj*, vol. VII, p. 103.

course one can argue that he was merely going along with the ruler's plans of encouraging the people of the region to enrol in his service by showing them how much they would gain from their co-operation. But then the question arises: what does a judge have to do with such matters? As it was an exceptional case, no firm conclusions can be drawn from it other than that Mu'taṣim had great faith in the wisdom of this particular man.

One important feature of Mu'taṣim's reign demonstrates the increasing volume of trade through the Indian Ocean with East Africa, South and South-East Asia and the Far East. Indians had started piratical activities throughout the Persian Gulf and many of them had immigrated into the region of Baṣra and threatened its communications with Wāsiṭ to the north. Again Mu'taṣim moved fast and put an end to this double threat to the prospering trade.[1] Until the end of his reign he seems to have objected to a certain measure which the merchant *wazīr*, Ibn al-Zayyāt, did in fact introduce soon after his death when he must have had more freedom to act. This measure was the abolition of all taxes on merchandise coming in through the ports of the Persian Gulf.[2] It is arguable that this could have resulted in a reduction of prices, but as this trade was mostly in luxury goods it would have benefited only the rich. Moreover, Ibn al-Zayyāt could not have been unaware of his fellow merchants' gain from such a concession.

Mu'taṣim was succeeded by his son, Wāthiq, who ruled for five uneventful years 842–7/227–32. Everything continued as it had been under his father, and he does not seem to have been much interested in ruling. During his short life he left the administration to Ibn al-Zayyāt. On the military side he divided the responsibility for the defence of the empire between two of his most outstanding generals, Ashnās in the west and Ītākh in the east.[3] This arrangement had nothing to do with the domains of the Ṭāhirids who were in charge of the East in addition to policing Baghdād and the Sawād. When 'Abdullah b. Ṭāhir died, his son was duly appointed to succeed him in the same position with the same responsibilities.[4]

The only important development at this time was a delayed reaction in Baghdād to the continued imposition of Mu'tazilism.[5] Some of the leaders of the *abnā'*, supported by the same conservative ele-

[1] Ṭabarī, III, pp. 1166–8; Mas'ūdī, *Tanbīh*, p. 355; Bal., *Futūḥ*, p. 446.

[2] Ṭabarī, III, p. 1363; Ya'qūbī, *Tārīkh*, vol. II, p. 483.

[3] Ya'qūbī, *Tārīkh*, vol. II, p. 479.

[4] Ṭabarī, III, pp. 1338–9.

[5] Ya'qūbī, *Tārīkh*, vol. II, p. 482.

ments that had appeared during the civil war, organized a resistance movement against the inquisition.[1] Although this movement was soon suppressed and its leaders executed or imprisoned, it seems to have had repercussions far reaching enough to change the course of events in the following years.

[1] Ṭabarī, III, pp. 1343–9.

4

THE ORIGINS OF THE *IQṬĀʿ*

For the researcher in Islamic history the study of the next period of almost a quarter of a century 847–70/232–56 ought to be an easy task. There are detailed reports rich with information about the rapidly developing changes, especially in the heart of the empire. Yet, these very reports tend to confuse and blur rather than clarify the issues involved. This period is characterized by long and complicated fighting between the military forces of Baghdād and Sāmarrā and even among the forces in each of these centres. The names of the principal leaders involved in this bitter struggle are mentioned in the sources and so are the groups that supported them. As there were no regimental names as such, army groups were given various nomenclatures, but in some cases different groups were described by the same name. What is important is whether the particular group in question belonged to Baghdād or Sāmarrā, e.g. the *shākiriyya*. Without identifying each group and its leader no real understanding of the causes of the struggle can be obtained. As this period contained the germs of military and administrative *iqṭāʿ*, such an understanding is vital for the analysis of later developments. In their valuable studies on this subject neither Cl. Cahen nor A. K. S. Lambton has made the necessary effort to clarify these beginnings.[1]

Arabic sources like us to believe that Wāthiq was so little interested in ruling that he did not even want to take the trouble to nominate a successor.[2] A more plausible explanation is the fact that when he died at the age of thirty-four his son was a minor, but perhaps he also well knew that it was difficult to find a member of his family who would be able or willing to continue as he himself had done with the policies his father had initiated. After his death a meeting of the men who held the reins of power was called to decide the question of succession. The dominant member was the chief judge Aḥmad b. Abī Duwād; the others were the two most prominent

[1] Cl. Cahen, "L'évolution de l'*iqṭāʿ* du IXe au XIIIe siècle. Contribution à une histoire comparée des sociétés médiévales", *Annales: Économie, sociétés, civilisations*, VIII (1953), pp. 25–52; Ann K. S. Lambton, "Reflections on the IQṬĀʿ" in George Makdisi, ed., *Arabic and Islamic Studies in Honor of Hamilton A. R. Gibb*, Leiden, 1965, pp. 358–76.

[2] Yaʿqūbī, *Tārīkh*, vol. II, p. 483.

military commanders and three high civilian officials, including the *wazīr* Ibn al-Zayyāt. It is important to note that this was the first time that such a situation had arisen in a century of 'Abbāsid rule, and that it set a precedent for later generations. In this meeting the military commanders did not seem particularly interested in the choice of any specific candidate, but surprisingly the civilians favoured the selection of the minor son of Wāthiq. Finally, in order to observe legality, the will of the chief judge prevailed, and Wāthiq's brother who was twenty-six years old was selected and given the title of Mutawakkil.[1]

Perhaps nobody was more surprised by the actions of the new ruler 847–61/232–47 than the selectors themselves, for it soon became clear that he had a mind of his own. In a matter of weeks he proceeded to make sweeping changes in the personnel of his administration. Ibn al-Zayyāt who had been in office as *wazīr/kātib* for twelve years, was dismissed, as were also his colleagues, some of whom were very wealthy merchants indeed. Mutawakkil must have realized that these men, who had continued their commercial activities while in office, had used their positions to amass huge fortunes for themselves and their fellow merchants, at the expense of the general public and the central treasury.[2] They were replaced by a team headed by Abū al-Faḍl al-Jarjarā'ī, a native 'Irāqī land-owner of ancient lineage. The significance of this team is that it combined members of the big land-owning families with other well-trained men who had served in previous administrations.[3] In other words, after getting rid of the corrupt merchants, Mutawakkil brought into government men with expertise in the affairs of the local rural communities, and supported them with others of special administrative talent.

On the military side he had even more radical plans which revolved around two main ideas. The first was to change the structure of the military forces in order to create a uniform standing army over which he would have direct control without the mediation of chiefs such as Afshīn. The second idea was a logical extension of the first; the autonomous powers of the Ṭāhirids in the East and their functions in Baghdād, the Sawād and Fārs were to be abrogated. Of course he knew only too well that he would meet strong opposition from very powerful elements throughout the whole empire, but he seems to have thought that by introducing them gradually he could eventually succeed in effecting these substantial changes.

[1] Ṭabarī, III, pp. 1368–9. [2] *Ibid.*, pp. 1376, 1379. [3] *Ibid.*, pp. 1373–9.

Mutawakkil perceived that the official adoption of Muʿtazilism and the subsequent fifteen years of inquisition had failed to produce tangible results. On the contrary, it had aroused stubborn opposition in the powerful conservative circles of Baghdād. In an attempt to win support for his plans, especially among these circles, he decided to drop this whole controversial issue and declare the official return to orthodoxy.[1] To emphasize his point he also made some anti-Shīʿite gestures;[2] and announced a discriminatory policy against non-Muslims in the empire. While most of the announced measures were of a symbolic nature, two were particularly offensive to non-Muslims; they were to be excluded from any appointments in government departments, and, more seriously, a tax was to be levied on their houses.[3] This last measure was widely resisted and when it was vigorously imposed resulted in insurrections in Syria.[4] On the other hand, the repeated announcements of these measures indicate that the government had difficulties in enforcing this policy.[5]

Turning his attention to the army, Mutawakkil's first step was to weaken its leadership. Fortunately Ashnās had died before Mutawakkil's accession to power and, with the acquiescence of the Ṭāhirids, the other powerful figure, Ītākh, was arrested in Baghdād on his way back from the pilgrimage.[6] Then came a sensitive and potentially dangerous problem, how to reduce the powers of the Ṭāhirids without appearing to renege on their agreement with Ma'mūn which had been in operation for almost thirty years. Time had helped to consolidate the Ṭāhirid presence in Baghdād, the Sawād and Fārs to the extent that they actually governed these and even adjacent regions also. The department of taxation in Baghdād was referred to as the "greater" in contrast to that of Sāmarrā.[7] Under the circumstances Ṭāhirid authority in the heart of the empire constituted a government within the government, and this was in addition to their control of the East.

A combination of circumstances and rivalries between the numerous members of the Ṭāhirid family helped Mutawakkil to implement his plans. Within a year no less than five Ṭāhirids holding key positions disappeared from the scene; two were murdered and three died.[8] Although the leading member of the family was alarmed enough to come from Khurāsān to Baghdād, Mutawakkil was

[1] *Ibid.*, pp. 1412–13.
[2] *Ibid.*, pp. 1307, 1324, 1326, 1379, 1403–4.
[3] *Ibid.*, pp. 1389–94.
[4] *Ibid.*, pp. 1420–4.
[5] *Ibid.*, p. 1419.
[6] Yaʿqūbī, *Tārīkh*, vol. II, p. 486; Athīr, vol. VII, p. 30.
[7] Yaqʿūbī, *Tārīkh*, vol. II, p. 488.
[8] Ṭabarī, III, pp. 1403–6.

astute enough to appoint other Ṭāhirids to the vacant positions and, without revealing his hand, to reduce the powers of the new appointees.[1] At the same time he proceeded with another subtle move which was designed to weaken Ṭāhirid authority in their regions, and to give him more direct control over the whole empire. He designated his three sons as his successors and decided on the titles they should assume when they came to power. The eldest, who was no more than thirteen years old, received the title Muntaṣir and was the immediate heir apparent. In due course he would be followed by his brothers Mu'tazz and Mu'ayyad respectively.[2] This was no innovation and could even be interpreted as a long term measure to ensure stability. This designation was accompanied by a declaration that had far-reaching and immediate consequences. The actual government of the empire was divided between these three children. Muntaṣir the heir apparent was put in charge of almost all the western half of the empire, with the exception of Syria which was assigned to Mu'ayyad. Mu'tazz was significantly given the responsibility for the East and as a camouflage Armenia, Ādherbayjān and Fārs were included in the bargain.[3] These appointments were not meant to be nominal because the declaration went into great detail assigning all the affairs of these regions to their prospective new rulers.[4] Of course the idea of dividing the empire between sons was not entirely new and a precedent had been set by Rashīd. But in this case the beneficiaries who were being charged with these responsibilities were minors for whose actions Mutawakkil himself was legally responsible. In other words he was using this as a means to give himself the right to interfere in any way he wanted in all the affairs of every province, particularly the East. The Ṭāhirids, in their already weakened positions, had no alternative but to accept the new arrangements, especially as they were allowed to keep their own military forces.

The next step was the dissolution of the army of Sāmarrā, and again this was done with great caution as part of the new arrangements. It was almost logical that each son should have a strong contingent to enable him to fulfil his responsibilities in his vast domains. Therefore the army of Sāmarrā was split into three divisions, each of which was dispatched with its child-ruler to a location in his regions. As all aspects of the administration of these regions,

1 *Ibid.*, p. 1410; Athīr, vol. VII, pp. 36, 43; Ya'qūbī, *Tārīkh*, vol. II, pp. 487–8.
2 Ṭabarī, III, pp. 1394, 1396–7.
3 *Ibid.*, pp. 1395–6.
4 *Ibid.*, pp. 1398, 1494.

including the fiscal affairs, were entrusted to these minors, it was necessary to appoint capable administrators.[1] Thus, in effect, the commanding officer of each division and the chief administrator were in charge of their respective regions albeit under the close scrutiny of Mutawakkil. This precedent gave birth to what can be best described as a military–bureaucratic alliance which was soon to become a troublesome feature in the politics of the empire.[2] Another precedent set at this time eventually developed into an institution that resulted in many serious problems. Although army stipends were deducted from revenues before sending them to the central treasury, the leaders of the divisions were given a land-grant, *iqṭā'*, for their own personal expenses and as a means to entice them to accept the move to their new regions. Even the Ṭāhirids were given such grants to compensate them for their losses, and probably also to equate them with their new colleagues in the provinces.[3] Of course *iqṭā'* was no new feature, but hitherto it had been granted to members of the ruling family and their favourite supporters for services rendered. Now it was granted to military leaders in areas where they exercised some administrative functions; this is the genesis of military–administrative *iqṭā'* to which we shall return later.[4]

Having thus consolidated his own position, Mutawakkil continued to carry out the rest of his plans. He dismissed his *wazīr* Jarjarā'ī, not because of any disagreements or faults but because he wanted to replace him by a man more useful for his purposes. The new *wazīr* was 'Ubaydullah b. Yaḥyā b. Khāqān whose qualifications were long experience and proven loyalty in the service of the 'Abbāsids. Although he was a Khurāsānian by origin and therefore not from the same category as his predecessor, his associates and the new appointees to the various departments were men of the same background as Jarjarā'ī.[5] In order to ensure the effectiveness of his own control Mutawakkil revived the office of chief comptroller, under a different title, and gave it more authority. To this office he appointed a well-trained administrator who was directly responsible to him.[6] However, very soon this arrangement proved unworkable for it gave the chief comptroller virtual authority over the trusted *wazīr* and his associates. The former was swiftly dismissed and the power

[1] *Ibid.*, pp. 1398–400.

[2] See below, pp. 94, 116.

[3] Ṭabarī, III, p. 1452.

[4] See below, pp. 95, 109.

[5] Ṭabarī, III, pp. 1407, 1441; Ya'qūbī, *Tārīkh*, vol. II, p. 485.

[6] Ṭabarī, III, pp. 1440–1.

of the latter vastly increased to include effective control over all departments.[1]

Ibn Khāqān, with his new powers, was instrumental in helping his master to proceed with a most important stage of his plans – the recruitment and organization of a new army. All the members of this army were directly attached to Mutawakkil as his *shākiriyya*, i.e. their allegiance was only to him as their sovereign. For obvious reasons such an army could not be recruited from Ṭāhirid territory in the East; furthermore this region was having its own new troubles. Therefore, it had to be recruited from the western regions such as Syria, Jazīra, Jibāl, 'Irāq, Ādherbayjān, Armenia and the Caucasus; even some *abnā'* from Baghdād enlisted alongside this conglomeration of Arabs and non-Arabs from all these different regions.[2] While this operation was in progress Mutawakkil decided on his next step; to move from Sāmarrā altogether. His first choice was Damascus, and he moved there in 858/244, but as this move brought Sāmarrā to the point of open revolt, he hurried back there after only a few weeks in Damascus.[3] However, a year later he started building a new city just outside Sāmarrā. It was called Ja'farī, after his personal name, and its cost was two million dinārs, equivalent to fifty million dirhams at the exchange rate at the time.[4] Although it is reported that most of the population of Sāmarrā moved to the new city where shops and similar *mustaghallāt* were constructed, it is also reported that because of an engineering mistake the water supplies were not adequate, and it was subsequently deserted, almost as soon as it had been built, after the death of Mutawakkil.[5]

After the apparent success of all his plans and as he seemed to be in full control, Mutawakkil wanted to take the final step to ensure the complete success of his policies, but it was a step that brought about his downfall. He thought that he could integrate the old Sāmarrā forces into his new *shākiriyya* army, but he realized that to achieve this end he must first get rid of their leaders. He began by attempting to take back the land-grants he had given them; a move which only helped to reveal his hand.[6] As his intentions became very

[1] *Ibid.*, pp. 1441–7; Ya'qūbī, *Tārīkh*, vol. II, p. 488.
[2] Ṭabarī, III, pp. 1389, 1463; Athīr, vol. VII, pp. 32, 64; Mas'ūdī, *Tanbīh*, p. 361.
[3] Ṭabarī, III, pp. 1435–6; Ya'qūbī, *Tārīkh*, vol. II, p. 491.
[4] Yāqūt, *Buldān*, vol. II, p. 143.
[5] Ṭabarī, III, p. 1436; Ya'qūbī, *Tārīkh*, vol. II, p. 492; Ya'qūbī, *Buldān*, p. 267; Bal., *Futūḥ*, p. 298.
[6] Ṭabarī, III, pp. 1452–6.

clear they decided that it was time to get rid of him before it was too late, and through their accomplices they had him murdered in his new palace in Ja'farī. Fatḥ b. Khāqān, an uncle of the *wazīr* who happened to be with Mutawakkil at that time, was also murdered, while his nephew the organizer of the *shākiriyya* remained unharmed under their protection. Muntaṣir, the eldest son of Mutawakkil, whose sympathies had been with the leaders of the Sāmarrā army, was promptly installed as his father's successor. He immediately moved back to Sāmarrā where he ordered a general withdrawal of the Sāmarrā forces from the provinces to the capital. He also received the allegiance of the *shākiriyya* after some hesitation on their part.[1]

During the reign of Mutawakkil the Byzantine front which had been quiet for more than a decade suddenly flared up. This was mainly the result of the increased naval activities of the Byzantines in the eastern Mediterranean which culminated in a major attack on Dimyāṭ on the Egyptian coast in 852/238.[2] Consequently fortifications were built on the Syrian and Egyptian coasts; also the construction of a new navy was started in Egypt and naval operations against the enemy began on a rather small scale.[3] Meanwhile a counter-attack was mounted on the Byzantine front. Summer expeditions were resumed and continued every year under the vigorous leadership of an Armenian Muslim, 'Alī b. Yaḥyā.[4] Part of the Sāmarrā army was stationed there at Sumaysāṭ, and significantly the land-tax there was confined to the Muslim tithes, probably because these men or their leaders were granted agricultural lands there.[5] On the other hand, in other locations in the *thughūr*, a land-tax concession was abolished. This was partial or complete tax exemption, *īghār*, on lands which had been previously granted to settlers in these areas.[6]

In neighbouring Armenia and Ādherbayjān there were fresh troubles in the aftermath of Bābak's revolt. One of the Arab leaders who had supported Bābak and had been imprisoned in Sāmarrā was able to escape, and he organized a new revolt against the central government, probably because of the strict enforcement of taxes. He did not seem to have much support and the region was soon

1 *Ibid.*, pp. 1453, 1457, 1459–79.
2 *Ibid.*, pp. 1417–18; Ya'qūbī, *Tārīkh*, vol. II, p. 498.
3 Ṭabarī, III, p. 1449; Maqrīzī, *Khiṭaṭ*, vol. I, pp. 211, 214, vol. II, p. 191; Bal., *Futūḥ*, p. 118.
4 Ṭabarī, III, pp. 1414, 1419, 1420, 1426–8, 1434, 1436, 1437; Mas'ūdī, *Tanbīh*, p. 191.
5 Ṭabarī, III, pp. 1428, 1436, 1459; Bal., *Futūḥ*, p. 184.
6 Bal., *Futūḥ*, p. 171.

pacified.[1] Interestingly, his sons enlisted in the *shākiriyya* probably with some of their fellow-countrymen.[2] However, in Armenia, when the same tax-collecting methods were enforced, the result was a combined Arab and Armenian revolt. The Muslim leaders of this region, whether Arab or Armenian, had extensive connexions with the chiefs of the adjacent Caucasian regions, and they probably relied on their support of their cause. After considerable resistance from the rebels and arduous efforts on the part of the government the revolt was barely contained.[3]

In Syria the Christians of Ḥimṣ, supported by the Muslims, rose against the house-tax introduced by Mutawakkil. With little effort their local insurrection was quickly suppressed.[4] In Egypt the failure of the 832/217 revolt convinced the Egyptians of the futility of armed resistance, and at the same time allowed Muslims to control more of the countryside.[5] The introduction of the house-tax therefore had no repercussions there. This tranquil state of affairs gave the government the chance to introduce a measure which was made necessary as a result of the withdrawal of Church officials from the administration. In 856/242 the governor of Egypt appointed a headman, *mukhtār*, to every village in the province; a move which could only enhance the power of the administration.[6]

The good relations that Ma'mūn had established with the Nubians had been strengthened under Muʿtaṣim to the extent that the king of Nubia had had a house in Cairo and another in ʿIrāq, which probably involved the presence of agents in both places.[7] On the other hand the Beja, the indigenous population of the Egyptian–Sudanese Red Sea coast, who had had long established peaceful relations with the Arabs, began to attack Upper Egypt. Since the conquest of Egypt these people had adhered to a peace treaty with the Arabs according to which they had agreed to pay an annual tribute of 75 ounces of gold. They had also agreed to permit Arabs to settle in their territory and exploit the silver, gold and precious stone mines there. As is evident from the name of their king at this time, ʿAlī Bābā, some of them had accepted Islam, and there is every indication that they had continued to abide by the terms of their treaty. Nevertheless, it seems that as a result of the implementation

[1] Ṭabarī, III, pp. 1380–2, 1387–8; Yaʿqūbī, *Tārīkh*, vol. II, p. 486; Khurdādhbeh, pp. 119–24.

[2] Ṭabarī, III, p. 1389; Athīr, vol. VII, p. 32; see also above, p. 76.

[3] Ṭabarī, III, pp. 1407–8, 1414–16; Athīr, vol. VII, pp. 38–9, 44–5.

[4] Ṭabarī, III, pp. 1420–4.

[5] Maqrīzī, *Khiṭaṭ*, vol. II, p. 494.

[6] Kindī, *Wulāt*, p. 203.

[7] Maqrīzī, *Khiṭaṭ*, vol. I, p. 199.

of the policy of imposing taxes on mineral produce they had been obliged, together with the Arabs there, to pay the required fifth. They must have considered this not only an "over-tax" but also a breach of their treaty. Under Mutawakkil they ceased to pay the tribute and stopped the Arabs from mining in their territories. In 855/241 Mutawakkil had therefore sent an expedition which successfully restored the position of the Arabs there.[1]

Another minor upset which seemed to have no great consequences at the time but which was soon to have serious repercussions in the heart of the empire, was the start of the Ṣaffārid movement in the rather neglected region of Sīstān. As this was in Ṭāhirid domains the Ṭāhirids dealt with it without great difficulty at this stage.[2]

On the economic side there were no great changes and the finances of the empire were in good order as may be seen from the fact that by the end of Mutawakkil's reign the central treasury had a reserve of four million dinārs and seven million dirhams.[3] There is a report that Aḥmad b. al-Mudabbir, who had been in charge of the taxation department in Baghdād, was sent to "adjust" the taxes of the Damascus and Jordan districts.[4] We have no details about this adjustment but later actions of this man in Egypt show that he was a genius in devising new taxes.[5] On the other hand there is no indication of any change or unrest in these districts at this time. It is possible that this adjustment was made necessary as a result of a series of unusual natural disasters that happened around that time. Violent earthquakes occurred almost everywhere in the empire throughout the years 855–60/241–5. In Qūmis 45,096 people were killed in the earthquake of 856/242.[6] Some of the worst-hit areas were in Jazīra and Syria where whole towns were destroyed; in 859/245 Antioch lost 1500 houses and on the Syrian coast the sea level rose to a threatening height. Mutawakkil distributed three million dirhams among the unfortunate people of Syria.[7]

We have some significant statistics that indicate the increasing rate of conversion to Islam in 'Irāq. While the Arab Muslims of the region of Baṣra paid six million dirhams in taxes a year, the non-Muslims of Baghdād paid 130,000 dirhams and those of Wāsiṭ paid only 30,000 dirhams in poll-taxes.[8] With some simple calculations

[1] Ṭabarī, III, pp. 1428–31.
[2] Athīr, vol. VII, p. 43.
[3] Mas'ūdī, *Murūj*, vol. VII, p. 227.
[4] Ya'qūbī, *Tārīkh*, vol. II, p. 490.
[5] See below, p. 95.
[6] Ṭabarī, III, pp. 1433–4.
[7] *Ibid.*, pp. 1439–40; Ya'qūbī, *Tārīkh*, vol. II, p. 491.
[8] Khurdādhbeh, pp. 59, 125.

it can be estimated that there were roughly 4000 non-Muslim families in Baghdād and 1000 families in Wāṣit.

The murder of Mutawakkil at the hands of the military leaders presaged a decade of unprecedented instability in the heart of the empire. Muntaṣir was installed by the murderers of his father to do their bidding and he was more than willing to concur. The army of Sāmarrā was reconstituted in the capital as it had been under Mu'taṣim, and all Mutawakkil's arrangements were declared invalid. The meticulous system he had set up to rule over all his domains without the cumbersome interference of the Ṭāhirids was completely abolished, and they regained all their lost privileges. To remove any remaining doubt Muntaṣir deposed his two brothers from the line of succession in favour of his own child.[1]

Two men emerged as Muntaṣir's chief aids. The first, Utāmish, was one of the leaders of the Sāmarrā army; and the other was Aḥmad b. al-Khaṣīb, an administrator and a member of an 'Irāqī land-owning family.[2] The latter arranged for a solution to the pressing problem of how to deal with the rival *shākiriyya* army. The decision was taken that it could be best deployed on the Byzantine front, and Waṣīf, a prominent general from Sāmarrā, was appointed in charge of this operation. Significantly his chief lieutenant was an uncle of Ibn Khāqān, the organizer of this army. Although our sources represent Waṣīf's appointment to this task as an attempt by Aḥmad b. al-Khaṣīb to get rid of a rival, it could not have been so. There was neither the occasion nor the time for such rivalry to take place. Their respective spheres of competence were completely different, and time was too short to allow such rivalry to occur. Furthermore, when Waṣīf was instructed to plan to stay four years at his base in Malaṭya, he showed no sign of disagreement.[3]

It must have been a great shock to everyone concerned when Muntaṣir died of a heart attack at the age of twenty-five after a reign of only six months. Again a council was hastily convened to decide on a successor. The desire to observe legality excluded Muntaṣir's minor son and the unwillingness to have a strong ruler precluded the choice of a capable candidate. With the implausible excuse that the military leaders did not wish to have in power any son of Mutawakkil, whom they had so recently murdered, a grandson of Mu'taṣim, who was barely eighteen years old, was selected and given the title Musta'īn 862–6/248–52.[4]

[1] Ṭabarī, III, pp. 1485–95. [2] Ya'qūbī, *Tārīkh*, vol. II, p. 493; Ṭabarī, III, p. 1480.
[3] Ṭabarī, III, pp. 1480–1; Athīr, vol. VII, p. 72. [4] Ṭabarī, III, p. 1501.

Utāmish was elevated to the position of *wazīr*, and Aḥmad b. al-Khaṣīb was appointed *kātib*.[1] In this arrangement there was still a recognition of the principle of the separation of military and financial affairs. Utāmish, however, had different ideas about the whole system of government, and decided that in order to put these ideas into effect he should have supreme control of both. After being in office for one month Aḥmad b. al-Khaṣīb was dismissed and exiled to Crete; Utāmish continued as *wazīr* but appointed a *kātib* as his own administrative assistant.[2] In this move lies the genesis of the later office of *amīr al-umarā'* and indeed, for all practical purposes, Utāmish held such a position though without this title, as it had yet to be invented.[3] He was determined to do everything in his power to preserve the ascendency of the Sāmarrā army, and consequently he was not particularly keen on the continued existence of the *shākiriyya* army in any form. The problem acquired a certain urgency because most of this army had returned to Sāmarrā with Waṣīf after the death of Muntaṣir. It was also compounded by the fact that other military leaders, namely Waṣīf and Bughā, saw no reason why the two armies should not be integrated into one powerful army. They had worked with the *shākiriyya* and found that with proper handling and leadership they could only add to the total strength of the military forces of the empire. For the moment a compromise was reached by which some of the *shākiriyya* were dispatched under the leadership of Bughā to deal with some minor disturbance in the Jibāl region, while Waṣīf remained in Sāmarrā with the rest.[4]

With remarkable professionalism Utāmish proceeded to reorganize the Sāmarrā army in groups consisting of ten men, companies of fifty, and battalions of a hundred, and all under appropriate officers at various levels. He also declared that while all stipends were assured and payment secured at regular times, all anomalies, inflated family allowances and irregular increases, were annulled. Most important, he proclaimed that no military personnel would be permitted, under any circumstances, to take part in tax-collecting in any form.[5] Although this was a reasonable plan, it raised objections from those affected by it. In less than a year Utāmish was murdered and all his decrees were revoked.[6]

At this stage Waṣīf and Bughā gained control of the situation. As

[1] *Ibid.*, pp. 1502–3.
[2] Ṭabarī, III, p. 1508; Mas'ūdī, *Murūj*, vol. VII, p. 324.
[3] See below, p. 157.
[4] Ṭabarī, III, pp. 1503–4, 1508, 1510–15; Athīr, vol. VII, pp. 79–81.
[5] Ṭabarī, III, p. 1799.
[6] Ya'qūbī, *Tārīkh*, vol. II, p. 496.

they did not have the same notion of supreme control as Utāmish, a well-trained bureaucrat was appointed to take charge of the administration.[1] Because of their own experience they were opposed neither to stationing contingents of the army in the provinces, nor to the still incipient military–administrative *iqṭā'*. However they became convinced that granting estates to military leaders would only arouse bad feelings among their own men in addition to antagonizing the general population, as indeed was the case in Kūfa. Bāghar who had actually dealt Mutawakkil the last blow, had been granted estates near Kūfa and the result was a pseudo-Shī'ite revolt there.[2] When Bughā's allies, who were among the most respectable men of the area and an early example of the military–bureaucratic complex, tried to interfere with the affairs of the agent of Bāghar, the latter threatened mutiny.[3] Bughā and Waṣīf had him murdered and all hell broke loose.[4] They lost any support they might have had from the Sāmarrā army and as they were supported by the *shākiriyya*, an open conflict began between the two armies.[5] Waṣīf used all possible means to assuage the feelings of the Sāmarrā forces, including releasing from prison the long forgotten son of Afshīn, but to no avail.[6] Even the support of public opinion in addition to that of the impotent Musta'īn did not make much difference to the declining position of Waṣīf and Bughā. Realizing that their situation in Sāmarrā was relatively weak they descended on Baghdād where they hoped to have the support of the Ṭāhirid forces. Musta'īn had no alternative but to join them.[7]

The conflict became one between Sāmarrā and Baghdād. To their credit the leaders of the former tried first to negotiate with their adversaries, but the latter, confident in their strength, refused any terms and began to mobilize all their forces.[8] They called for reinforcements from all the regions under their control and gathered all the *shākiriyya* in Baghdād. They also sent out instructions to the various districts that the revenues should be carried to Baghdād and not to Sāmarrā.[9] Sīma al-Sharābī emerged as the leader in Sāmarrā. The second part of the name of this man is an epithet that expresses the real nature of the construction of the Sāmarrā army.

Sharābī is often taken to mean cup-bearer which is utterly wrong.

[1] Ṭabarī, III, pp. 1512, 1514, 1531.
[2] *Ibid.*, pp. 1515–18, 1535.
[3] *Ibid.*, pp. 1535–6, 1541; Mas'ūdī, *Murūj*, vol. VII, p. 111.
[4] Ṭabarī, III, pp. 1537–8.
[5] *Ibid.*, p. 1539.
[6] *Ibid.*, pp. 1533, 1555.
[7] *Ibid.*, pp. 1539, 1542.
[8] *Ibid.*, pp. 1543–4.
[9] *Ibid.*, pp. 1550, 1552.

As it occurs frequently among the names of military leaders at this time, we are asked to believe that the natural order of affairs then was to promote favourite cup-bearers to the rank of generals. Of course this fits in very well with the mistaken theories of slave armies, but it also shows almost deliberate negligence in handling the source material. It has been noted that this name occurs in various forms, Sārbānī, Shārbānī, Sharābī, Shārbāmyānī and others which cannot be clearly identified, thanks to copyists and editors. It is not methodologically sound in this area however to take one form of a name and leave all others out of consideration.[1] In any case, in this instance all forms lead to a precise identification and that is Shārbāmyānī, i.e. a follower of the prince of Bāmyān; other forms are the result of the common Arabic practice of shortening long names when forming relative adjectives, *nisbas*, from them as, e.g., ‘Abdī and ‘Abqasī from ‘Abdulqays.

Reference has been made to the presence of the prince of Bāmyān earlier in Sāmarrā, and Sīma was obviously one of the leading figures among his followers.[2] In due course he attained a commanding position in the hierarchy of the Sāmarrā army. Having emerged as the leader of these forces he started planning for the inevitable fight against Baghdād. A son of Mutawakkil was brought out of prison and proclaimed a rival ruler with the title of Mu‘tazz. The new ruler's brother Abū Aḥmad, the future formidable Muwaffaq, was put in charge of the expected military operations; he was given the assistance of a *wazīr* though the effective control of the bureaucracy in Sāmarrā remained in the hands of Sīma's secretary. Sīma himself was put in charge of the postal service and the seal which under the circumstances can only mean that he had direct access to and control over correspondence with the provincial governors concerning the all important revenues. Finally, another general was appointed to assist, and probably watch over, Abū Aḥmad, and the whole of the army advanced on Baghdād; only Sīma and a few men stayed behind to hold the fort.[3]

They converged upon Baghdād, a siege was begun and the city was soon suffering from food shortages. When occasionally fighting broke out neither side gained an advantage over the other and Ibn Ṭāhir, the governor of Baghdād, began to realize the weakness of his position. Once more the *‘ayyārs* appeared on the scene as the local

[1] *Ibid.*, pp. 1550, 1687, 1688, and the variant readings in the footnotes; Sourdel, p. 294.

[2] See above, p. 64.

[3] Ṭabarī, III, pp. 1544, 1550, 1594.

population was recruited to fight the enemy but to no avail.[1] Abū Aḥmad, on his part, saw the stalemate and started making overtures to Ibn Ṭāhir.[2] It took the latter some time to overcome the opposition in his own camp, and only after threatening to throw in his lot with Sāmarrā, was he able to open negotiations.[3] Finally terms were agreed; the *shākiriyya* would continue as a separate force in Baghdād, and in return, the Ṭāhirid governor would be given one third of the revenues of Sāmarrā for their expenses.[4] Muʿtazz the rival ruler was accepted by all parties, while Mustaʿīn was deposed and exiled to Wāsiṭ.[5] The fate of Waṣīf and Bughā was not so easily decided. On the one hand Ibn Ṭāhir did not want them to remain in Baghdād; on the other hand they understandably dreaded returning to Sāmarrā. Their prestige among their former colleagues came to the rescue, and it was decided that they should be rehabilitated. Waṣīf was appointed governor of Jibāl and Bughā governor of Ḥijāz, but of course they were kept in Sāmarrā, and only their representatives were sent to their respective regions.[6] However, as they could not desist from intrigues to regain their lost power they practically brought about their own murder.[7]

In Baghdād, Ibn Ṭāhir, who had apparently asked for troops from the East when his position had been in jeopardy, was now faced with a difficult situation. Although these troops arrived long after the fight had finished, they still required to be paid. He knew that if he were to pay them, this could only be done at the expense of either his old troops or the *shākiriyya*. When he turned to Sāmarrā for more financial help, he was plainly told that it was his own problem, to which he had to find a solution from his own resources. He tried to stretch these as much as possible to satisfy all these men, but this only added to his problems. The *shākiriyya* did not see why their interests should be sacrificed for the interests of new arrivals. Open fighting started but the Ṭāhirid forces prevailed and the *shākiriyya* quickly dispersed.[8]

Muʿtazz seems to have thought that with some manipulation he could be master of his army and wield real power. With astonishing boldness he arrested his brother Abū Aḥmad who had just won him

[1] *Ibid.*, pp. 1552, 1564, 1586, 1588, for the term *ʿayyār*; for the details of the fighting, pp. 1550–1628.

[2] *Ibid.*, pp. 1628–30.

[3] *Ibid.*, pp. 1630–7.

[4] *Ibid.*, p. 1640.

[5] *Ibid.*, pp. 1640, 1645, 1670.

[6] *Ibid.*, pp. 1658–60.

[7] *Ibid.*, pp. 1687–96.

[8] *Ibid.*, pp. 1660–71, 1725–35; Athīr, vol. VII, pp. 113–14, 136; Yaʿqūbī, *Tārīkh*, vol. II, p. 501.

a victory, and had helped to maintain his position in Sāmarrā. He also deposed his other brother Muʿayyad, his heir apparent according to the will of their father Mutawakkil. A few months later both were banished to Wāsiṭ, and eventually ended up taking refuge with the Ṭāhirids in Baghdad. Less fortunate was the deposed Mustaʿīn who was murdered in exile in Wāsiṭ on the orders of Muʿtazz.[1]

In order to control the army, the first step was to try to win the loyalty of its most powerful generals. For this purpose Muʿtazz introduced a new feature in government, which was not quite military–administrative *iqṭāʿ* though not too far from it. Each general was appointed as the governor of a province to which he sent, as his personal representative, one of his trusted subordinate officers accompanied by some of his troops. Neither general nor representative was granted any estates and indeed they were strictly kept out of any intervention in the fiscal affairs of the province, for which an independent official was appointed. The significance of this system was that, while it maintained the principle of the separation of military and fiscal affairs, it allowed the governor in the capital a priority claim over the income from his province as a guarantee for the pay of his men. The best known example of this system is Bāykbāk whose deputy in Egypt was Aḥmad b. Ṭūlūn, who was obliged to leave the fiscal affairs in the firm hands of Aḥmad b. al-Mudabbir, one of the most astute experts in such matters.[2]

The liaison between the generals and the administration was through the office of the *wazīr*, Aḥmad b. Isrāʾīl, whose job was to supervise the collection of taxes and the disbursement of revenues. He also had to satisfy the generals which proved to be a difficult task, for very soon he fell out with one of them, Ṣāliḥ b. Waṣīf, who did not hesitate to arrest the hapless *wazīr*. At this point an open struggle started between Muʿtazz and the generals. He wanted to keep the military out of fiscal affairs as much as possible, while they demanded full control of both military and fiscal affairs. The bureaucrats also became divided between those who supported Muʿtazz, and others who were willing to serve under the generals. In the event the military won and Ṣālih b. Waṣīf took charge of all affairs. In no time Muʿtazz was deposed and replaced by one of his nephews who took the title of Muhtadī.[3]

1 Ṭabarī, III, pp. 1668–70, 1693; Athīr, vol. VII, pp. 116, 122.

2 Ṭabarī, III, pp. 1685, 1697; Maqrīzī, *Khiṭaṭ*, vol. I, pp. 99, 103; Yaʿqūbī, *Tārīkh*, vol. II, p. 508.

3 Ṭabarī, III, pp. 1647, 1706–11; Athīr, vol. VII, pp. 112, 131; Yaʿqūbī, *Tārīkh*, vol. II, p. 504; Masʿūdī, *Murūj*, vol. VII, pp. 379, 397–8; Masʿūdī, *Tanbīh*, p. 365.

There was some hesitation in Baghdād about accepting the new arrangements in the capital and paying allegiance to the new ruler. This was not important in itself, for the prompt arrival of the customary bonus, paid at the accession of a new ruler, overcame any objections.[1] But the fact that there was some support in Baghdād for Abū Aḥmad to replace his deposed brother, was a portent of developments that were to take place very soon.[2] Meanwhile things did not remain quiet in Sāmarrā. Another general, Mūsā b. Bughā, who was on a minor policing operation in the Jibāl region, was alarmed by the developments in the capital and decided to go back there. On his arrival, Ṣāliḥ b. Waṣīf simply went into hiding and Bāykbāk, yet another general, took over his responsibilities. The situation was thrown wide open, and the struggle that had started under Muʿtazz was resumed all over again. Furthermore, Mūsā b. Bughā who was extremely unwilling to accept the succession of Muhtadī, wanted to depose him but did not or could not offer an alternative.[3]

At last, the men of the army themselves grew tired of the endless differences of their generals, and many of them decided that in their own interest they should support Muhtadī in order to enable him to impose a solution on the continuing crisis. Their support was conditional on his meeting certain demands. This emphatically confirms that their main concern was that they should receive their stipends regularly and on time. These demands, that clearly explain the causes of all the problems, were that:

(1) all affairs of government should revert to the control of the *Amīr al-Mum'inīn*;

(2) the re-organization that had been introduced by Utāmish, to put the army on a professional basis, should be reinstated;

(3) all allowances for women and children should be stopped;

(4) stipends should be paid regularly every two months;

(5) no general should be allowed to interfere in any form in the fiscal affairs of the provinces;

(6) all land-grants should be annulled;

(7) the *Amīr al-Mum'inīn* himself should be responsible for promotions in the army;

(8) he should also appoint one of his brothers as commander-in-chief.[4]

[1] Ṭabarī, III, pp. 1714–15.

[2] See below, p. 92.

[3] Ṭabarī, III, pp. 1736–40, 1787–96.

[4] *Ibid.*, pp. 1796–9; Athīr, vol. VII, pp. 151–3.

As Muhtadī was not able to meet all these demands, fighting broke out again and an attempt was made to depose him. He called on those men who had sought to support him and, with surprising ease, had some of the generals arrested and Bāykbāk killed. However, in the ensuing fighting Muhtadī was wounded and died after a reign of only eleven months 869–70/255–6.[1] Under the circumstances, and while the moderate elements had the upper hand in Sāmarrā, a son of Mutawakkil was brought out of prison and proclaimed successor with the title Muʿtamid.[2] The choice of Muʿtamid was apparently a compromise that put an end to the fighting and paved the way for reaching agreement on other arrangements which will be discussed in the following chapter.

While all these disturbances were taking place in the heart of the empire, and in spite of the gradual weakening of the Ṭāhirids, remarkably little happened in the provinces to decrease the authority of the central government. In Ḥimṣ insurrections occurred in 863/248 and 864/250 but were easily suppressed.[3] In Mawṣil, the people of the region elected their own governor but as they continued to pay allegiance to the ruler in Sāmarrā, there was no cause for alarm.[4] Summer expeditions were regularly carried out against the Byzantines.[5] In Fārs, a take-over by the local commander of the Ṭāhirid forces did not upset the province. Realizing the growing power of Ṣaffār's movement in Sīstān, the central government confirmed him as governor of Fārs, and added the threatened region of Kirmān to his domains.[6]

The only serious problem arose in Ṭabaristān, where Mustaʿīn had granted land which had been public property to the Ṭāhirid in charge of the region.[7] Naturally this aroused the wrath of the local population. A man of ʿAlawid descent who had taken refuge among them, led their rebellion and was able for a time, in 864/250, to drive the Ṭāhirid forces out of the area and even occupy Rayy itself. Another ʿAlawid captured Qazvīn and Zanjān in 865/251 while the central government forces were barely able to protect Hamadān. A strong contingent of the Sāmarrā army under the command of

1 Ṭabarī, III, pp. 1799–1810, 1815–34; Athīr, vol. VII, pp. 154–61; Yaʿqūbī, *Tārīkh*, vol. II, pp. 505–6; Masʿūdī, *Tanbīh*, p. 366.
2 Ṭabarī, III, p. 1831.
3 *Ibid.*, pp. 1508, 1533.
4 Azdī, *Mawṣil*, p. 88.
5 Ṭabarī, III, pp. 1534, 1577, 1581, 1615, 1697.
6 *Ibid.*, pp. 1698–9; Yaʿqūbī, *Tārīkh*, vol. II, p. 495; Iṣṭakhrī, p. 144.
7 Ṭabarī, III, pp. 1524–5; Athīr, vol. VII, pp. 85–6.

Mūsā b. Bughā was dispatched to deal with these rebels. Both ʿAlawids were forced to flee into the mountains, and government control was temporarily re-established in this region.[1] When the rapid developments in Sāmarrā alarmed Mūsā enough to force his return to the capital in 869/255, fresh troubles started in the region and indeed in the rest of the empire.

[1] Ṭabarī, III, pp. 1526–33, 1583, 1643, 1686, 1693, 1698, 1736.

5

REGIONAL ECONOMIC CONFLICTS

The lack of viable political institutions to rule the empire and the failure to establish well organized military forces to defend it had brought some traumatic experiences to Islamic society. Although these problems had yet to be solved they were pushed into second place by economic crises. It was not that the government was suffering from monetary deficits or lack of reserves; nor was it that the general population had to endure poverty because of a deficiency of natural resources. These were ample in most regions, and the occasional famines that occurred were not of long duration. Indeed there were clear signs of prosperity and progress in all walks of life, whether in industry and commerce or arts and sciences, that could have justified calling this era the Golden Age of Islam.

The economic problems of this affluent multi-racial empire were the result of the cumulative effects of bad management in all fields, at all levels and of all regions. The symptoms were the absence of equal opportunities not only as between the various sectors of society, but also as between the diverse regions of the empire. The central government acted very much like a colonial power whose only interest was to exploit its domains without regard to the interests of its subjects. It was a classic example of a loosely associated economic bloc where the central areas reap all the benefits while the outer areas make all the sacrifices. The government saw all its duties and responsibilities in terms of enforcing tax-collection, the revenues of which were to support a growing and corrupt bureaucracy and an almost useless army. When it came to public services the government did not seem to consider that these fell within the realm of its responsibilities. Even necessary repairs to the delicate irrigation systems which had been previously paid for by the government were now charged to the users who had to pay for them over and above the required taxes.[1] We are told that hospitals were built in major cities, but the cost of maintaining the only hospital in Baghdād was the dismal sum of thirty eight and one third dinārs a day, and this was to cover all expenses including the wages of the resident

[1] Ṭabarī, III, p. 2153.

physicians in addition to the cost of medicaments. The insignificance of this hospital becomes clear when we know that the daily wages of the men in charge of the hunt amounted to seventy dinārs, and the daily cost of feeding and stabling the ruler's horses was four hundred dinārs.[1] It should also be realized that *bīmāristān*, hospital, must have been a euphemism for such an institution, which was more of a lunatic asylum than anything else. It can be easily discerned that the patients were from the more affluent strata of society, so that in effect the government was relieving them of the burden of taking care of their less fortunate kin.

The corrupt practices started by the Barmakids continued to permeate all ruling circles and were perfected to an art. Members of the 'Abbāsid family acquired more and more estates as their numbers multiplied with amazing rapidity. Government officials, many of whom came from families with big landholdings, took advantage of their appointments to enhance their own wealth and that of their masters. They continually devised illegitimate means of evading their taxes at the expense of the small landowners, many of whom were thus forced to give up their holdings and join the various protest movements which were sprouting in the heart of the empire. Meanwhile, the flourishing commercial life of the cities attracted the accumulated wealth of both the big landowners and government officials and the interests of both groups became completely intertwined. The order of the day was hoarding and speculation in commodities by men in government service, and even female members of the ruler's household were involved in such operations. These malpractices were so widespread that they were officially accepted as the norm, and accordingly every high official was obliged to pay a monetary fine or even had all his wealth confiscated at his dismissal. This most unusual method of taxation could not have been completely effective since it did not prevent the same official from seeking office time and again, happily prepared to accept the consequences.

The wealth of the empire and the private fortunes of the rich generated an unprecedented volume of international trade, especially in luxury goods, with all known parts of the world. China, South East Asia, India, Africa, Western Europe as far north as Scandinavia, Eastern Europe, Russia and Southern Europe from Byzantium to Spain were all partners in this trade. Imports into the empire included silks and brocades; furs and skins such as panther, sable,

[1] Ṣābī, *Wuzarā'*, pp. 18–20.

grey squirrel, ermine, mink, fox, beaver, spotted hare and goat; shagreen; fur-caps; felt; all sorts of spices and aromatics; drugs; musk; camphor; aloes; woods, especially ebony and teak; amber; rubies; gold; tin; wax; honey; hazel nuts; coconuts; fish-glue; fish-teeth; ink; paper; swords; armour; arrows; locks; gold and silver utensils; crockery; trinkets; slaves and all kinds of animals such as tigers, panthers, elephants, peacocks, falcons, swift horses, sheep and cattle. Much of this trade was for local consumption as well as for re-export. For export also were the products of the most developed industry of the empire, textiles of every kind be it linen, cotton, silk or wool, piece-goods or finished items of all sorts. Practically every region and every town had its own brand of cloth, clothes, tapestries, cushions, upholstery or carpets.

The shores of the Indian Ocean, Persian Gulf, Arabian, Red, Black, Caspian and Mediterranean Seas were studded with busy ports, all involved in imports and exports to and from various parts of the world. The flow of this trade was greatly helped by the development of a highly sophisticated banking system that allowed payment by cheques or letters of credit anywhere, even in enemy territory. New overland routes leading into and out of the empire were chartered by intermediaries who found fresh opportunities to bring in the products of far-away lands. The regions through which this trade passed naturally had an interest and competed for a bigger share in such commerce, according to their respective locations at the importing or exporting end. These competing, and sometimes conflicting, interests demanded some sort of harmonization, if not complete integration, into a wider economic entity. As this was not done the competing regions began to look exclusively after their own interests; alliances were made, and efforts were spent to secure the flow of trade into or out of a given region. Merchant navies were built and control over inland routes was sought; the more inlets a region had the better for its prosperity, and if it could also have some outlets so much the better.

The central government added to the complexity of the situation by imposing inter-regional taxes in addition to the taxes imposed on international trade at the port of entry. A new office was created, *ṣāḥib ṭarīq*, an official in charge of a route, who was not only charged with ensuring public safety, but also with collecting the taxes on internal trade.[1] Of course this new tax increased the wealth at the centre of this economic complex but it further separated the interests

[1] Ṭabarī, III, pp. 1889–2039, 2106, 2107, 2114.

of the regions from that of the central government. Moreover, the central government did not make much effort to rectify the most damaging fault in the tax-system; the inequity of the burden as between rural and urban taxes continued and even worsened, because of the enormous wealth of the ever-expanding urban communities. Although sporadic attempts were made to remedy this situation, as we shall see, vested interests were too strong to dislodge. The tension between rural and urban communities mounted and were certainly exploited by revolutionary movements in the empire.[1]

The compromise that brought Mu'tamid to office in 870/256 involved his brother Abū Aḥmad. It will be recalled that the latter had played an important role in the struggle between the forces of Sāmarrā and Baghdād. He had also played an essential part in the final reconciliation of the two sides. Although Mu'tazz, the beneficiary of this action, did not seem to have appreciated the help of Abū Aḥmad and had banished him to Wāsiṭ, the latter's going to Baghdād is an indication of his ties there. As part of their plan to reform the military forces, the men of Sāmarrā had demanded that Muhtadī should appoint one of his brothers in charge of the army.[2] It fell to Mu'tamid to carry out this wish and Abū Aḥmad's military experience and association with both Baghdād and Sāmarrā made him an ideal choice for this task. For the first time, the responsibility for the military forces was taken away from an 'Abbāsid ruler and given to another experienced member of the family, who was neither a son nor in the direct line of succession to the current ruler. Furthermore he was given a title, in the same fashion as the 'Abbāsid rulers, Muwaffaq, i.e. successful with the help of God. This situation has led some scholars to describe him as "regent", but this could not have been the case because Mu'tamid was neither a minor nor incapacitated; he was for twenty-two years the *Imām*, *Amīr al Mu'mimīn* and *Khalīfa* of God. Muwaffaq's appointment was made in response to the demand of the army to keep the generals under strict control, and to ensure the separation of military and fiscal affairs even at the highest level. Another part of the compromise was to appoint as *wazīr* 'Ubaydullah b. Yaḥyā b. Khāqān, the organizer of the *shākiriyya* under Mutawakkil. As he had worked with the military before, he was acquainted with the problems involved. His full co-operation with Muwaffaq helped to bring some stability to an otherwise chaotic situation.[3]

[1] See below, p. 126.

[2] See above, p. 86.

[3] Ṭabarī, III, pp. 1839, 1915.

It was becoming clear that the Ṭāhirid power base in the East was being eroded, their position in Baghdād and the western regions under their control weakened. Muwaffaq was put in charge of these regions over the Ṭāhirids with Baghdād as his base.[1] This necessary step aroused the apprehensions of some of the Sāmarrā forces who saw it as a resurrection of the forces of the rival city. Under the circumstances, Mu'tamid was forced to intervene to alleviate these fears. He appointed his son Mufawwaḍ as his heir apparent and gave him a share of power in Baghdād with Muwaffaq, who himself was appointed second in line of succession.[2] However, the death of the co-operative *wazīr* deprived the government of his experience in dealing with the military, and made way for further complications. To replace him Mu'tamid appointed Ḥasan b. Makhlad b. al-Jarrāḥ whose choice was apparently an attempt to appease a faction of the Sāmarrā forces. It did not take long for another faction, led by the powerful general Mūsā b. Bughā, to arrive at the capital, at which Ḥasan simply went into hiding. His replacement was an interesting choice, Sulaymān b. Wahb, a very experienced administrator who came from a long line of officials that had been in government service since the Umayyad period. Of more significance was the fact that his son 'Ubaydullah had the unusual function of being the *kātib* of Mūsā b. Bughā, Mufawwaḍ and Muwaffaq at the same time.[3] This was not because of a sudden scarcity of administrators; it was an attempt to co-ordinate if not to combine the administration of Baghdād with that of Sāmarrā. This ingenious solution did not seem to lessen the fears of the opposing faction of the Sāmarrā forces, and they forced Mu'tamid to dismiss Sulaymān and re-instate their favourite Ḥasan. Muwaffaq's reaction indicates the seriousness of this move, for he marched on Sāmarrā and forced his brother, after a week of negotiations, to reverse his decision. The result was that the militant faction of the Sāmarrā army, led by Mūsā b. Utāmish, left the capital and scrambled for positions on the *thughūr* of Jazīra.[4] This was practically the end of Sāmarrā and its forces, 877/264. It does not serve any purpose to go into the details of their last struggle to survive. Suffice it to say that Mu'tamid, who had lost all but his title, was sent down to Wāsiṭ five years later in 882/269.[5]

Of course, the fall of Sāmarrā allowed Baghdād to regain its position at the centre of the empire, but this did not mean a return

[1] *Ibid.*, p. 1841.
[2] *Ibid.*, p. 1890.
[3] *Ibid.*, p. 1915.
[4] *Ibid.*, pp. 1926–7.
[5] *Ibid.*, p. 2068.

to the situation as it had been fifty years earlier. The events, policies, changes and developments intervening had had their impact on everybody concerned. After some jostling for positions the outcome was the emergence of two distinct parties, each backing completely different policies. Supporters of these parties permeated all levels of leadership in society from the ruling family down to government officials, military leaders, merchants and landowners. Perhaps the best representatives of these parties were the Jarrāḥ and the Furāt families. Members of these two families succeeded each other in the most important position in government for generations. In a real sense they were the leading politicians of their times who, when in power, had their protégés and disciples appointed to subordinate positions in government in order to propagate their policies. On the right stood the Jarrāḥs who had a conservative approach to all matters, especially with regard to taxation. They wanted the land to bear the main burden of taxes, and the towns to continue in their privileged position. They were also for the exploitation of the regions to the advantage of the central government. In order to achieve this end and still have firm control over the regions they were, in varying degrees, in favour of the wide application of military–administrative *iqṭā*ʿ in all corners of the empire. It is no wonder that the first prominent Jarrāḥ, Ḥasan b. Makhlad, had been the favourite of the militant Sāmarrā forces. The military–bureaucratic complex, born in the provincial administrations as a result of the manipulations of Mutawakkil, had gravitated towards the centre, and found its promoters among this party. However, at this stage, neither the military nor the bureaucrats dominated each other, but it was almost inevitable that in due course the former should get the upper hand over the latter.

To the left were the Furāts who were definitely against military–administrative *iqṭā*ʿ in any form and were keenly aware of the dangers of such a system. In order to keep the military out of fiscal matters the Furāts were willing to do their utmost to assure them of regular and reasonable stipends. They were also determined to put an end to the corrupt practices of their colleagues in government service. These reformist ideas can equally be discerned in their approach to fiscal affairs where they tried to acknowledge regional interests vis-a-vis those of the central government. In the reactionary milieu of Baghdād it was almost a compliment that they should be accused of being Shīʿites, and it is an indication that they were inclined towards greater equality in taxation as between urban and rural areas.

During the life time of Muwaffaq, who proved to be a most pragmatic statesman, the two parties worked together and their policies were applied simultaneously, albeit in different regions. On the one hand there is no indication that new taxes were imposed in Baghdād at this time. On the other hand a most extensive tax programme was carried out in Egypt by Aḥmad b. al-Mudabbir who was in charge of its fiscal affairs. Furthermore, the central government re-affirmed his authority in these matters and his complete independence from Aḥmad b. Ṭūlūn, the representative of the incipient military–administrative *iqṭā'*; and against the latter's opposition even salted fish was taxed.[1] At this stage, Muwaffaq's policy was that the military should be strictly kept out of the fiscal affairs of the central government in Baghdād, and that all matters whether military or fiscal should remain in the hands of a civilian under his own firm control. For this task he appointed an efficient administrator, Ṣā'id b. Makhlad, as his own assistant, *kātib*.[2] In the regions, Muwaffaq tried to maintain the separation of military and fiscal affairs as much as possible. However, he tolerated the application of full military–administrative *iqṭā'* in some areas as it was the only way to support government control there. This meant that some trusted military commanders were appointed as governors of certain regions with complete authority over all matters including fiscal affairs, and in exchange, they undertook to pay fixed sums to the central treasury.[3] Meanwhile, he had to meet serious troubles resulting from the breakdown of Ṭāhirid power in the East and the stand of some regions in defence of their own interests.

The first problem was in Sīstān where the Ṣaffārids had now consolidated their strength. The origin of their movement has been explained as the action of bands of brigands who, after establishing themselves in their region, were finally able to take control of a great part of the empire. We are told that they were Khārijites, yet there is no indication whatever of Khārijite thought in their movement. The valiant efforts of C. E. Bosworth do not prove any tangible connections between the Ṣaffārids and the early Khārijites of the Umayyad period; and heresiographers' evidence should not be taken as more than an attempt at making neat classifications of sects and groups without regard to history.[4] Indeed the descendants

1 Maqrīzī, *Khiṭaṭ*, vol. I, pp. 103, 107, 316; Kindī, *Wulāt*, p. 214; Ya'qūbī, *Tārīkh*, vol. II, p. 508.
2 Ṭabarī, III, p. 1930; Athīr, vol. VII, p. 265.
3 Ṭabarī, III, pp. 2039, 2048, 2114, 2115; Ṣābī, *Wuzara'*, p. 11.
4 C. E. Bosworth, *Sīstān Under The Arabs*, Rome, 1968, pp. 37–42, 87–91, 109–23.

of the early Khārijites were, at this very time, literally millionaires and strong supporters of the 'Abbāsids.[1] The sources that describe the Ṣaffārids as Khārijites use this term in its widest sense, simply to mean rebels against the established government. This is exactly what the Ṣaffārids were.

It is important to realize that this movement took place in western Sīstān, one of the least inviting and most neglected regions of the empire. Although it was first conquered in 652/32 Arab rule there had never been very secure. This was due to the failure of the conquerors to make any progress eastwards in the kingdom of Zābulistān.[2] For more than two centuries this kingdom had defended its independence with great zeal against the repeated attempts of the Arabs to gain a foothold in its territories. This resistance had forced the Arabs to by-pass the region and concentrate their advance eastwards through the coastal areas in the south into the province of Sind where they had been able to establish a strong presence. Eventually, they were probably more than glad to leave Sīstān to the care of the Ṭāhirids. The latter did not show any particular interest in the region more than the usual obligation to defend it against outside attacks. In fact we are told that they, the Ṭāhirids, were traditional rulers whose main concern was with the long established families in their regions.[3] In other words they contented themselves with enforcing the treaties of capitulation concluded at the time of the conquest with the *dihqāns* there. As these *dihqāns* were by definition the big landowners it is possible to conclude that the economy was mostly based on agriculture. Although the east–west trade route across Asia continued to bring some of this valuable trade to Soghdiana whence it was carried west through Ṭabaristān to Baghdād, a good deal of this trade had begun to find its way by sea from China to the Persian Gulf and the ports of the Arabian Sea. At the same time the trade route from Soghdiana to Balkh and then across the Hindū-Kush into India had been obstructed by the formidable power of Zunbīl the king of Zābulistān. The conspicuous absence of contacts between Sind and Khurāsān suggests that an economic boycott was mounted against the obstinate enemy. Such a boycott would certainly have its repercussions in the neighbouring region of Sīstān and the Ṭāhirids with their traditional concern would not be disturbed enough to take measures to alleviate the effects of the economic slump there. Under the circumstances a

[1] Iṣṭakhrī, p. 142.
[2] Shaban, *'Abbāsid Revolution*, pp. 23, 28, 54.
[3] Athīr, vol. VIII, p. 5.

breakdown of public order was inevitable, and as a result of the weakening power of the Ṭāhirids the situation went out of control. Bands of men spread all over the region either pillaging or demanding protection money from their more fortunate countrymen. The euphemism Khārijites is perfectly suitable to describe these men. On the other hand the settled communities, in self-defence, began to form their own militia which came to be known to us as *'ayyārs*, Home Guard, or *mutaṭawwi'a*, volunteers; and clearly there is no contradiction between these two terms. As some of the bandits were persuaded to join this militia the term Khārijites was used to describe what was basically the same people. Accordingly, there is no sectarian significance whatever in this episode, and this is proved by the fact that after the quick eclipse of the Ṣaffārids we do not hear about any traces of Khārijism in Sīstān.

The Ṣaffārids, then, originated from these bands of men who went through a process of change from outlaws to militia. The attainments of one or other of the leaders of such groups must end by giving him authority over his peers and in due course the talents for leadership of the Ṣaffārid Ya'qūb were recognized in this way.[1] He was able to organize his followers into a strictly disciplined military force. This organization may explain the use of the term *'ayyār* in this situation. An able recruit who was willing to join Ya'qūb had to give up all his personal belongings which were sold; the returns went to the treasury but were credited to the man. He was then given all necessary equipment which, however, remained the property of Ya'qūb. As all his personal needs were taken care of, such a soldier did not receive any stipends while in service. If he were honourably discharged he was given his accumulated earnings, otherwise he had to return all the equipment, receiving no money at all except what had been credited to him at the time of recruitment.[2] With such an organized army Ya'qūb was able not only to establish his uncontested control over Sīstān but also to invade Rukhkhaj and finally bring down the stubborn kingdom of Zābulistān, 870/256.[3] Significantly the following step was to push down to the Makrān–Kirmān coast and, as well put by one source, to control the extremities of Sind and Hind.[4]

This coastal area, now known as Balūchistān, is even more arid than Sīstān, and any effort to expand in this direction would seem

[1] Iṣṭakhrī, pp. 246–7; Ḥawqal, pp. 419 20.
[2] Mas'ūdī, *Murūj*, vol. VIII, pp. 47–9.
[3] Athīr, vol. VII, p. 226; Ṭabarī, III, p. 1883.
[4] Iṣṭakhrī, p. 247.

certainly wasteful. Yet this coast and its extension to the Persian Gulf had suddenly become the bone of contention between various parties. We recall that the 'Abbāsids had long been aware of the value of the revenues from the taxes on the trade coming through the southern shores of the empire. We also remember that Mu'taṣim had found it necessary to send land and sea expeditions to the remotest parts of these coasts to remove any threat to the flow of this prospering trade. The central government continued to consolidate its control over this trade which came mainly through the ports of Ṣuḥār, Ubulla, Baṣra, Sīrāf and of course Daybul at the mouth of the Indus River in Sind. The arid Kirmān–Makrān coast between Sīrāf and Daybul was not considered worth the trouble of a similar effort there, but this was where private enterprise came to the rescue. Some of the seafaring Arabs from the Azd of 'Umān moved into these areas, acquired good landing sites, built citadels and established themselves at suitable points along this coast. Ships unloaded their goods at these private harbours in return for a certain fee which was probably lower than the usual tax-rate.[1] To the advantage of these entrepreneurs the central government did not see any justification for interference especially as it did not have firm authority in the area. Some of these Arabs, interestingly enough, were called Ṣaffārids. It is not suggested here that the Ṣaffārids of Sīstān were of Arab origin, though the possibility cannot be totally excluded. It may be too much of a coincidence that they should have a two year war with their namesakes on the coast.[2] It is not a coincidence, however, that part of the population of wealthy Fārs were also after the control of arid Kirmān. Sensing the danger of Ṣaffārid designs and realizing that no help was forthcoming from the central government, these people decided it was time to defend their interests and took matters into their own hands. Led by Muḥammad b. Wāṣil, they defied the government, deposed its representative, started the attack on the Ṣaffārids, joined forces with Baghdād against them and continued the fight even after the government had reconciled itself to accepting the terms of their common adversary.[3] It is a remarkable fact that Muḥammad b. Wāṣil was of a genuine lineage of Umayyad Khārijites who had long since settled in Iṣṭakhr in the heart of Fārs, where they and their descendants had eventually

[1] *Ibid.*, pp. 116, 117, 140–1; Yāqūt, *Buldān* vol. II, pp. 543–4, vol. III, p. 298; vol. IV, p. 444.

[2] Iṣṭakhrī, p. 141; Yāqūt, *Buldān*, vol. II, pp. 543–4.

[3] Ṭabarī, III, pp. 1839, 1858, 1859, 1887–90, 1908, 1912.

acquired tremendous wealth.[1] Of course, heresiographers and certain modern scholars do not pay much attention to complicated details which might interfere with their simplistic outlook.

It cannot be over-emphasized that at the time of the rise of the Ṣaffārids there were many other regional uprisings. Although there may be no apparent connection, the Ṣaffārid movement cannot be understood in isolation from the others. Another most important movement at the time was the Zanj revolt. It is a sad comment on research in Islamic history that, in spite of the proximity of the territories where these two movements took place, no attempt has been made to examine their relationship, and instead efforts have been wasted on examining imaginary relationships with movements whose force was long spent. It is a curious fact that the two movements never made any attempts to ally themselves against their common enemy, the central government, and instead actually fought each other.[2] This seemingly illogical behaviour can only mean that each movement considered the elimination of the other to be of advantage to it. As we will soon see, their origins were different but their objectives were not entirely dissimilar – control of a longer stretch of the shores of the Arabian Sea and the Persian Gulf.

The rise of the Ṣaffārids brought about the final collapse of the Ṭāhirids in the East. With the exception of Soghdiana, in almost all other districts local strong men tried to emulate the Ṣaffārids and gain control of their own regions.[3] It was practically impossible for the central government to cope with this situation by its own military forces alone. The presence of the Sāmānids, the faithful protégés of the Ṭāhirids, in Soghdiana and the stability of their rule in this region offered a viable solution to the government's predicament. They were acknowledged to be directly in charge of their region and its vicinity down to the River Oxus. Ya'qūb the Ṣaffārid was given charge of the rest of the Ṭāhirid domains to the south of the river, in addition to a subsidy from the central government to enable him to carry out the fight against the rebels.[4] To establish his authority in these troubled regions, Ya'qūb knew that he first had to deal with the Shī'ite Ḥasan b. Zayd who was actively trying to re-assert his position in Ṭabaristān with the help of the local population. As this proved increasingly difficult and as he was faced with a hostile population in every direction, Ya'qūb realized that he was

[1] Iṣṭakhrī, p. 142.
[2] Ṭabarī, III, pp. 1914–15.
[3] *Ibid.*, pp. 1874–5, 1883, 1931, 2017, 2039.
[4] *Ibid.*, p. 1841.

at the losing end of the bargain with the central government.[1] Furthermore, he was actually shielding the Sāmānids, the real winners in the whole situation. He decided to turn back and pursue his plans in the south. The central government tried to negotiate with him and entice him to co-operate by offering him some nominal appointment in Baghdād. He over-estimated his bargaining position and asked for too high a price which the government could not have given even if it had agreed to it. Ya'qūb demanded authority over the Sāmānids in order to obtain their help against the rebels. When negotiations failed he boldly advanced on Baghdād, but again this was a gross over-estimation of his own power and Muwaffaq had no difficulty in inflicting a severe defeat on him not too far from Baghdād in 875/262.[2] Turning back, Ya'qūb tried to demonstrate his rule over Fārs. However the resistance of the local population led by Muḥammad b. Wāṣil, a defeat by the Zanj, and trouble in his own backyard put an end to his ambitions.[3] Yet, after his death in 879/265 his brother 'Amr was able to negotiate with the central government and secure the terms Ya'qūb had sought. This was because the Sāmānids were not doing anything to check the efforts of former Ṭāhirid protégés and remnants of their forces to regain the domination of Khurāsān.[4] The Shī'ites of Ṭabaristān took advantage of this situation to extend their influence in this region. To the disappointment of the central government 'Amr failed to make any progress against these rebels especially since they had joined forces in opposition to him. On the other hand this very failure, in addition to the mounting pressure from Ṭabaristān, persuaded the Sāmānids to act. With a little effort they restored order in these regions and drove 'Amr out of Khurāsān.[5] Thus they replaced their patrons, the Ṭāhirids, as masters of the whole East, while the Ṣaffārids continued for centuries in their little enclave in Sīstān.

In the meantime the other movement in southern 'Irāq had been gathering momentum to the extent of becoming a real threat to Baghdād. This was the Zanj revolt, one of the most misunderstood episodes in Islamic history. Since Nöldeke first wrote about it almost a century ago and introduced the notion that it was a slave revolt, this idea has prevailed and has never been reconsidered.[6] Although he was writing only "sketches", these outdated misconceptions have

[1] *Ibid.*, pp. 1840, 1880, 1883–5, 1940–1, 1993.
[2] *Ibid.*, pp. 1891–4, 2113.
[3] *Ibid.*, pp. 1895–6, 1908, 1914, 1993, 2112.
[4] *Ibid.*, pp. 1931–2.
[5] *Ibid.*, pp. 1941, 1993, 2039, 2123; Athīr, vol. VII, pp. 256–7.
[6] Th. Nöldeke, "A Servile War in the East" in *Sketches from Eastern History*, tr. by J. S. Black, Edinburgh, 1892, pp. 146–75.

been slavishly regurgitated by modern scholars. Perhaps the temptation of the romantic idea of a slave revolt in a slave-ridden society is too much to resist, or that wading through the considerable amount of valuable material in the sources is thought to be an unnecessarily cumbersome task. As it happens this is one of the best reported events of the period and by no lesser authority than Ṭabarī himself, who witnessed some of its developments and quotes directly the accounts of some of the participants, notably Muḥammad b. Ḥasan b. Sahl, who was a leading figure in the revolt.[1]

It was not a slave revolt. It was a *zanj*, i.e. a Negro, revolt. To equate Negro with slave is a reflection of nineteenth-century racial theories; it could only apply to the American South before the Civil War. The facts are that in Islamic society there were white as well as black slaves and that slave labour was not a factor in the economy as it had been in Rome. In the Islamic world slaves were mostly employed in domestic housework and of course as concubines. All the talk about slaves rising against the wretched conditions of work in the salt marshes of Baṣra is a figment of the imagination and has no support in the sources. On the contrary, some of the people who were working in the salt marshes were among the first to fight against the revolt.[2] Of course there were a few runaway slaves who joined the rebels, but this still does not make it a slave revolt. The vast majority of the rebels were Arabs of the Persian Gulf supported by free East Africans who had made their homes in the region. Along with such Negroes there were Arabs from the clans of Bāhila, Hamdān, Iyād, ʻIjl, Qays, ʻAbdulqays, and the numerous clans of Tamīm were strongly represented.[3] Furthermore, this Arab–Negro alliance was well represented in the leadership of the revolt.[4] The founder of the movement was undeniably an Arab whether he was of ʻAlawid descent as he claimed, or from ʻAbdulqays as his opponents asserted.[5] More important is the fact that among the leaders we find Negroes as well as Arabs and the astounding fact that the latter were from the ʻAbbāsid "establishment" itself. Mention has already been made of Muḥammad b. Ḥasan b. Sahl, who, though not exactly an Arab, was none other than the son of one of Ma'mūn's closest associates.[6] But the various Muhallabite

[1] Ṭabarī, III, pp. 1742–2098. [2] *Ibid.*, p. 1752.

[3] *Ibid.*, pp. 1743, 1744, 1746, 1751, 1756, 1759, 1760, 1770, 1777, 1850, 1902, 1903, 1925, 1998, 2016; Athīr, vol. VII, pp. 202, 204, 248, 255, 283; Masʻūdī, *Tanbīh*, pp. 392–3.

[4] Ṭabarī, III, pp. 1751, 1763, 1766, 1769, 1778, 1779, 2095.

[5] *Ibid.*, pp. 1742–3; Masʻūdī, *Murūj*, vol. VIII, p. 31; Ibn Ḥazm, *Jambara*, p. 57

[6] Ṭabarī, III, pp. 2135–6.

leaders represent a prestigious Arab line who had served the Umayyads and the ʿAbbāsids with great distinction in many capacities.[1] Even Jews were among the supporters of the revolt.[2] If more proof is needed that it was not a slave revolt, it is to be found in the fact that it had a highly organized army and navy which vigorously resisted the whole weight of the central government for almost fifteen years. Moreover, it must have had huge resources that allowed it to build no less than six impregnable towns in which there were arsenals for the manufacture of weapons and battleships.[3] These towns also had in their mammoth markets prodigious wealth which was more than the salt marshes could conceivably produce. Even all the booty from Baṣra and the whole region could not account for such enormous wealth.[4] Significantly the revolt had the backing of a certain group of merchants who persevered with their support until the very end. Ṭabarī makes it very clear that the strength of the rebels was dependent on the support of these merchants.[5] Under the circumstances it is hardly surprising that the rebels did not have a concrete ideology, albeit they had a purpose which certainly was not the freeing of the slaves, for they continued to have their own.

The bone of contention was the African trade, and this issue had its effects not only on the Persian Gulf but also in all the regions of North Africa, Egypt, the Red Sea coasts, Syria and even the *thughūr* on the Byzantine borders. The demand for African products was not a new feature of this era. Carthage had made its fortunes by trading in these products, the Abyssinians had sent them to Byzantium and the Makkans had greatly benefited from this trade. The demand for these products had never diminished, but the routes of the trade had changed because of wars, political situations and the interests of middlemen. Before the Arab conquest of North Africa the Byzantines had control of all the coast, and the trade had been easily carried north across the Sahara by many routes. New excavations at Garama in Libya testify to the existence, before Islam, of a great trade centre there, almost halfway between the terminals of the shortest north to south route from Chad to Tripoli.[6] The conquest and the subsequent century of revolts, unrest and fighting had put an end to the flow of this trade to the coast.

[1] *Ibid.*, p. 1745; Athīr, vol. VII, p. 283.
[2] Ṭabarī, III, p. 1760.
[3] *Ibid.*, pp. 1878, 1899, 1932, 1953, 1971, 1974, 2042–3, 2062.
[4] *Ibid.*, pp. 1959, 1964, 1966, 1971, 1975, 2032, 2053, 2055–6, 2068, 2078.
[5] *Ibid.*, pp. 1783, 1835; Athīr, vol. VII, p. 262.
[6] M. S. Ayyūb, *Jerma*, Tripoli, 1969, pp. 91–127.

When the ʿAbbāsids came to power and the Aghlabids established their rule over Tunisia – then called Ifrīqiyya – 800/184, this region like Libya and Egypt continued its basically agricultural economy, and no attempt was made to revive the long-forgotten trade. But the Berbers, the indigenous population of North Africa, remembering its lucrative profits, were now free to resume this activity. This manifested itself in the rise of new political entities in north-west Africa; the Rustamids in what is now western Algeria in 777/160; and the Idrīsids in what is now Morocco in 789/172. These small states were little more than trading companies formed at the terminals of well-known trade routes across the Sahara. The Rustamids were Khārijites and the Idrīsids Shīʿites, the main difference in economic policy between them being their respective systems of taxation. The Khārijites were for a measure of *laissez-faire*, i.e. lower taxes on trade. They obviously needed the intermediaries to bring the trade to them and in such a case the imposition of taxes would be counter-productive.[1] The Shīʿites favoured a higher rate of taxation either because some local minerals were involved or because they had better access to the trade that came to them along easier routes.[2] Another difference between the Shīʿites and the Khārijites was the fact that among the former there was a noticeable Arab element while the latter were almost purely Berbers. It is worth noting that while Egypt and Tunisia were under the firm control of the ʿAbbāsids and the Aghlabids, Tripolitania, which was at the terminal of the shortest but most difficult route across the Sahara, remained a strong bastion of the Khārijite Berbers.[3]

It should be pointed out that the most guarded trade secrets of the time were the places where the product originated and the routes across difficult terrains. Intermediaries knew only too well that these secrets constituted all their know-how, and accordingly many practices and customs were developed to preserve them. In some areas foreigners were not allowed to cross certain territories although they were welcome to trade at market places established for this purpose close to the borders.[4] In other places goods were brought across a river and left there over-night to enable the foreign trader

[1] Ḥawqal, pp. 67–9, 153–5; Maqdisī, p. 29; Yaʿqūbī, *Buldān*, pp. 252, 345; Bakrī, *Al-Mughrib* . . ., ed. De Slane, Paris, 1911, pp. 68, 139.

[2] Yaʿqūbī, *Buldān*, pp. 356–7; Bakrī, pp. 76–7, 161; ʿIdhārī, vol. 1, pp. 232–3; see also my forthcoming study on Spain and North Africa.

[3] Kindī, *Wulāt*, p. [illegible]; Maqrīzī, *Khiṭaṭ*, vol. 1, p. 320; Yaʿqubī, *Buldān*, p. 352; Ḥawqal, pp. 67–9.

[4] Maqrīzī, *Khiṭaṭ*, vol. 1, pp. 190, 199; Ḥawqal, p. 51.

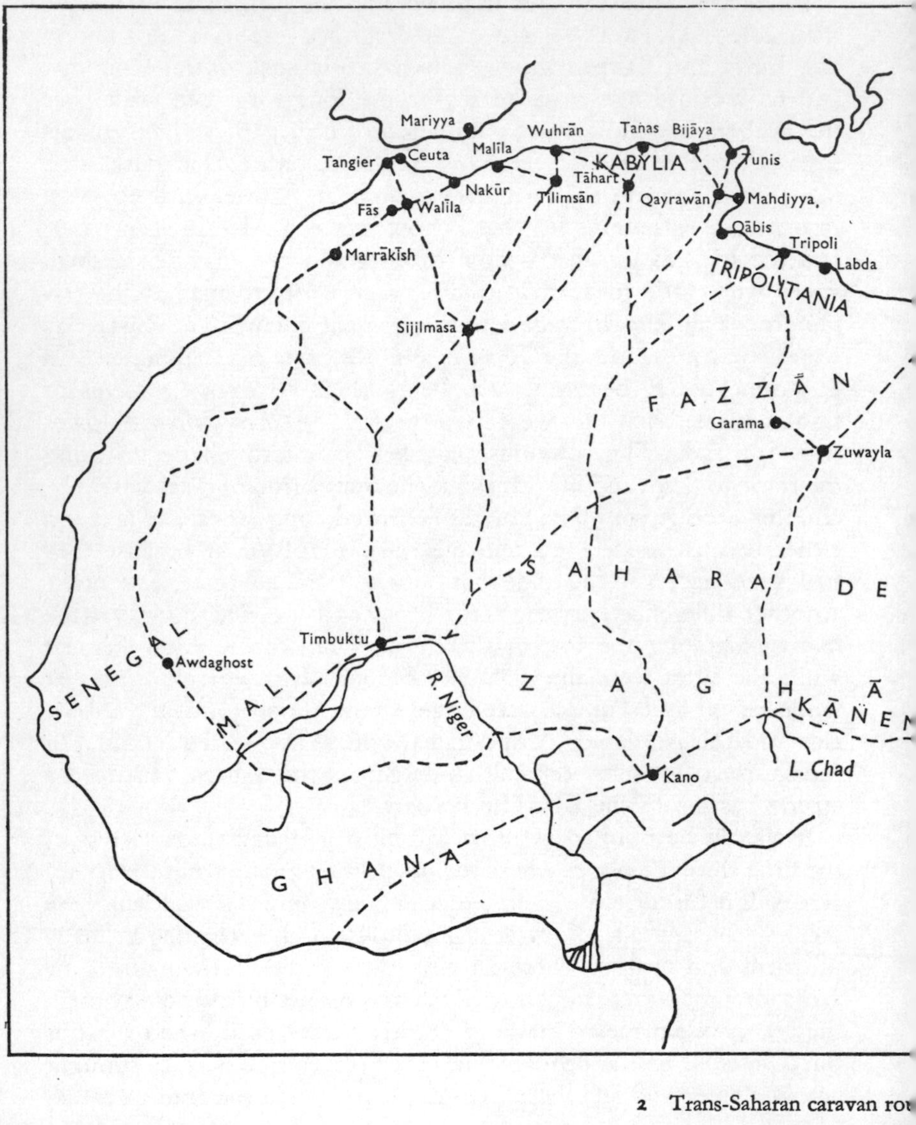

2 Trans-Saharan caravan rou

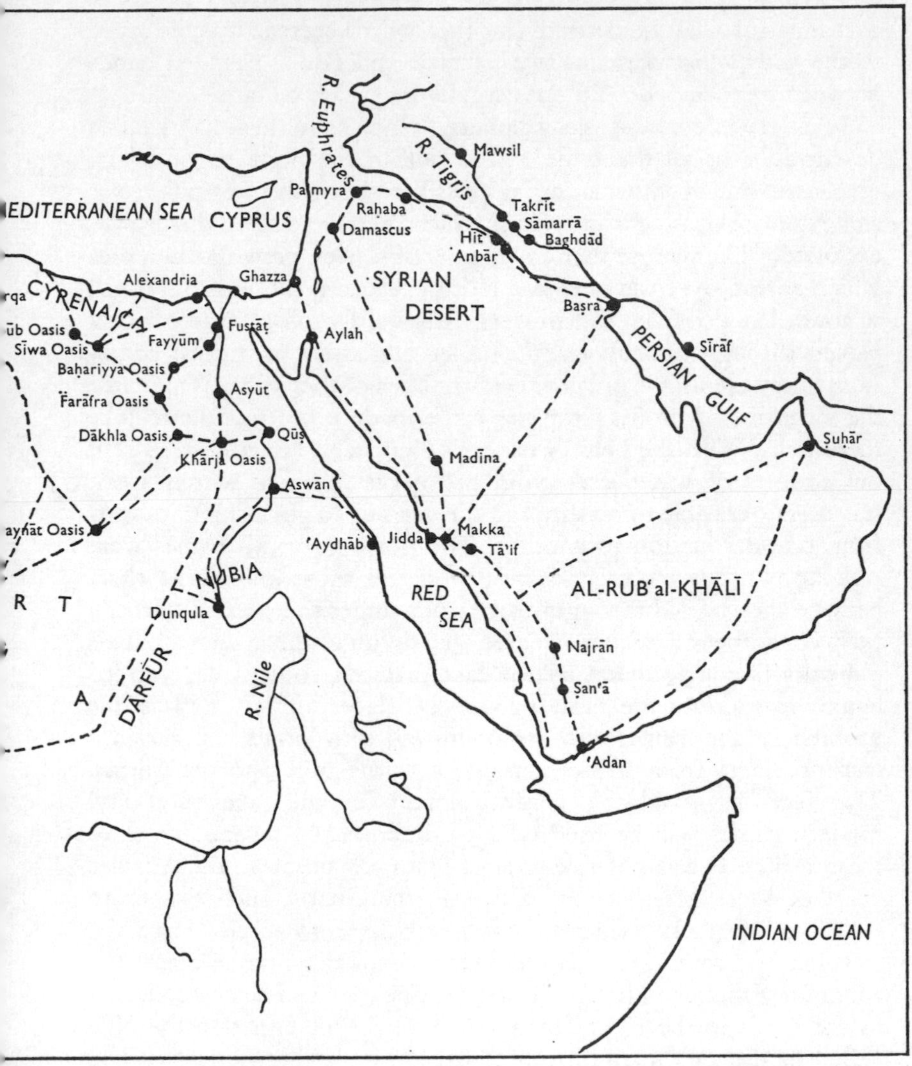
R. Euphrates
R. Tigris
Mawsil
Palmyra
Rahaba
Damascus
Takrīt
Sāmarrā
Baghdād
Hīt
Anbār
EDITERRANEAN SEA
CYPRUS
Alexandria
Ghazza
CYRENAICA
SYRIAN
DESERT
Basra
Fustāt
Fayyūm
Aylah
Siwa Oasis
Bahariyya Oasis
Farafra Oasis
Asyūt
Dākhla Oasis
Qūs
Khārja Oasis
PERSIAN GULF
Sīrāf
Madīna
Suhār
Aswān
Jidda
Makka
'Aydhāb
Tā'if
NUBIA
RED SEA
AL-RUB'al-KHĀLĪ
Dunqula
DĀRFŪR
R. Nile
Najrān
San'ā
'Adan
INDIAN OCEAN

to leave what he considered a fair amount of his own goods in exchange for what he desired. In other words secrecy was observed to the extent that bargains were struck and goods changed hands between partners who did not actually meet face to face.[1]

Arab travellers and geographers, who have left us detailed descriptions of all the trade routes within the domains of Islam, give us as much information as possible about the feasibility, use and extent of outside routes from which they were often themselves excluded.[2] The picture that emerges is of a wide network of routes which spread over the northern half of Africa not only from north to south but also from east to west. Admittedly most of these routes passed through difficult terrain under extremely hazardous conditions and were usable only for certain times of the year. All the same the incentive of profits from the trade made it worthwhile to take these risks. With the help of expert guides who knew how to sniff out sources of water and avoid the perils of these barren areas, travellers were able to go through the various stages of their journey from one destination to another. The north to south routes were well known but the east to west were the most difficult to chart because they passed through many lands under the control of many peoples, none of whom wanted to divulge their secrets. This difficulty is compounded by the fact that our sources use various names to indicate the same groups of places and, to add to the problem, these names can be confused with other things since ancient differs from modern usage, e.g. the Nile and the Sudan. Therefore, to avoid this confusion and for the sake of clarity, modern names will be used here to describe the several stages of these routes. It was possible to start from any point on the Atlantic coast of West Africa, be it in Senegal or Ghana, and advance to Kano in Northern Nigeria, and from there to Chad. Here the traveller had a multiplicity of choices; he could go north across the Sahara to Fazzān and then to Tripoli; or he could advance north-east to the Oasis in the Egyptian desert, and thence either to the Nile valley or the Egyptian–Libyan coast. An easier choice from Chad was to proceed slightly south-east in order to skirt the desert and then almost straight east to Dārfūr in the Sudan. From here it was

[1] Marvazī, p. 49.

[2] Yāqūt, *Buldān*, vol. III, pp. 142, 159–60, 261, vol. IV, pp. 260, 432, 486, vol. V, pp. 242, 392; Khaldūn, pp. 94, 98–9; Ya'qūbī, *Buldān*, pp. 334, 335, 345; Maghribī, *Jughrāfiyā*, pp. 91, 96; Mas'ūdī, *Tanbīh*, p. 331; Iṣṭakhrī, p. 45; Ḥawqal, pp. 15, 16, 60, 61, 92, 101, 153, 154, 155; Bakrī, pp. 9, 14, 15, 180, 182; Maqrīzī, *Khiṭaṭ*, vol. I, pp. 4, 182, 193–7, vol. II, pp. 257, 263.

an easy journey into Nubia and then north to Egypt or east to the ports of the Red Sea. From ʻAydhāb, the most important of these ports at the time, it was an easy crossing to the ports of Ḥijāz, which were only a short distance from Makka and Madīna, and then ultimately to Baghdād. Of course, it was also easy to sail from ʻAydhāb to any other port on the East African, Arabian and Persian Gulf coasts. All the peoples along these routes were interested in the profits from the trade passing through their territories, and although relations were usually good, conflicts frequently arose. Piratical activities in the Persian Gulf, increasingly vicious attacks on trade caravans at all points *en route* from Makka to Baghdād by impoverished nomads, the sudden rise of antagonisms between Makka, Madīna and Jidda, and above all the Zanj revolt, were all contemporaneous manifestations of such conflicts.[1]

In the case of the Persian Gulf the seafaring Arabs of the region had an astonishingly wide range of international relations. They had an established colony as far east as Canton; and an enterprising merchant from Sīrāf managed to overcome all the barriers and pay a visit to west-central Africa.[2] Arab relations with East Africa since antiquity need no proof. Over the ages many Arabs have settled and become part of the population there, and although we do not know when this process started, there is no reason to believe that it was a one-way practice. On the contrary, the secrecy on the African side, the open-door policy of the empire, the expansion of trade and the clamour for African goods, certainly stimulated the setting-up and growth of East African colonies in all the trade centres of the Gulf. Many of these immigrants became Muslims and established close relationships with the indigenous population of the region. Others were not assimilated to such an extent, but their interest in trade would have been stronger owing to their bonds with their native lands.[3] Such a situation gave these people and their partners in the Gulf a virtual monopoly over the importation of African goods into the area. Any outside competition in this field through newly activated trade routes such as that via ʻAydhāb would certainly represent a very serious threat to the prosperity of these monopolists. To add to their distress a change in the government's taxation policy was put into effect at this time. We remember that early in Wāthiq's reign 847–61/227–32, taxes on trade coming through the Gulf ports

[1] Ṭabarī, III, pp. 1931, 1941, 2008, 2025, 2026, 2039.
[2] Marvazī, p. 42.
[3] Ṭabarī, III, 1744, 1751, 1752, 1757, 1758, 1763–4, 1766, 1769, 1771–2, 1837.

had been abolished. The new taxation policy of Muwaffaq did not allow such leniency and, if the new taxes imposed in Egypt were a guide, it can be easily perceived that stringent new taxes were re-imposed on all these goods, and considering that they were imported from non-Muslim territory, the rate could have been as much as 20%.[1] The appointment of Ibrāhīm b. al-Mudabbir, the brother of the organizer of the new tax system in Egypt, to supervise tax collection in Baṣra is a vivid attestation to the tax-collecting methods there.[2] Any merchant who is suddenly confronted with such a tax in addition to a drastic decline in his trade, cannot be expected to sit back and hope for the best. The Arabs of the region whose interests were certainly involved and who, under similar circumstances earlier, had begun to attack trade caravans would surely rise again in defence of these interests. Without this combination of wealth and manpower, the Zanj revolt would not have been possible.

With remarkable efficiency and expedition the rebels swiftly established their control over most of the Persian Gulf coast, and extended it inland to secure their food supplies. Special vehemence was reserved for the port of Baṣra which they practically destroyed. Their choice of sites fo rtheir own new towns and their meticulous knowledge of the intricate waterways of the region in addition to their great skill in naval warfare were all utilized to strangle the Baṣran economy and drive all the in-coming trade through their own channels.[3] Wāsiṭ, the major bottle-neck on the way north to Baghdād, was completely cut off from any road or waterway leading south to the Gulf coast. Furthermore, the rebels occupied Kūfa in order to secure the alternative inland route to the north.[4] They expelled government forces from all these areas and easily withstood the onslaught of the successive expeditions that Muwaffaq sent against them. Realizing the grave dangers of this situation, he decided to mobilize all his financial and military forces against this audacious enemy. For the army he introduced yet another re-organization which was in effect an amalgamation of previous measures. It is characteristic of his pragmatism that his plans took into consideration all aspects of the existing conditions. Perhaps the most important step was that he was able to integrate most of the military forces in such a way that racial differences were set aside. This involved re-grouping

[1] See above, p. 95; Ṣābī, *Wuzarā'*, p. 248.

[2] Ṭabarī, III, p. 1838; Abbār, p. 162.

[3] Ṭabarī, III, pp. 1767–8, 1772, 1776, 1783, 1835, 1836, 1848–9, 1855–6, 1866, 1991, 2032, 2053, 2096.

[4] *Ibid.*, pp. 1883, 2013.

the men, placing non-Arabs under Arab commanders and vice versa.[1] This simple device put an end to the internal squabbles within the army. All that remained to ensure its stability was to secure the financial resources in order to guarantee to the men regularity of their stipends. For this purpose Muwaffaq allowed for the first time the full application and formal institution of military–administrative *iqṭāʿ*. As explained before this meant that military commanders were appointed governors of certain regions and given complete authority over the all important fiscal affairs there and, in return, they assured the central treasury of the payment of an agreed sum from the revenues of their respective regions. This was applied in areas where government rule needed to be more firmly established, or in areas such as Egypt where the revenues were of vital importance to the central treasury. Thus Aḥmad b. Ṭūlūn was given a free hand in Egypt, and relieved of the restrictive presence of the fiscal supervisor Aḥmad b. al-Mudabbir who was transferred to Syria.[2] The Ṣaffārid attack and the Zanj revolt helped Muwaffaq to carry out his plans against considerable opposition spear-headed by his own son, the future Muʿtaḍid. The latter's subsequent imprisonment on his father's orders is a clear sign of the gravity of the situation.[3]

The problems of Ibn Ṭūlūn in his domains were no less complicated than those of Muwaffaq and also had a great deal to do with the African trade. The revenues of Egypt were ample enough to satisfy Ibn Ṭūlūn and the central treasury to the extent that he abolished all the tax innovations that had been so recently introduced by Ibn al-Mudabbir. The central government was so happy with his management of Egypt that it added southern Syria up to Damascus to his domains. His problems stemmed from the *sūdān*, i.e. the Negroes, the *thughūr*, his son ʿAbbās and Tripolitania. At a first glance these various problems seem entirely unrelated, yet they were all directly connected with the sources, routes and markets of the African trade.

The sudden and conspicuous appearance of the *sūdān* amongst the armies of Ibn Ṭūlūn in Egypt calls for an explanation. Some sources like us to believe that he bought as many as 40,000 Negro slaves and made soldiers out of them to build up an empire of his own.[4] Buying such a number of slaves, let alone training them to be an effective fighting force in a completely unfamiliar territory, would

[1] *Ibid.*, pp. 1920, 1921, 1975, 1977, 1981, 1988, 2016, 2020, 2039, 2083, 2097.
[2] Maqrīzī, vol. I, p. 319; Yaʿqūbī, *Tārīkh*, vol. II, pp. 508–9; Kindī, *Wulāt*, pp. 214–17.
[3] See below, p. 113.
[4] Maqrīzī, *Khiṭaṭ*, vol. I, p. 315.

certainly have required more time than the few years that preceded their appearance in Egypt and subsequently in Syria and on the Byzantine borders in the early years of Ibn Ṭūlūn's rule 868–84/254–70. Other sources more accurately inform us that he "enlisted" these *sūdān* in his army.[1] Curiously enough Muḥammad 'Alī, the ruler of Egypt in the early nineteenth century, did the same thing and we know that when he unsuccessfully deployed such men in these very areas against the Ottomans, the failure of the experiment was attributed to the fact that these men had no motive to fight in a foreign land. Under Ibn Ṭūlūn, however, these *sūdān* fought well and for a good reason not too difficult to understand. The key is in the use of the term *sūdān* to describe people who were as negroid as the Zanj. In the terminology of the time these designations were not used at random; they were meant to define certain groups of mankind. The Zanj were the population of East Africa and extending from there into Central Africa. To the north there were the Ḥabasha, i.e. the Abyssinians, and still further north was the land of the Beja. West of these, to the south of Egypt, the country of the Nubians extended south to Central Africa and west into West-Central Africa. From what is now the western Sudan to the shores of the Atlantic were the lands of the *sūdān*, many of whom were also known by their tribal names or according to the names of their localities.

We are here concerned with the Zaghāwa, the name of a tribe and its territory which bordered the south of the Sahara and extended west from what is now the western Sudan across Chad, Niger and Northern Nigeria to Upper Volta.[2] Through these regions passed an important trade route that started from Ghana and continued all the way to the Egyptian Oases and then either to the Nile valley or to Tripolitania. It is significant that this route had been in use until Ibn Ṭūlūn cut it at the Oases.[3] He did so, not because he did not want the trade, but because he wanted more control over it. The vast Egyptian desert and the troublesome Khārijites of Tripolitania demanded constant surveillance, and this would be much easier if the trade could be diverted to a more controllable route. The good relations with the king of Nubia, who had had his Nubia House in Fusṭāṭ since the days of Mu'taṣim, provided the solution. Although he did not allow Egyptians to enter his territory and all trading with them was done at the borders, it was a different matter to solicit his

[1] Kindī, *Wulāt*, p. 214.
[2] Khaldūn, pp. 94, 98; Yāqūt, *Buldān*, vol. III, p. 142.
[3] Ḥawqal, p. 153.

co-operation in allowing the Zaghāwa to pass through his lands. After all they had been by-passing Nubia altogether and going from Chad to the Egyptian Oases, and it could only be to his advantage to bring more trade to his kingdom. For Ibn Ṭūlūn, Aswān was an ideal control point from which merchandise could be transported north up the Nile or east to 'Aydhāb, a secure outlet to the Red Sea and further. For the Zaghāwa the Nubian route was a much safer one that would save them from the hazards of the desert. Once this was established, their increasing presence in Egypt was almost a logical consequence and a clear indication of their interest in widening the scope of their trade. Ibn Ṭūlūn would have no objection to such an expansion which could only enhance the wealth of his domains. This common interest created the opportunity for military as well as economic co-operation which explains the enlistment of the *sūdān* in the army of Egypt.

Between them these two parties commanded major sources for African goods, the greater part of an important trade-route and outlets on the Red and Mediterranean Seas. The addition of southern Syria to Ibn Ṭūlūn's governorship gave them more outlets, as it was no secret that the ports on the Syrian coast were trading with Byzantium through Cyprus. To take full advantage of these sea outlets, no time was wasted in building a strong merchant navy for Egypt.[1] However, it was soon realized that the best exporting outlets were through the markets of the *thughūr*. While Baghdād was busy fighting the Ṣaffārids and the Zanj there was a perfect chance to try and capture these areas. For this task Ibn Ṭūlūn dispatched an expedition of the *sūdān* led by their powerful chief Lu'lu'. The intrepid resistance of the population of Tarsus and Antioch to these intruders is the most telling proof that they knew what their losses were likely to be.[2] On the other hand the Byzantine emperor showed his goodwill towards Ibn Ṭūlūn by sending him gifts and releasing from captivity a nephew of Afshīn.[3] This last personal gesture can be taken to mean that the emperor knew that there was a special relationship between the Afshīn and Ṭūlūn families. This affinity in addition to the fact that Ibn Ṭūlūn had in his service both the son of the *jabghū*, the ruler of Ṭukhāristān, and Toghj, a prince from Farghāna, ought to put to rest the fictitious story that Ṭūlūn was of slave origin.[4]

[1] Kindī, *Wulāt*, p. 234.

[2] Ṭabarī, III, pp. 1929, 1939–40, 2025, 2028–9; Mas'ūdī, *Murūj*, vol. VIII, pp. 68, 71.

[3] Ṭabarī, III, p. 1931.

[4] *Ibid.*, p. 2037; Maqrīzī, *Khiṭaṭ*, vol. I, pp. 313, 319.

The resistance of the *thughūr* convinced Lu'lu' of the futility of continuing his attacks on this front. At the same time he also realized that if the Zanj were to win their fight against Baghdād, they would be in a much better competitive position to dominate the greater share of the African trade. Without any hesitation and against the wishes of Ibn Ṭūlūn, Lu'lu' and his followers turned around and joined Muwaffaq against the Zanj.[1] Ibn Ṭūlūn's efforts in person to capture the *thughūr* came to naught, especially as he had opposition to his plans from within his own ranks. His brother had refused to take part in the whole venture.[2] His son 'Abbās had a positive plan of his own which he proceeded to put into practice while his father was on the Byzantine frontier. He marched west into Tripolitania and proclaimed Ṭūlūnid rule in this troublesome region, and from there he vied with the Aghlabids to command as much as possible of the North African coast.[3] His logic must have been inspired by the fact that the latter had at last got involved in the lucrative African trade, and started exporting direct to Europe from the bases in Sicily which they had conquered a few years earlier.[4] In his judgment it was probably better to spend the effort overcoming a competitor rather than to secure outlets for a market which was accessible already. His father had to cut short his campaign and return to Egypt to deal with him.

The reconciliation of father and son and the death of the former soon after, in 884/270, did not put an end to Ṭūlūnid ambitions to capture the *thughūr*. Ibn Ṭūlūn was succeeded by another son, Khumārawayh, who immediately resumed the campaign, but this time the dauntless population there had the active support of Baghdād. Muwaffaq, who had suppressed the Zanj revolt only months earlier in 883/270, was able to spare some of his troops and dispatch them to the rescue. After three years of fighting neither side had won a decisive victory, and the stalemate led to a compromise agreement. Muwaffaq realized that the regions of Damascus and Palestine preferred to remain under Ṭūlūnid rule and that their economic interests lay with Egypt. On the other hand it became clear to Khumārawayh that capturing the *thughūr* was out of the question, and that the interests of the people there were in the flow of trade coming from the Gulf and Baghdād. Therefore he gave up

[1] Ṭabarī, III, p. 2025; Kindī, *Wulāt*, p. 224.

[2] Kindī, *Wulāt*, p. 215.

[3] *Ibid.*, pp. 220–4; Ṭabarī, III, pp. 1932, 2011; Maqrīzī, *Khiṭaṭ*, vol. I, 320; Athīr, vol. VII, pp. 195–225.

[4] Athīr, vol. VII, p. 196.

all his ambitions there, and in return Muwaffaq confirmed him and his descendants as rulers over Damascus and Palestine as well as Egypt for thirty years. Eventually the Ṭūlūnids agreed to pay the central treasury either 200,000 or 300,000 dinārs a year.[1] Compared to the 750,000 that Aḥmad b. Ṭūlūn had paid for Egypt alone, it meant a great loss for Baghdād.[2] However the real casualties of this agreement were Lu'lu' and his Zaghāwa *sūdān*; he was imprisoned and his followers absorbed into Muwaffaq's army.[3] The remaining *sūdān* in Egypt reacted to these developments by rebelling in 887/273 but they were easily subdued.[4]

Having freed himself from all these major problems, Muwaffaq began to reassert the authority of the central government wherever possible. His change of policy was signified by the dismissal of Ṣā'id b. Makhlad in 885–6/272. In his thirteen years in office, this man, who had been first appointed only as a *kātib*, had been allowed a good deal of authority to enable him to handle the affairs of the central government on behalf of Muwaffaq in his protracted absences on various campaigns. Indeed he had had an advantage over the military leaders as is evident from the fact that he had led military expeditions, and had been granted the title *dhū al-riyāsatayn*, i.e. one having authority in two capacities.[5] In his stead Muwaffaq appointed Ismā'īl b. Bulbul, a man long associated with Ṣā'id's administration as *wazīr* to the impotent Mu'tamid. All the same, on his appointment, Ismā'īl assigned the Furāt brothers to various departments concerned with fiscal affairs.[6] This new team was well suited to apply Muwaffaq's new policy, the core of which was the repudiation of military–administrative *iqṭā'*. He was so determined to revoke this system which had been practically forced upon him that he used his army against such governors as refused to give up their positions.[7] When his son Aḥmad opposed these measures, he did not hesitate to throw him into prison.

In the last months of his life Muwaffaq was a very sick man and his long-forgotten brother, the nominal ruler Mu'tamid, was in no position to exercise any authority. This confused situation allowed

[1] Kindī, *Wulāt*, pp. 233–40; Maqrīzī, *Khiṭaṭ*, vol. I, p. 321; Ṭabarī, III, pp. 2106, 2108, 2116, 2132.

[2] Kindī, *Wulāt*, p. 214.

[3] Ṭabarī, III, p. 2112; Ṣābī, *Wuzarā'*, pp. 11–12.

[4] Athīr, vol. VII, p. 298.

[5] Ṭabarī, III, pp. 1930, 2040–9, 2083, 2109; Mas'ūdī, *Murūj*, vol. VIII, pp. 61–2.

[6] Ṭabarī, III, pp. 1931, 2104, 2110, 2123; Ṣābī, *Rusūm*, p. 51; Abbār, p. 180.

[7] Ṭabarī, III, pp. 2115–18, 2131.

the supporters of Aḥmad to bring him out of prison and install him as a *de facto* ruler. Within a few months after the death of both Muwaffaq and Mu'tamid in 892/278 he was formally invested as a successor under the title Mu'taḍid. Ismā'īl was arrested, the Furāts went into hiding and the Jarrāḥs eventually came to power.[1]

[1] *Ibid.*, pp. 2118–23, 2131 2133; Abbār, p. 175.

1. What were regional econ. interests?
2. How did they differ from central govt? →
3. Why was treasury empty?
4. Was taxation agrarian?
5. Was agrarian prod. ∇?
6. Was " investment ∇?

Answers??:

1. Regional econ. interest – lower land tax.
2. Revenues were not sent to Baghdad?
3. Yes.
4. Yes. } Wars consumed revenues of centre.
5. Yes

1. Did (from 850–900) military stipends Δ faster, greater than land revenue production? (Apparently – yes)

6

THE BREAKDOWN OF THE CENTRAL GOVERNMENT (I)

So far the central government had managed to muddle its way through successive crises and challenges from the provinces and had continued to rule without any solid foundations. Its wealth had helped it to recruit military forces adequate to impose temporary solutions for the many problems in its vast domains. When military measures had failed half-hearted political concessions had been made in the hope that they could be revoked in due course. Any long term policies that had been introduced had had the single aim of strengthening central control without taking regional interests into consideration. The maintenance of this political order depended on the continued flow of revenues from the provinces into the coffers of the central treasury. The increasing tendency in these provinces to take a stand in defence of their economic interests had begun to have its impact on the revenues of the central government and this in turn had affected its ability to mobilize its forces to maintain its rule.

It is most significant that when Mu'taḍid came to power in 892/279, there were no reserves in the central treasury for the first time in its history.[1] This critical situation demanded immediate rectification. In his ten years' reign, his efforts were doomed to failure because he did not or could not depart from the basic principles of the political orthodoxy of his ancestors. It is no wonder that the seeds of self-destruction inherent in these policies continued to germinate, and caused his successors even more insoluble problems that eventually brought about the collapse of the central government. Military–administrative *iqṭā'* became the only vehicle of maintaining control over the provinces and led to the appearance of *mutaghallibūn* or *aṣḥāb al-aṭrāf*, i.e. military leaders who defied the central government and for all practical purposes became independent in some of the outer regions. To contain this movement the government needed more money to pay more men to fight for the preservation of its integrity in the remaining territories under its direct control. As the

[1] Ṣābī, *Wuzarā'*, pp. 9–10.

money had to come from these latter regions a new method of tax collecting, tax-farming, was introduced to ensure the flow of the badly needed revenues. Members of the military–bureaucratic complex were quick to endeavour to utilize this new system to their advantage, and allowed each other to exploit the situation to enrich themselves. Their growing land-holdings in addition to the increasing burden of taxation forced many small farmers out of their lands. The outcome of this dislocation of the rural population was a growing horde of nomads who vented their grievances by attacking caravans and attempting to dominate the network of the inland trade routes. This serious threat to the all-important trade created new conflicts and unusual alliances between unexpected partners. Prompted by vested interests among its own circles, the central government had to act to find forces to protect trade. Military–administrative *iqṭāʿ* was extended to include even the income from inter-regional taxes imposed on the trade passing along the important trade routes. It was also used to pay for the services of military groups from the outer regions who flocked into the heart of the empire, attracted by these free-for-all conditions. One of these groups, the Daylam, from the indigenous population of the Caspian regions were to play a major role in the downfall of the central government. Meanwhile, revolutionary movements of a Shīʿite character found fertile ground among the rural communities and hastened the break up of the empire.

The symptoms of all these ailments had been present during the rule of the strong man Muwaffaq, whose pragmatism had helped to save the empire as well as to check these weaknesses. Having overcome his formidable adversaries, he had begun to think in terms of a long term policy but gout and elephantiasis had only added to his difficulties in this respect. We do not know what this policy would have been, yet his moves to put an end to military–administrative *iqṭāʿ* indicate his awareness of the dangers of a system that he had tolerated for the sake of expediency. He must have been aware also that there would be strong resistance from powerful conservative circles to any attempt to change the prevailing conditions. It is ironical that he himself had, to some extent, helped to consolidate the powers of these circles in order to win their support in his earlier difficult years. The resulting balance of power in the empire was to the advantage of these circles and they did not like to see it disturbed.

Muʿtaḍid, who had opposed his father's departure from his first policies, was also a strong man, but pragmatism was certainly not one of his characteristics. Indeed he was essentially a conservative who was willing to accept only minor tactical changes in order to preserve the established order. In his reign 892–902/279–89 he completely failed to take note of the very obvious signs of unrest in his domains, and made no attempt to meet the crying need for change everywhere. Instead, he satisfied himself by using every possible device to tighten his personal control over every component of his government. To such a conservative ruler the policy of the separation of military and fiscal affairs was not only a political dogma but also a means to acquire the management of both. Nevertheless, in spite of all the measures he took to secure this objective, his short-sighted policies procured just the opposite result.

Mu'taḍid inherited a relatively strong and unified army which had been rid of the scourge of racial differences, and he had a grand plan for the proper use of it. This plan involved dividing the army into three main forces, each of which had a special function. The first division constituted the elite of his forces and was to act as a standing army, stationed in Baghdād to take part in ceremonial occasions and to be dispatched to meet any emergency. These men fell into two categories, infantry and cavalry. The infantry were mainly from the *sūdān*, and eventually some Daylamites joined them. As they were stationed in barracks built for the purpose of housing them and because of their particular duties, they were called *maṣāffiyya*. The cavalry who, by the nature of things, were more involved in ceremonies and more effective in fighting, were not only better equipped but also a more distinguished calibre of men. Many of them were the sons of generals, chiefs and comparable leaders;[1] some of them were Arabs while others were not, and amongst the latter there was a noticeable Khazar element.[2] They were all housed in the palace and performed the duties of the personal guards of the ruler. Because of these various factors they were described by different appellations, *fursān*, cavalry; *khāṣṣa*, elite; *ḥujariyya*, living in rooms; *ghilmān*, servants and *mamālīk*, slaves of the ruler. This last term gave rise to some reports that they were bought, but as we know that they were of such distinguished origins such reports can be easily dismissed. Any one of these men who showed special abilities was promoted to the rank of *fatā Amīr al-Mu'minīn*, i.e. a brave youth in service of the ruler.[3] They were all in the charge of a *khādim*, a high

[1] Ṣābī, *Rusūm*, pp. 71–2.

[2] Athīr, vol. VII, p. 376; Ṭabarī, III, p. 2263.

[3] Ṭabarī, III, p. 2265.

ranking official of the palace. Their stipends were paid from the central treasury, and to begin with this cavalry force was no more than a hundred men, although their numbers increased very rapidly.

The second division of Mu'taḍid's army was also composed of cavalry and infantry, but of men of less ability. They were known as *'askar al-khidma*, servicemen and also as *shurṭa*, police force. Their duties were to maintain public order in Baghdād and its immediate vicinity. They were also charged with the responsibility of securing the safety of the main routes leading into the city. In charge of them was also a *khādim*, and this means that they were under the direct control of the ruler. Their stipends, which were less than those of the elite forces, were also paid by the central treasury.

The third division comprised the least able men, a fact which is confirmed by the appellation *'askar al-dūn*, inferior forces. Their function is indicated by their other name *ma'ūna*, auxiliary body. Under the leadership of their generals, they were sent out to the provinces to enforce government authority, police their areas, and support the fiscal administrators when needed, to enable them to collect overdue taxes from recalcitrant subjects. This does not mean that they were allowed to interfere in fiscal affairs, because although they were to receive their stipends from the revenues of the provinces in which they were stationed, a special civilian official *munfiq*, bursar, was appointed to supervise the distribution of stipends in order to ensure the strict separation of military and fiscal affairs.[1]

In charge of the central government Mu'taḍid appointed a *wazīr*, 'Ubaydullah b. Sulaymān b. Wahb, an old hand associated with Muwaffaq's early administration. He also happened to be a grandfather of Mu'taḍid's wife and could therefore be expected to be a more loyal agent.[2] Significantly this *wazīr* was given authority over the generals of the third army division in the provinces.[3] In other words, a trustworthy civilian representing the ruler and in charge of fiscal affairs, was assigned the responsibility and given the power to keep the military out of fiscal affairs in the provinces where they were stationed. To fulfil these strenuous duties the old *wazīr* had the assistance of his son Qāsim, the ruler's father-in-law, who was appointed as liaison officer between his father and his son-in-law.[4] These meticulous arrangements were thought to be enough to bring

[1] Ṣābī, *Wuzarā'*, pp. 11–17, where the details of this organization are elaborated in the current official language; for the term *munfiq* see, Ṣābī, *Wuzarā'*, p. 158; Miskawayh, vol. I, p. 153.

[2] Baṭrīq, p. 74.

[3] Ṭabarī, III, pp. 2152, 2155; Mas'ūdī, *Murūj*, vol. VIII, p. 114.

[4] Ṣābī, *Wuzarā'*, p. 20.

stability to the empire, but as they were not accompanied by any measures to tackle the various regional problems, the whole plan fell apart at the first shock.

The first problem that was particularly pressing was an empty central treasury. By coincidence the death of the Sāmānid governor of the East early in 892/279 offered a solution, as it seems to have encouraged many groups to encroach on Sāmānid domains. Once more, remnants of Ṭāhirid forces in Khurāsān and the Shī'ites of Ṭabaristān tried to take advantage of what seemed to them to be a lapse of Sāmānid power, in order to re-assert themselves in their regions.[1] Further south, the Ṣaffārid 'Amr b. Layth also thought that he had a chance of dislodging the Sāmānids altogether. The central government, which had earlier confirmed the rule of the Sāmānids over the whole east in lieu of the Ṭāhirids and presumably on the same conditions, namely granting them a subsidy from the central treasury, was now more than ready to strike a bargain with the Ṣaffarids. These were ready not only to forsake the subsidy but also to pay Mu'taḍid four million dirhams a year in exchange for assigning Sāmānid domains to them.[2] Although the Ṣaffārids had some initial successes against the combined forces of Khurāsān and Ṭabaristān they were eventually routed by the Sāmānids. 'Amr was captured and pointedly sent to Baghdād. Mu'taḍid was put in the humiliating position of having to confirm the Sāmānid Ismā'īl b. Aḥmad over the East, and resume paying him the subsidy of between three and ten million dirhams to enable him to continue his efforts against the Ṣaffārids.[3] Although this venture did not bring much of the hoped-for revenue to Baghdād, it brought there some of the remainder of the Ṭāhirid forces of Khurāsān; a factor which added to the financial difficulties of the central government.[4]

The astute *wazīr* had to find the badly needed money especially as the central government had to face new challenges which will be explained presently. Although, by all accounts, he was a capable man he seems to have been of limited imagination. Or at least, his abilities were more in the administrative than in the fiscal field. First, he saw that because of the complexity of the lunar calendars taxes were being demanded in April for crops that were harvested in June. As this anomaly was bound to interfere with the revenues it was easily adjusted to the satisfaction of everyone concerned.[5] He

[1] Ṭabarī, III, pp. 2135, 2151.
[2] *Ibid.*, pp. 2135, 2151, 2183, 2188.
[3] *Ibid.*, pp. 2194, 2203, 2204.
[4] *Ibid.*, p. 2141.
[5] *Ibid.*, p. 2143; Mas'ūdī, *Tanbīh*, p. 216.

took another step which involved a further complex matter; the inheritance laws of Islam. Before the stringent administration of Muwaffaq these matters had been left to the discretion of the judges, but the government had then created a special department for inheritance affairs. Its purpose had been to acquire for the treasury any legacies which, according to the strict application of the law, would have had no claimants. As there must have been many ways to evade such meddling by government, the expenses of running such departments would have been more than the revenues. Sensibly, they were abolished and inheritance problems returned to the discretion of the judges.[1] Another interesting measure introduced for the sake of economy at that time was a five-day week for government employees. In addition to Fridays they were also allowed Tuesdays, unfortunately without pay.[2] All these measures might have saved the government some money, but obviously more action was needed to satisfy the needs of the central treasury.

With surprising agility the old *wazīr* brought out of prison the Furāt brothers, who had gone into hiding at the accession of Muʿtaḍid and had subsequently been arrested, and appointed them his advisers on fiscal matters.[3] They went to work and almost instantly revenues began to roll in. As we know they were not in favour of military–administrative *iqṭāʿ*, but they knew that the *qabāla* system had been working efficiently in Egypt since it had been introduced there by Ma'mūn. It has to be remembered that this was not a tax-farming system and that safeguards were injected into it to avoid the harmful results of tax-farming.[4] Under the compelling circumstances in Baghdād and because of the availability of men of immense fortunes whose interests were tied to those of the government, it was thought appropriate to introduce tax-farming in the areas under the direct jurisdiction of the central authority. The Furāt brothers approached a certain Aḥmad b. Muḥammad of the tribe of Ṭayy and offered him the concession for the districts around the capital, including the trade routes leading into the city, in exchange for the guaranteed payment of 7000 dinārs a day to the central treasury; the total being 2,520,000 dinārs per annum.[5] They also took advantage of the succession of a new Ṭūlūnid governor in Egypt and southern Syria in 896/283 to renegotiate the terms of the

[1] Ṭabarī, III, p. 2151; ʿArīb b. Saʿd, *Ṣilat Tārīkh al-Ṭabarī*, ed. M. J. de Goeje, Leiden, 1897, p. 18.
[2] Ṣābī, *Wuzarā'*, p. 22.
[3] *Ibid.*, p. 10.
[4] See above, p. 120.
[5] Ṣābī, *Wuzarā'*, p. 11.

previous agreement with Muwaffaq. The lump sum that the Ṭūlūnids had to pay for their military–administrative *iqṭā'* was practically doubled to 450,000 dinārs per annum, and they had to give up their right of access to Qinnasrīn, a trade link with Jazīra.[1] These apparently innocuous arrangements introduced in good faith by the Furāts had far-reaching and certainly unintended results in all corners of the empire. They provided the shock that tumbled down the house of cards that Mu'taḍid had so meticulously built. Almost every one of the military leaders stationed in the provinces demanded or seized control of fiscal affairs in his region. Long-established local dignitaries, nomadic chiefs, wealthy merchants and big landowners led a flood of uprisings hoping to get the same privileges or to protect their local interests. Mu'taḍid first tried to regain control by using his elite force but this proved impossible, and in one case after another he had to yield to the full application of military–administrative *iqṭā'*.[2] The tax-farmers made use of their profits to have their own private armies which were probably a necessity for them.[3] Thus the distinction between tax-farming and military–administrative *iqṭā'* became theoretical. The members of the military–bureaucratic complex were not slow to introduce new corrupt practices to enhance their wealth and power. First, government officials went in as partners of tax-farmers and in no time the *wazīr* himself was a tax-farmer.[4] Needless to say the Furāt brothers were replaced by the Jarrāḥ brothers who were better suited to the new conditions.[5] It is also significant that, at this point, the commander of the second division, the police force of Baghdād, was allowed to intrude into the fiscal affairs of the central government.[6]

As would be expected, the *thughūr* were a major target for leaders who had any significant military strength and wanted to establish their dominions in these outlying regions. Another Afshīn, a descendant of the princes of Ushrūsana, by name Muḥammad b. Dīvdād b. Dīvdast but better known as Ibn Abī al-Sāj, who along with his followers had been in the service of the 'Abbāsids since the early days of Sāmarrā, forced Mu'taḍid to concede to him Armenia and Ādherbayjān as a military–administrative *iqṭā'*.[7] Local Arab

[1] Ṭabarī, III, pp. 2185–7; Athīr, vol. VII, p. 340.
[2] Ṭabarī, III, pp. 2136–46.
[3] Muḥammad b. 'Abdilmalik al-Hamdānī, *Takmilat Tārīkh al-Ṭabarī*, ed. A. Y. Kan'ān, Beirut, 1961, p. 20.
[4] Maqrīzī, *Khiṭaṭ*, vol. I, p. 82; Miskawayh, vol. I, p. 16.
[5] Ṭabarī, III, p. 2190.
[6] *Ibid.*, p. 2192.
[7] *Ibid.*, pp. 1222, 2185.

chiefs like the Ḥamdānids, about whom we shall hear later, captured strongholds at profitable points in the *thughūr* of Jazīra.[1] Other Arabs of the region satisfied themselves by simply collecting their own taxes on the passing trade.[2] In Tarsus, one of the most important trade centres of the *thughūr*, where merchants from every town in the empire had their own resident agents, a new situation developed which involved the whole northern frontier from the Mediterranean to Central Asia.[3] Also involved were all the peoples interested in trade between the Islamic empire, Byzantium, Russia and Europe as far afield as Sweden. The wealthy merchants of Baghdād who had their fingers in every pie were also interested, and so was Mu'taḍid whose mother, grandmother and great grandmother were of Byzantine origin. It is not surprising that he spoke fluent Greek.[4]

The problem in Tarsus was that some elements in the community had started and were actively pursuing piratical activities against the Byzantines in order to discourage them from trading with the Syrian ports through Cyprus.[5] These activities aroused the ire of the Syrians, the Egyptians and the Byzantines. Further east the Arab chiefs who had established themselves at Sumaysāṭ, Mārdīn and Āmid were contending with each other for a bigger share in the trade and were also in direct competition with Tarsus. As they had better access to the trade coming up the Tigris and the Euphrates they were inclined to try to maintain good relations with Baghdād. Their neighbours to the east in Armenia and Ādherbayjān were more interested in the trade coming from Europe through the regions of the Caucasus. Although some of this trade had always been shipped across the Caspian to the flourishing ports of Gurgān and Ṭabaristān it had never represented a serious threat to the busier inland route across the Caucasus. The threat came from a completely unexpected quarter, the domains of the Sāmānids. Previously the Ṭāhirids had never shown any interest in trade and had witnessed the decline of the trans-Asian traffic almost with equanimity. The Sāmānids with their bases in the land of the Soghdians, the enterprising people who had dominated commercial intercourse with China, had a different outlook towards trade. As it was obvious that the sea-route around Asia had attracted most of the Chinese trade, these entrepreneurs directed their attention to the other trade that had been flowing

[1] *Ibid.*, pp. 2141–5, 2185.
[2] *Ibid.*, p. 2138; Athīr, vol. VII, p. 252.
[3] Iṣṭakhrī, p. 64.
[4] Ṣābī, *Rusūm*, p. 89; Mas'ūdī, *Murūj*, vol. VIII, pp. 108, 113.
[5] Ṭabarī, III, p. 2185; Mas'ūdī, *Murūj*, vol. VIII, p. 77.

through the Caucasus regions from areas as far away as the Baltic shores. The thousands of Islamic coins, dating from the first to the fourth centuries of the Islamic era, that have been found in Scandinavia and along the course of the Volga, testify to the continued interest of various peoples in this extensive trade. As in the case of the east–west African trade, the European trade was carried out through various intermediaries amongst whom the Slavs, the Bulghārs and Khazars were most prominent. Like their contemporaries in Africa, these peoples were just as jealous of their trade secrets and just as determined to prohibit foreigners from crossing their lands. Each intermediary group benefited from transporting the merchandise across its own territory, in addition to the taxes imposed at the point of entry. With their special expertise and being in close proximity to the terminus of this trade at the mouth of the Volga, the Sāmānids could not have had much difficulty diverting this trade around the east side of the Caspian to the *entrepôt* of Khwārizm.[1] As good merchants they would have had an innate abhorrence of taxes and tariffs especially if they wanted to capture the greater share of this trade. Indeed we hear only about a tax imposed at the crossings of the Oxus, which at this time was not considered a border. Furthermore as it was at the negligible rate of one dirham per donkey, mule or horse load and two dirhams per camel load, and considering that these loads were mostly luxury goods, it could hardly have been more than the ferry fare. This is confirmed by the fact that the same report speaks about a payment ot half a dirham to one dirham at the various overnight stopping-places *en route*.[2]

Significantly these crossing points were used to discourage some of the slave trade. A special licence from the authorities in addition to a levy of 70 to 100 dirhams was required for the transport of every young male Turkish slave. For female Turkish slaves no licence was needed but a levy of 20 to 100 dirhams was assessed according to age. As this could not have been introduced on humanitarian grounds, the only conceivable reason is that the Sāmānids were particularly anxious not to offend the Turkish nomads surrounding their territories, who were involved in their trade schemes, and from amongst whom these slaves were mostly captured. Indeed the fact that only Turkish slaves were singled out for this

[1] Iṣṭakhrī, pp. 218, 221, 225, 226, 299; Khurdādhbeh, p. 154; Rusteh, p. 141; Ibn Faḍlān, *Risala*, ed. S. Dahhān, Damascus, 1959, pp. 74, 98, 103, 145; also see below, p. 149.

[2] Maqdisī, p. 340.

treatment supports this conclusion. Another interesting use of these crossing points was to stop the smuggling of silver ore from the rich mines of Central Asia into the heart of the empire. This makes economic sense because the value of silver was rising rapidly as against gold. Therefore, all baggage was inspected and silver was returned to Bukhārā where it could better serve the purposes of the expanding trade.[1]

Faced with this complex situation and in order to be able to cope with it, Mu'taḍid had to decide on priorities. While he was interested in the flow of trade, he was not concerned with nor was he in favour of any particular route. His main responsibility was to contain the situation and stop it from further deterioration. There was no reason to fight the Sāmānids; he had conceded Armenia and Ādherbayjān to Ibn Abī al-Sāj and had no desire whatever to fight the Byzantines, and he had just concluded a reasonable agreement with the Ṭūlūnids. Therefore his immediate problems were limited to securing the vital link with the eastern regions from Baghdād to Rayy, to restoring some sort of order in the troublesome *thughūr* of Jazīra, and to terminating the unnecessary provocations of the Byzantines by Tarsus. With remarkable energy he proceeded towards these objectives. His own military efforts did not bring about the desired results on the eastern front, and he had to fall back on the political acumen of his *wazīr* who was dispatched to Rayy. There, through further application of military–administrative *iqṭā'*, the *wazīr* was able to bring some stability back to the surrounding regions.[2] Mu'taḍid himself turned to Jazīra where he had a measure of military success mainly because his opponents were divided amongst themselves. The strongholds of Sumaysāṭ, Āmid and Mārdīn easily fell into his hands, and the alliance between the Arabs and the Kurds of the region could not sustain the pressure from his elite forces. The Arab Shī'ite Ḥamdānids who had co-operated with the "Khārijite" Kurds turned against their allies and joined forces with Mu'taḍid to subdue the latter. For this flexibility they were rewarded by a military–administrative *iqṭā'* in the region of Mawṣil, where they had had their strongholds. The Ḥamdānid forces thus became part of the central government's third division, and in this role they were soon to play an important part in support of Baghdād's and, of

[1] All this information is included in Maqdisī's report, quoted in the previous note, which was completely misunderstood by W. Barthold, *Turkestan Down to the Mongol Invasion*, London, 1928, pp. 239–40.

[2] Ṭabarī, III, pp. 2140–1, 2147, 2152, 2155–6, 2161, 2178.

course, their own interests. Other Arabs who had been in control of strongholds of the *thughūr* followed the Ḥamdānid example and surrendered to Mu'taḍid. To ensure their continued allegiance he stationed a strong contingent, led by his own son the future Muktafī, at Raqqa, and returned to Baghdād.[1]

As for the problems posed by Tarsus, Mu'taḍid thought that with some persuasion the pirates there would desist from their controversial activities. For this task and to sort out the problems of the aftermath of his military operations, he sent, as his own representative, his best informed high official, the post-master general of all the north-west regions.[2] Nothing happened in Tarsus, but a serious disturbance started in Ādherbayjān. Waṣīf, probably an Armenian Muslim, who had a considerable following in Ibn Abī al-Sāj's army, disagreed with his chief about the new arrangements for the region. Being a native he was in a better position to imagine the extent of the loss they would suffer as a result of the drying up of their trade. Therefore he led his followers in a march on Malaṭya, one of the forward strongholds of the *thughūr*, and had no difficulty in establishing himself there. The Byzantines had no objection to anybody literally setting up shop closer to their territory, and thus took no action against Waṣīf. But Mu'taḍid was quick to realize that Malaṭya's prosperity would be at the expense of the other markets further south and east in Jazīra. The upshot would be the dislocation of the arrangements he had so recently contrived there. Without wasting a moment he mobilized all his forces, including the Arabs of Jazīra, and led them in person against Waṣīf. In desperation, Waṣīf tried to take refuge with the Byzantines but was swiftly intercepted and captured, and his army quietly absorbed into the government's forces.[3] Mu'taḍid then made a grand tour to inspect all the *thughūr*. In Tarsus he took a most extraordinary step, yet a most significant one; he ordered the destruction of its entire Muslim fleet that had operated against the Byzantines. Fifty expensive warships went up in flames, and many parties were satisfied at least for a time.[4]

In the last three years of his life Mu'taḍid was confronted with a new problem, but one that had been simmering for generations. He must have been puzzled by the sudden explosion in southern 'Irāq, an area which had been so recently pacified. Perhaps in his own way

[1] *Ibid.*, pp. 2108, 2141–5, 2149–51, 2185–7.
[2] *Ibid.*, p. 2184.
[3] *Ibid.*, pp. 2195–8; Mas'ūdī, *Murūj*, vol. VIII, pp. 196–9.
[4] Ṭabarī, III, pp. 2199–200.

he, like Marie Antoinette, wondered why people were shouting for bread. He had just stumbled on a new political order for the empire and was probably hoping for an era of tranquillity. Instead, there was an explosion that was to reverberate in almost all corners of the empire. It was bound to happen and there had been signs of its coming, but reactionary circles were too blinded by their interests to take note of these forewarnings. Confident in their power and certain of government support they were too arrogant to consider the slightest change which was not to their advantage. Thus, they practically asked for the coming revolution.

Although this revolution took place in separate regions and almost certainly under different leaders, there were three distinguishable common features in its eruptions; regional interests, rural disaffection, and Shī'ism. The establishment of military–administrative *iqṭā'* had not been motivated by the consideration of regional interests. It was promulgated for the benefit of the central government and the satisfaction of the military–bureaucratic complex. Moreover, the presence of separate and strong military forces in the regions, such as those of the Ṭūlūnids in Egypt, would surely work to the disadvantage of the weaker regions. To protect their vital interests the latter had no alternative but armed revolt against the established order.

As always, the rural communities had patiently endured the injustices imposed upon them in the hope that some day, somehow, salvation would come. They had had to find new ways and means of evading the constantly increasing burden of taxation, while the affluent members of the urban population had been unscrupulously busy multiplying their untaxed wealth. Any attempt to redress this glaring inequity had been easily brushed aside by the powerful vested interests. The introduction of tax-farming must have caused the long suffering tax-payers to despair of any prospects of relief. The rapid spread of big land-holdings had been mostly at the expense of the peasantry and the small landowners, many of whom had been driven out of their properties. The upsurge in the number of nomads in areas bordering the fertile lands of Syria and 'Irāq was a direct result of this dislocation of population. Many of them had supported the Zanj revolt against their oppressors and had been eagerly waiting for another opportunity to vent their grievances.

From its very inception Shī'ism had been the traditional opposition party, and as such had been the vehicle for various protest movements. It has already been explained and it cannot be over-stressed that during the Umayyad period the various Shī'ite sects had had nothing in common, other than the necessity of an *Imām*, to be chosen from the members of the House of the Prophet to occupy the office of *Amīr al-Mu'minīn.*[1] The absence of a concrete Shī'ite ideology, and the diversity of their opinions on the many aspects of the one thing upon which they had agreed, had helped to emphasize the sectarian nature of Shī'ism. On the other hand, the collective will of the Muslim community to preserve its unity had been so strong that it had forced the 'Abbāsids to set themselves apart from Shī'ite sectarianism.[2] Furthermore, the fact that Shī'ite sects had identified themselves with regional interests, whether in Kūfa or Merv, had deprived Shī'ism of the universality that Sunnī orthodoxy had so strongly claimed. The descendants of 'Alī through his martyred son Ḥusayn, the grandson of the Prophet, had had the strongest claims for the latter's legacy, and until the failure of the revolt of Zayd in Kūfa in 740/122,[3] they had been willing to fight for their rights. The appearance of other members of the House of the Prophet leading separate Shī'ite movements had not affected the legitimate rights of the Ḥusaynids. The victory of the 'Abbāsids, themselves heirs to the claims of a third son of 'Alī who was not even a grandson of the Prophet, had allowed the descendants of Ḥasan to overcome their ancestor's lapse in abdicating in favour of the Umayyads, and put forward their own claims. This had manifested itself in the revolt of the Pure Soul in the reign of Manṣūr.[4] Henceforth the Ḥusaynids, satisfying themselves with their legitimacy, remained the quietist party, while the Ḥasanids continued to lead the activist party.

The last spasm of the Ḥusaynids had been expressed in their co-operation with Ma'mūn in his shilly-shallying attempts to effect a general compromise. However, the imposition of orthodoxy by Mutawakkil had, at last, convinced this anachronistic main line of Shī'ite leaders of the futility of their claims. The "disappearance" of their twelfth *imām* in 878/265 had, in effect, marked the giving up of these claims, and accordingly their party had become known as the Twelvers. In contrast, the Ḥasanids had already established a dynasty in Morocco, the Idrīsids, beginning 789/172, which can barely be described as Shī'ite but had succeeded, to some extent, in acquiring bases in Yaman and Ṭabaristān. In these latter regions these Ḥasanids had called themselves 'Alawids in order to emphasize

[1] Shaban, *Islamic History*, pp. 179–81.

[2] See above, p. 8.

[3] Shaban, *The 'Abbāsid Revolution*, pp. 132, 148.

[4] See above, p. 14.

their claims as sole heirs to their ancestor's legacy, or Zaydites, an epithet that evoked memories of the struggle of their cousins the Ḥusaynid Zaydites of Kūfa, and stressed their determination to continue to fight for their claims. Significantly the 'Abbāsids applied the term Ṭālibids to all descendants of 'Alī indicating that, in their view, there was no meaningful difference between any of them, thus in effect equating the grandsons of the Prophet through his daughter Fāṭima with their half-brother who could not claim such a distinguished lineage.[1]

Amidst all this an insignificant Shī'ite sect, which had deviated from the main line of the Twelvers as a result of a disagreement about the succession of the seventh *imām*, was thrust on to the scene. They were called Seveners and also Ismā'īlīs after the name of their chosen *imām*, and it is with these that we are now concerned. Their movement, which eventually developed into a radical social, economic, philosophical and religious revolution, started as a secret society soon after the occultation of the twelfth *imām* of the main line. Subsequently it manifested itself in five separate regions; Kūfa, Syria, Baḥrayn, Yaman and North Africa in that order. At the same time there was supposed to be a headquarters in Salamiyya, a small village bordering the desert not far from the site of ancient Palmyra.[2] While in Kūfa, Syria and Baḥrayn they were called Qarāmiṭa, in Salamiyya they called themselves Ismā'īlīs, and some of them in the Syrian desert called themselves Fāṭimids. In North Africa they encouraged the latter appellation.

A great deal of research has been done on the origins, and nature of these groups, the connexions between them or independence from each other, yet we are still very much in the dark about all these things. Indeed little progress has been made since they were first discussed in 1886.[3] Perhaps it serves a purpose to remember that these movements were active over eleven centuries ago under circumstances where their survival, let alone their success, ultimately depended on the maintenance of absolute secrecy at the incubatory stage. It is more important, and perhaps more instructive, in trying to solve these vexing questions, to examine the particular milieu of each of these movements and to establish the nature of the support each had, a most important ingredient in any revolution. It is just as important to scrutinize all the economic conditions of Ismā'īlī

[1] Ṣābī, *Wuzarā'*, p. 20.
[2] Yāqūt, *Buldān*, vol. III, pp. 55, 240–1.
[3] M. J. de Goeje, *Mémoire sur les Carmathes du Bahraïn et les Fatimides*, Leiden, 1886.

strongholds in relation to the wider economic situation of the Islamic and the international scenes. In this respect a little more than lip service has been paid to the Fāṭimids, while the other Ismā'īlīs have not been considered worthy even of such meagre treatment.

The callousness of the central government and its obdurate refusal to take cognizance of the two burning issues of the time, regional interests and rural disaffection, gave the Shī'ites the opportunity to revive their movement in a revolutionary form as champions of both causes. Their long association with regional uprisings and their complete identification with the oppressed made them ideally suited for this role. Nonetheless, the sectarian nature of Shī'ism, in addition to the inherent connection with regional interests, were bound to allow for various approaches to solve the problems involved. The highly sophisticated Fāṭimid ideology was a far cry from the crude notions of the Qarāmiṭa of Kūfa. Other contemporary non-Ismā'īlī Shī'ites like the Ḥamdānids, the Zaydīs of Ṭabaristān and the Būyids, had their own ideas and solutions for the same problems. It is most significant that all these Shī'ite regimes which, for some decades, dominated the greater part of the Islamic lands, found no room for co-operation among themselves, and indeed were busy fighting each other in defence of their respective local interests.[1]

There is no reason to doubt that there were Ismā'īlī headquarters in Salamiyya from which agents were sent to exploit the situation in troubled areas; this fits well with Shī'ite activities before this time. But it is not possible to detect a master-plan according to which these agents would operate, nor is it easy to piece together the confused reports about the identity and relations of the members of this subversive network. They all moved wide and fast, had disciples and relatives who perpetuated their activities, and appointed their own agents even in government circles,[2] with little apparent direct connexion with Salamiyya. Ḥamdān Qarmaṭ, the most famous of these sub-agents, is reported only to have kept up correspondence with his supposed masters which could not have amounted to much in the way of contact.[3] It has been wrongly assumed that he gave his name not only to his own movement but to others as well. Endless speculations have accordingly been made about the Arabic, Aramaic or Nabaṭī origins of the various forms of the word Qarmaṭ. The

[1] See below, pp. 167–8.
[2] Ṭabarī, III, p. 2179.
[3] Maqrīzī, *Itti'āẓ al-Ḥunafā'*, ed. J. Shayyāl, Cairo, 1948, p. 223.

term first appeared to describe a group who had supported the Zanj revolt, the reference being to the Qarmāṭiyyūn and to Nubians who could hardly speak Arabic.[1] The geographer Maqdisī also associates these two peoples and considers that they were *sūdān*.[2] Reliable lexicographers tell us that the Qarmāṭiyyūn (sing. Qarmaṭī) were a specific race.[3] It does not need much imagination or etymological explanation to realize that the people in question were from Garama, the ancient Libyan trade centre.[4] It becomes clear, then, that these Qarāmiṭa were remnants of the Zanj revolts who, under the circumstances, were ready to take part in any revolt, especially in this area and of course Baḥrayn. It should be pointed out, however, that this participation was only a minor element, but being a common one, it was enough to give these movements this peculiar name.

The movement in Kūfa, where the first Qarāmiṭa appeared and disappeared, spread among the peasants of the Sawād but did not have the support of the Arab nomads in the desert.[5] It was specifically a reaction to the newly imposed tax of one dinār a year per man, which had been decreed by Aḥmad al-Ṭā'ī who had the tax-farming concession and held a military–administrative *iqṭā'* of most of the region.[6] The preachings of their leader Ḥamdān seem close enough to those of the Ismā'īlīs. His grandiose plans to establish a fortified base were probably inspired by the Zanj tactics and were not enough to provoke the central government to take action.[7] But one measure is most important as it is an indication of Ismā'īlī thinking and a portent of things to come. For the first time in Islamic history an income tax of 20% was introduced and this was effected by this relatively insignificant man.[8] The movement was tolerated for roughly ten years 890–901/277–88 but then Ṭā'ī and his men were able with little effort to bring it to an end. Ḥamdān disappeared with his movement.[9]

The second movement of the Qarāmiṭa broke out in Baḥrayn in 899/286 under the leadership of Abū Sa'īd al-Jannābī. This man who was from Fārs, certainly had no direct or indirect relation with Salamiyya, and the attempts of some sources to establish a connexion between him and Ḥamdān are not convincing.[10] Intellectually he may not have been as talented as Ḥamdān, but tactically he was

1 Ṭabarī, III, pp. 1756–7.
2 Maqdisī, p. 242.
3 *Lisān*, s.v. *qrmṭ*.
4 See above, p. 102.
5 Ṭabarī, III, pp. 2117, 2124, 2198, 2202; Maqrīzī, *Itti'āẓ*, pp. 208–9.
6 Ṭabarī, III, pp. 2126, 2127, 2198.
7 Maqrīzī, *Itti'āẓ*, p. 213.
8 *Ibid.*, p. 210.
9 Ṭabarī, III, pp. 2202, 2206.
10 *Ibid.*, p. 2188; Maqrīzī, *Itti'āẓ*, p. 214; Ḥawqal, p. 295.

certainly more gifted. His support came mainly from amongst the nomads of East Arabia whom he organized into an army powerful enough to maintain a base in Baḥrayn and pose a threat to Baṣra.[1] The central government was not particularly alarmed but was prompted to take action by pleas from its representatives there. In 891/278 Mu'taḍid sent an expedition of 2000 men who were utterly routed by Abū Sa'īd and his Qarāmiṭa.[2] Surprisingly the latter did not follow up their victory by advancing towards Baṣra, and instead they satisfied themselves with consolidating their strength in Baḥrayn. In 900/287 the old *wazīr* died and a year later Mu'taḍid himself also died. Both were succeeded by their sons, Qāsim b. 'Ubaydillah and Muktafī respectively, Qāsim being the grandfather of Muktafī. Needless to say the policies of the central government continued unchanged, but it had to cope with the third movement of the Qarāmiṭa.

This time there is no doubt that the movement had no direct relation with Salamiyya and indeed was probably in competition with it. It was organized by a disciple of Ḥamdān, Zakrūyeh, who had gone underground after the collapse of the Kūfa peasant movement.[3] He found his support among the nomads of the Syrian–'Irāqī desert and particularly from the clans of Kalb, once a pillar of Umayyad rule. They were now reduced to transporting goods along the caravan route from Kūfa to Damascus, skirting the desert via Palmyra.[4] It is significant that other nomads of the clans of Asad, Ṭayy and Tamīm from the vicinity of Kūfa, who had no interest in this particular route, refused to join the movement.[5] It is also important to realize that this route was part of Ṭā'ī's responsibility, and it is more than likely that the men engaged in work along it were also subjected to the tax of one dinār per year.

Taking advantage of the death of Mu'taḍid, these men, led by Yaḥyā son of Zakrūyeh, rose in arms and swiftly established their domination of this important trade route. In the process they defeated the government forces on the 'Irāqī side of the desert and the Ṭūlūnid army of Damascus on the Syrian side.[6] The latter must have shown some apathy in fighting the Qarāmiṭa because the Damascene merchants, whose interests were directly involved, pleaded with their colleagues of Baghdād to persuade the govern-

[1] Ṭabarī, III, pp. 2188, 2192; Maqrīzī, *Itti'āẓ*, pp. 215–16.
[2] Ṭabarī, III, pp. 2188–9, 2192–3; Maqrīzī, *Itti'āẓ*, p. 218.
[3] Ṭabarī, III, p. 2217; Maqrīzī, *Itti'āẓ*, p. 224.
[4] Ṭabarī, III, pp. 2217–18.
[5] *Ibid.*, p. 2217.
[6] *Ibid.*, pp. 2219, 2221; Maqrīzī, *Itti'āẓ*, pp. 225–6.

ment to intensify its efforts against this relentless enemy.[1] While the authorities were trying to comply with this request, the Qarāmiṭa were joined by a respectable group called Banū al-Aṣbagh.[2] A few years earlier a member of this family had been influential in maintaining good relations between Mu'taḍid and the *thughūr*.[3] It can therefore be inferred that members of this family had some interest in the flow of trade through at least the 'Irāqī side of the route controlled by the Qarāmiṭa. The important thing here is that the adherence of this group coincided with a methodical change in the movement. First, the leader, Yaḥyā, was proclaimed as the *Shaykh*, Elder, a fact that indicates the existence of some sort of collective leadership. At the same time he claimed a Ḥusaynid descent and the Aṣbaghids began to call themselves Fāṭimids, which was almost certainly meant to include all the leadership of the movement.[4] We do not have any evidence to substantiate the claims of the Aṣbaghids that they were descendants of Fāṭima, the daughter of the Prophet, or for this matter of any other significant person of that name. But the fact that this claim was not disputed, even by a Jarrāḥ member of the administration, is in itself a proof of its validity.[5] The meaning of this is that these men had the combined prestige of being descendants of Ḥusayn and Ḥasan, the only sons of Fāṭima. The significance of such a claim from a Shī'ite point of view is that it associates the legitimacy of the Ḥusaynids with the activism of the Ḥasanids to the exclusion of all other 'Alawid claimants, and to the utter abasement of the 'Abbāsids.

When the *Shaykh* Yaḥyā was killed, soon afterwards, in the fighting against the government forces, he was succeeded by his brother Ḥusayn, the Man with the Mole, who took not only the title of *Amīr al-Mu'minīn*, but also nine other messianic titles including that of *Mahdī*. Furthermore, he gave honorific and significant titles to at least two of his aides.[6] After reaching an agreement with Damascus and imposing the payment of tribute on it, he directed his attacks towards the north occupying Salamiyya and destroying it in the process.[7] Alarmed by this threat, the government mobilized all its forces, and Muktafī himself went out to Raqqa to muster support for these efforts against the Qarāmiṭa. The Arabs of the *thughūr*, especially the Ḥamdānids, who were cut off from both

[1] Ṭabarī, III, p. 2222.
[2] *Ibid.*, p. 2219.
[3] *Ibid.*, pp. 2137, 2148.
[4] *Ibid.*, pp. 2118–19.
[5] *Ibid.*, p. 2257.
[6] *Ibid.*, pp. 2219, 2225, 2232–4; Maqrīzī, *Itti'āẓ*, pp. 231–2.
[7] Ṭabarī, III, pp. 2225–6; Maqrīzī, *Itti'āẓ*, p. 227.

Damascus and Kūfa, gave their whole-hearted aid and effective military help.[1] The *wazīr* who remained behind in Baghdād appointed the *kātib* Muḥammad b. Sulaymān, who was the head of the department of army affairs, to put together and lead an expedition which constituted men recalled from the regions for this purpose.[2] A contingent was sent down to Baḥrayn as a precaution against any move by the Qarāmiṭa there.[3] The Ṭūlūnids seem to have been in two minds as to what attitude they should take towards a movement which did not seriously threaten their interests, and was in fact directed against their competitors in Syria. After some internal struggle, there emerged a party in favour of co-operation with Baghdād, and accordingly a Ṭūlūnid army led by the prominent general, Badr, advanced against the Qarāmiṭa from the south.[4] This pincer-movement was more than enough to defeat them. Their leader was captured, his forces dispersed and the government's authority restored over the Syrian–'Irāqī desert at least for the time being.[5]

The next move, emanating from Baghdād almost immediately, was rather surprising. The army of Muḥammad b. Sulaymān was ordered to attack Egypt and in a matter of months was able to terminate Ṭūlūnid rule there in 905/292.[6] Two remarkable factors contributed to this easy victory; the defection of Badr and his men to the central government's side, and the deployment of the rebuilt naval forces of Tarsus in co-ordination with the army's attack on Fusṭāṭ, the Ṭūlūnid capital.[7] The presence of the Ḥamdānids in the army attacking Egypt indicates that they had as much interest in bringing down the Ṭūlūnids as the people of Tarsus, who did not hesitate to sail all the way across the Mediterranean for the same purpose.[8] The leader–organizer of the expedition, Muḥammad b. Sulaymān, had, himself, an interesting history. Twenty years earlier, he had been in the service of Lu'lu' who had defected with his *sūdān* from the army of Aḥmad b. Ṭūlūn to fight the Zanj along with Muwaffaq.[9] His intimate knowledge of Egypt and the intricate problems involved must have qualified him for this particular task. After his victory, he was particularly interested in destroying any

1 Ṭabarī, III, pp. 2231–2.
2 *Ibid.*, pp. 2236, 2240–2.
3 *Ibid.*, p. 2232; Ṣābī, *Qarāmiṭa*, p. 23.
4 Ṭabarī, III, pp. 2219, 2251, 2253; Maqrīzī, *Khiṭaṭ*, vol. I, p. 322; Kindī, *Wulāt*, pp. 242–3.
5 Ṭabarī, III, pp. 2232–45.
6 *Ibid.*, p. 2248.
7 *Ibid.*, pp. 2251–2; Maqrīzī, *Khiṭaṭ*, vol. I, p. 322.
8 Kindī, *Wulāt*, pp. 246–7.
9 Maqrīzī, *Khiṭaṭ*, vol. I, p. 327.

remaining power of the *sūdān* in Egypt.[1] He also made a special effort to dislodge the rest of the Ṭūlūnid forces in the country, including Badr whose defection had facilitated the government's victory.[2] The latter was known as Ḥamāmī and although one source explains this epithet as pigeon-keeper, it is more credible to relate this powerful leader to Dhāt al-Ḥamām, a big market town on the coast to the west of Alexandria.[3] Earlier there had been some troubles to the west of the Delta in which the Berbers of the nearby desert had been involved in support of an army faction, and apparently the latter had also been Berbers.[4] All this leads us to believe that Badr was a Berber who represented interests different from those of the *sūdān*. In other words the controversy involving Aḥmad b. Ṭūlūn and his son 'Abbās had not completely subsided.[5] Six months after the fall of the Ṭūlūnids, the party supporting the cause of the *sūdān* revolted. The government forces withdrew to Alexandria and significantly Badr was called upon to subdue the rebels.[6] In terms of general policy Baghdād, aware of the crumbling power of the Aghlabids and the incipient Fāṭimid movement in North Africa, decided to fortify the position of its forces in Egypt. Before his return to Baghdād, Muḥammad b. Sulaymān laid the foundations for direct control over all Egyptian affairs by the appointment of two independent representatives of the central government to take charge of military and fiscal matters.[7] This was, of course, a departure from military–administrative *iqṭā'*, but it was an exception forced by the circumstances.

Meanwhile, the Qarāmiṭa of Syria thought that they had an opportunity to recover their position. They regrouped their forces and were even joined by some of the government troops of Damascus.[8] In a series of lightning attacks they terrorized all the urban communities bordering the Syrian–'Irāqī desert, and for two years 905–6/293–4 they attacked and plundered every possible passing caravan, including those returning from the pilgrimage. The great wealth of goods transported by the latter was far more than that needed for the simple functions of this religious occasion. Once

[1] *Ibid.*, p. 322.
[2] *Ibid.*, p. 327; Kindī, *Wulāt*, p. 248.
[3] Al-Sam'ānī, *Ansāb*, ed. D. S. Margoliouth, Leiden, 1912, f. 174; Athīr, vol. VIII, p. 17; Ya'qūbī, *Buldān*, p. 342; Bakīr, p. 3.
[4] Ṭabarī, III, p. 2153; Kindī, *Wulāt*, p. 242; Maqrīzī, *Khiṭaṭ*, vol. I, p. 322.
[5] See above, p. 112.
[6] Ṭabarī, III, pp. 2253, 2267; Kindī, *Wulāt*, pp. 259–63; Mas'ūdī, *Murūj*, vol. VIII. pp. 236–7.
[7] Kindī, *Wulāt*, p. 258; Ṭabarī, III, p. 2253.
[8] Tabarī, III, p. 2257.

more the Ḥamdānids distinguished themselves in supporting the government forces to bring a final defeat to these impudent marauders. This time old Zakrūyeh himself was wounded and captured. His death put an end to this particular movement.[1] The Qarāmiṭa of Baḥrayn, who had not made a move to support their fellow revolutionaries nor to take advantage of the government's plight, were left alone, and it was to be some years before they made their presence felt.

Throughout his reign 902–8/289–95 Muktafī was as interested as the Byzantine emperor Leo VI the Wise 886–912, in finding a *modus vivendi* between their respective domains. In 902/289 he sent presents to the latter, and in 903/290 and 907/294 Leo responded by sending a peace mission headed by his own brother-in-law.[2] These cordial relations were not disturbed by the hostile activities of the hawks on both sides of the borders.[3] Indeed measures were taken to bring such elements under control. On his part Muktafī appointed a Ḥamdānid over all the Mawṣil regions, and the latter proceeded to subdue the Kurdish and Arab nomads of the area.[4] On the other hand, Leo cut off the support of the Byzantine military base at Konya to the extent that its garrison was forced not only to cease operations, but also to seek refuge in Tarsus, of all places.[5]

In the eastern regions Muktafī was not so fortunate, because the difficulty of the problems there was compounded by the absence of any agreement on a unified approach to tackle them, even within the parties concerned themselves. To begin with, his *wazīr*, who was also his own grandfather, happened to have had the tax-farming concession of Fārs and Kirmān in exchange for the sum of four million dirhams.[6] This kind of interest prompted him to persuade Muktafī of the advantages of reaching an accommodation with the neighbouring Ṣaffārids.[7] The powerful military commander in charge of the security of Fārs opposed this approach, and seems to have had the support of influential figures in Baghdād including Muktafī's uncle. In the ensuing struggle, the *wazīr* won and managed to have his two strong opponents murdered.[8] However, attempts to reach an agreement with the Ṣaffārids failed because of opposition within their own ranks, and soon enough defecting Ṣaffārid forces arrived at Baghdād.[9]

[1] *Ibid.*, pp. 2255–78.
[2] *Ibid.*, pp. 2223, 2236, 2277.
[3] *Ibid.*, pp. 2249, 2251, 2268, 2269, 2275; 'Arīb. p. 13.
[4] Athīr, vol. VII, pp. 293–4.
[5] Ṭabarī, III, pp. 2251, 2275–6.
[6] Miskawayh, vol. I, p. 16.
[7] Ṭabarī, III, p. 2222.
[8] *Ibid.*, pp. 2209–15.
[9] *Ibid.*, pp. 2233, 2255.

When the aged *wazīr* Qāsim died in 903/291, he was replaced, on his own recommendation, by 'Abbās b. Ḥasan who had a clear interest in the affairs of the Sāmānids. The new *wazīr* was a loyal disciple of his patron and therefore his policies were in essence a continuation of the latter's.[1] The central government had never been completely satisfied with the arrangements with the Sāmānids. Encouraging the Ṣaffārids had been one way of changing these arrangements, but as this had failed the authorities in Baghdād had been watching for other means to bring about the desired effect. Soon, the opportunity presented itself in the form of a series of insurrections in Rayy, Ṭabaristān and Gurgān.[2] The diversion of the northern trade to Khwārizm had adversely affected the prosperity of the regions under Sāmānid domination. With some subtle manipulation, the central government could at least try to regain these regions. Such hopes were curtly dashed as the Sāmānids were quick to use their military forces to subdue the insurgents.[3] As a result Pārs, the former Sāmānid governor of Gurgān and 4000 of his men, had to flee to Baghdād. Their arrival there had been anxiously expected by the disconcerted *wazīr* when Muktafī died and more urgent problems now had to take precedence.[4]

[1] Ṣābī, *Wuzarā'*, pp. 229, 360–1.
[2] Ṭabarī, III, pp. 2208–9.
[3] *Ibid.*, pp. 2216 2220–1.
[4] Miskawayh, vol. 1, p. 4.

7

THE BREAKDOWN OF THE CENTRAL GOVERNMENT (II)

The anxiety of the *wazīr*, 'Abbās, before the death of Muktafī had not been without good reason; he had known, for some time, that there would be a crisis of succession. Muktafī, who died at the age of thirty-two, had been in failing health for several months, if not longer. As his children were too young, he had expressed the wish that he should be succeeded by his brother, Ja'far, who had just reached puberty.[1] Having been in office for four years, the experienced *wazīr* was convinced that the absence of strong leadership would simply take the lid off the whole situation. There were three separate military forces; one in the provinces and two in Baghdād. The former, which constituted the third division, was dispersed in various regions and was not a cause for compelling worry. But the other two, the elite force of the first division and the police force of the second division, were concentrated in the capital. From the time of their formation they had been under the direct command of strong rulers who had used them effectively as instruments of the central government. A boy of thirteen could not be expected to take personal charge of these vital forces; that would leave their commanders in virtual mastery of the government. The fact that one of these commanders was the maternal uncle of the boy ruler could only add to the apprehensions of the *wazīr*. The latter had hoped that the arrival of Pārs and his army of 4000 men would enable him to enforce the choice of a more mature ruler. When Muktafī died before the arrival of this army, the *wazīr* had no alternative but to accept the proclamation of Ja'far to succeed his brother under the title of Muqtadir, 908–32/295–320.[2]

In less than four months all the *wazīr*'s fears had come true. Some army commanders arranged a *coup d'état*, killed the unfortunate *wazīr*, deposed Muqtadir and replaced him by another 'Abbāsid with the title of Murtaḍā. In 24 hours a counter-coup by the elite first division reversed the situation and reinstated Muqtadir, the

[1] 'Arīb, pp. 21–2; Miskawayh, vol. 1, pp. 2–3.
[2] Miskawayh, vol. 1, p. 4.

child ruler.[1] From this turmoil emerged four strong men who retained their positions and held the reins of government between them for almost twenty-five years – Naṣr al-Qushūrī as commander of the first division; Gharīb al-Khāl, a leading general of this army, who was closely allied to Naṣr; Mu'nis al-Faḥl, as commander of the second division police force; and Mu'nis al-Khaṣiyy as commander of the third division. Naṣr, whose official titles were *ḥājib*, chamberlain, and *mawlā Amīr al-Mu'minīn*, was of Khazar origin from a village called Qushūra in the vicinity of Balanjar.[2] His recent arrival from his native land was betrayed by the fact that he did not speak Arabic well.[3] Gharīb was Muqtadir's maternal uncle, hence al-Khāl, the Uncle.[4] His association with Naṣr and the fact that neither he nor his sister are described by any source as Armenians or Greek, makes it more than probable that he was also a Khazar.

The other two personages together are interesting. As they were namesakes various epithets were used to distinguish them from one another. One was *khāzin*, bursar, versus *khādim*, high official; both terms allude to their respective previous activities. Because of his military achievements Mu'nis, the commander of the third division, was also called *muẓaffar*, victorious, and in his old age he became known as *kabīr*, elder. However, they were popularly known as al-Faḥl, the virile, and al-Khaṣiyy, the emasculated. Although this had nothing to do with their sexual prowess, scholars, failing to see the vivid contrast of these names, have taken *khaṣiyy* to mean literally "eunuch". Consequently another aspect of the slave society theories has been blown up out of all proportions and has created a good deal of confusion. The use of the official title *khādim* to describe Mun'is in addition to the term *khaṣiyy* has led to the unfounded conclusion that both words mean "eunuch". This confusion is compounded by the fact that in North Africa and Muslim Spain some officials had the status of *khādim* along with the military rank of *ghulām* or *fatā*. As they also had the physical attribute of *khaṣiyy*, all these terms have been taken to mean "eunuch" also. Therefore we find "eunuchs" as generals, high officials and even rulers. The scholars who have introduced this idea and come to this astounding conclusion have been influenced by the institutions of the Roman, Byzantine and Ottoman courts where harems and eunuchs participated in palace

[1] *Ibid.*, pp. 5–8; Ṭabarī, III, pp. 2280–2; Ṣābī, *Wuzarā'*, pp. 87–8; 'Arīb, pp. 26–9.

[2] Ṣābī, *Wuzarā'*, p. 154; Maqdisī, pp. 51, 355 and variant readings in the footnotes thereof; Yāqūt, *Buldān*, vol. I, p. 489; *Takmila*, p. 29.

[3] Ṣābī, *Wuzarā'*, p. 92.

[4] Ṣūlī, *Akhbār al-Rāḍī*, ed. J. H. Dunne, London, 1935, p. 5.

conspiracies and attained a measure of political power in these societies. Be that as it may, a eunuch is the embodiment of man's cruelty and inhumanity towards his fellow man. Such a frustrated and abused male may crave for power, conspire or be entrusted with confidential tasks, but he certainly cannot lead armies or rule governments. Anyone who has any doubts about that would only have to see a eunuch to realize this, and until recently it was possible to see in Egypt such pitiable specimens who had outlived their Ottoman masters.

What is being disputed here is the wide use of eunuchs in Islamic society and what is denied is their attainment of any power. The palace of Muqtadir in Baghdād was run by women and there is no indication whatever that Mu'nis had anything to do with it.[1] He was called *khaṣiyy* not because he was castrated but because he could not grow a beard.[2] To the Arabs male virility was, and to some extent still is, represented by wearing a beard. Men were punished and humiliated by publicly shaving off their beards. Arab geographers and travellers never tire of telling us of the various habits of wearing or shaving hair in other parts of the world.[3] In short, beardless men were considered less than normal and this abnormality had to be attributed to the physical defect characteristic of eunuchs.[4] Therefore, any man who did not grow a beard was commonly described as *khaṣiyy*. Ibn Khayyāṭ, an author who died 854/240, tells us about an Arab, Sa'd of the tribe of Azd, who had been in charge of Kūfa in 745/127 and who was called *khaṣiyy*. Then this careful author explains that he had been called thus because he had not had a beard.[5] The most famous and certainly not castrated *khaṣiyy* was Sa'd b. Qays b. 'Abāda. His father had been a powerful leader in Madīna during the Prophet's lifetime and he himself stood by 'Alī's side until the very end. However, this unusually big and brave man, like Mu'nis, had no beard and accordingly he was known as *khaṣiyy al-anṣār*, the eunuch of the Madīnan helpers of the Prophet!![6]

We have no indications at all about the origins of the bearded Mu'nis, but the ready links the beardless Mu'nis had with the Byzantines suggest that he may have originated in their territories.

1 *Takmila*, p. 31; Athīr, vol. VIII, p. 74.
2 Athīr, vol. VIII, p. 123; *Takmila*, p. 51; Miskawayh, vol. I, p. 160.
3 Rusteh, p. 129; Bakrī, pp. 175, 179; Ḥawqal, pp. 397, 482; Iṣṭakhrī, p. 226; Mas'ūdī, *Tanbīh*, p. 168.
4 Maqdisī, p. 242.
5 Ibn Khayyāṭ, *Tārīkh*, ed. A. D. Umary, Baghdad, 1967, p. 430.
6 Iṣfahānī, *Maqātil al-Ṭalibiyyīn*, ed. S. S. Ṣaqr, Cairo, 1949, pp. 71–2.

Perhaps it is of interest to note that there were no conflicts between these two leaders. However, their conflicts and alliances with the other two leaders Naṣr and Gharīb, dominated the scene and in fact created the conditions for the Būyid take-over. These conflicts were complicated by the fact that during Muqtadir's minority his mother, probably prompted by the desire to protect him, took an active part in the affairs of state. In addition to her alert brother Gharīb, her sister and uncle too did not remain idle either. In the turbid atmosphere of the long reign of Muqtadir there were no less than fifteen changes of *wazīrs* and five *coups d'état*. In order to be able to present the history of this period, make sense and keep things in perspective, the following analysis will be made in terms of two different policies as represented by the protagonists the Jarrāḥs and the Furāts. This is not to over-simplify the issues but rather to clarify them, and not at the expense of leaving out any *wazīr*. For if he who was holding office was not a Jarrāḥ or a Furāt by name, he was so by association. In the very few appointments when this was not exactly the case, the policies followed then can be identified to the right or left of the two main parties.

Reference has already been made to the opposing views of these two groups and it is clear that their differences had remained basically the same.[1] Some changes had become unavoidable because the domination of the government by the military had introduced a new factor in the situation. The Jarrāḥs, the conservatives who had always been for the wide application of military–administrative *iqṭā'*, had become completely subservient to the military. In order to serve their masters better they became converts to the cause of "good management", almost with the same degree of conviction as the Conservatives in Britain today. The strict measures of the Jarrāḥs generally worked to the advantage of the rich and powerful who could easily evade them. The Furāts were not exactly socialists although they were accused of worse things by their opponents. It is farcical that Naṣr, who could not even pronounce the word properly, should accuse them of being Qarāmiṭa.[2] Surely they did not and could not introduce any revolutionary changes, yet by trying to lessen the woes of tax-farming and military–administrative *iqṭā'*, they were in effect supporting the cause of the tax-payer. They openly declared that tax-farming was evil and that in any case it should not be granted to the military or government officials.[3] Furthermore, they strongly asserted their conviction that the

[1] See above, p. 94. [2] Ṣābī, *Wuzarā'*, p. 92. [3] *Ibid.*, pp. 71, 258.

military should be subject to the civil authorities.[1] On the other hand they accepted corruption in government circles as a fact of life. Therefore they allowed it as a lesser evil, but at the same time tried to utilize it to the advantage of the treasury by demanding for the latter a share in the amassed gains.[2] While there is no record that the Furāts did anything to remedy the iniquities of urban and rural taxation, the Jarrāḥs added to the gravity of the situation by abolishing taxes on the import–export trade.[3] The merchants of Baghdād were more than ready to lend money to the government while the Jarrāḥs were in power, but of course at the handsome interest of at least 12% a year. The strict prohibition of usury in Islam was overlooked by the severest of the Jarrāḥs, the so-called "good vizier" ʿAlī b. ʿĪsā.[4]

The Furāts first came to power in 908/296 in the wake of the counter-coup that reinstated Muqtadir. As the Jarrāḥs had supported the first coup against the latter, it was almost natural to appoint a Furāt as *wazīr*.[5] The finances of the central government were in a comfortable state; the public treasury had a reserve of 600,000 dinārs while the private treasury of the ruler had 15 million dinārs.[6] With some necessary manipulation the *wazīr* and his brothers used the latter to meet the demands on the former.[7] Although Furāt satisfied the needs of the ruling circles in Baghdād, he fell out with some of the military commanders as he showed some unexpected determination in trying to bring them in line. One of them was summarily executed as a result of his attempts to interfere in the *wazīr*'s domain.[8] But the beardless Mu'nis was too strong a figure for such treatment and to his credit he was not averse to letting the *wazīr* carry out his responsibilities. Mu'nis was only interested in securing the wages of his men but the *wazīr* had different ideas about how this should be done, and indeed questioned the wisdom of having the third division as a separate force from the first. This had been an acceptable arrangement when the ruler himself had been able to command the first division. Under the new circumstances Furāt left the second division, now numbering 9000 men, to police Baghdād and its vicinity, and took some steps to combine the other two divisions.[9] His plan was to reduce the number of the first division in Baghdād to the minimum needed for ceremonial occasions

[1] *Ibid.*, p. 72.
[2] *Ibid.*, pp. 220–7.
[3] *Ibid.*, p. 286; Miskawayh, vol. 1, pp. 228–9.
[4] Ṣābī, *Wuzarāʾ*, p. 81.
[5] *Ibid.*, p. 88; Tabarī, III, p. 2282; Miskawayh, vol. 1, p. 5.
[6] ʿArīb, pp. 22–3.
[7] Miskawayh, vol. 1, p. 108.
[8] Miskawayh, vol. 1, p. 12.
[9] *Ibid.*, p. 20.

and scatter the rest in the provinces, whereby the central treasury would be relieved of their expenses. Indeed when Pārs and his 4000 men who had been anxiously awaited in Baghdād, finally arrived there, they were quickly directed to Jazīra where they could balance the Ḥamdānids' growing strength and extract their stipends from them.[1] The appointment of the Khazar Tigin al-Khāṣṣa, i.e. of the elite force, as governor of Egypt in 910/297 was not a coincidence.[2] It means that some of the forces of the first division were now given the function of the third division in the provinces. General Mu'nis would not be expected to object to a move that would ultimately enhance his own forces, as long as acceptable arrangements were made to secure the high stipends of the elite force. But he and Furāt did not see eye to eye on this crucial point, and the latter was forced out of office in 912/299 after holding power for three years and eight months.[3]

At this point a solution was urgently needed for this delicate problem, and for this task Muḥammad b. 'Ubaydillah b. Yaḥyā b. Khāqān was brought out again and appointed *wazīr*. Although aged and almost senile he was the descendant of a long line of experienced administrators and his own father had been involved in a similar situation fifty years earlier in Sāmarrā and Baghdād.[4] To counteract his weaknesses, his son was appointed as his assistant and, most unusually, a trusted *khādim* with strong army connections was made an overseer, not only over all departments but also over the *wazīr* himself.[5] Within a year the old idiot, who had tried to please all parties concerned, had achieved just the opposite and exasperated everybody.[6] His dismissal in 913/301 coincided with the death of the bearded Mu'nis, the chief of police and also a strong force among the proverbial powers behind the throne.[7] This temporary lapse in the strength of the latter caused them to lose the initiative. Although the Mother, the Uncle and Naṣr were in favour of the return of the Furāts, they could not press their preference against the wish of the other Mu'nis, who had already decided on his choice. This was to be a Jarrāḥ team headed by the "good vizier" himself, 'Alī, b. 'Īsā, who had been taking refuge in Makka for the previous five years.[8]

1 *Ibid.*, p. 16.
2 Ibn Taghrībirdī, *al-Nujūm al-Zāhira*, Cairo, 1963–72, vol. III, p. 171.
3 Miskawayh, vol. I, pp. 20, 25; Athīr, vol. VIII, p. 51.
4 See above, p. 75.
5 Miskawayh, vol. I, pp. 23–5.
6 *Ibid.*, pp. 24–6; 'Arīb, p. 39; Ṣābī, *Wuzarā'*, pp. 262–3.
7 'Arīb, p. 45.
8 Ṣābī, *Wuzarā'*, pp. 30, 263; Miskawayh, vol. I, pp. 25, 27; 'Arīb, p. 42.

Soon enough, the "good management" of the Jarrāḥs came into play to the satisfaction of Mu'nis and his swelling forces. It has been pointed out that this military commander was one of the few of his kind who was not particularly keen on interfering with the fiscal affairs of the provinces wherein he operated; all he wanted was to secure the stipends of the men under his command. This reasonable attitude made the *wazīr*'s work less complicated and was the basis of the good relationship that lasted between the two men for two decades. By the device of appointing the infant son of the teenage ruler in charge of Egypt and Syria, with Mu'nis as his deputy, the revenues from these provinces were allocated to meet the latter's needs.[1] Naṣr was allocated the revenues from some districts in 'Irāq for the additional expenses of his police force which was mainly paid by the central treasury. With remarkable efficiency the *wazīr* proceeded to clear up the mess left by his predecessor. His principal aim was to balance the budget and to this end he was determined to take all the necessary steps. Cuts in all salaries and expenses paid by the central treasury were his major weapon in economizing on expenditure.[2] As for the receipts, he introduced a mixed bag of minor tax adjustments and major tax concessions. The adjustments were concerned with re-assessing the land-tax in some areas of Fārs and 'Irāq, sometimes in favour of the treasury and sometimes in favour of the tax-payer.[3] The concessions amounted to abolishing taxes on imports and exports, particularly at points where such trade was bound to pass through the hands of 'Irāqī merchants. Hence trade taxes imposed at Makka, all the ports of the Persian Gulf and the *thughūr* of Jazīra were annulled.[4] Our sources tell us, along with the copious praise they heap upon the pious *wazīr*, that all these just and desirable tax reforms had cost the central treasury the very moderate sum of 500,000 dinārs.[5] However, as these sources are always reticent about taxes on trade which they considered illegal, it can be concluded that this figure is meant to cover only the minor land-tax reforms. Considering that these very sources estimate the population of Baghdād, about that time, at 96 million, the validity of their calculations regarding the other figure comes very much into doubt.[6]

[1] Miskawayh, vol. I, pp. 32, 153.
[2] *Ibid.*, pp. 29, 34; Ṣābī, *Wuzarā'*, p. 282; Athīr, vol. VIII, p. 51; *Takmila*, p. 13.
[3] Ṣābī, *Wuzarā'*, pp. 286, 340, 343–6; Ḥawqal, p. 303; Iṣṭakhrī, p. 158; *Takmila*, pp. 12–13; Miskawayh, vol. I, pp. 27, 29–30; Ṣābī, *Rusūm*, pp. 67–8.
[4] Miskawayh, vol. I, pp. 28–9; *Takmila*, p. 13; Athīr, vol. VIII, p. 51.
[5] *Takmila*, p. 13; Miskawayh, vol. I, p. 29.
[6] Ṣābī, *Rusūm*, p. 20.

In spite of the good reputation he enjoyed in conservative circles, our *wazīr* does not seem to have gone far enough to satisfy the rigid Ḥanbalites of the capital.[1] He got himself involved in the controversial issue of *waqf*, endowment, establishment. We remember that the central government had objected to such institutions established in Egypt about a century earlier under the name *aḥbās*.[2] Although over the years they had begun to gain some general acceptance, the issue had not been completely resolved. Trying to establish a precedent, the *wazīr* persuaded Muqtadir to endow some of his properties in Baghdād and outside, for religious purposes.[3] The amount of money involved was insignificant but the principle was of great importance, for once it was accepted for religious purposes then it could be used for personal and family endowments. This innovation did not appeal much to the Ḥanbalites, nor was it easily accepted by the less conservative elements in Baghdād. Indeed, when the Mother, a little later, took advantage of it to protect some of her extensive properties against the unknown, or for that matter known and foreseeable, hazards of the time, there were riots in the city and demands that the deeds be invalidated.[4]

Another controversy, and one that the *wazīr* did not ask for, was over the question of the extravagant mystic Ḥallāj. His preachings, about which a great deal has been said, do not concern us here; what concerns us is the fact that he was involved in the highly charged political atmosphere of Baghdād. The conservatives saw in him a venomous enemy who was out to destroy the establishment. Others were intrigued by his theopathic phrases and saw him as a harmless, possibly deranged man who could not have brought down the established order even if he wanted. Such "saints" were common enough and could gather a considerable following but it would all soon dissipate itself. The *wazīr* was torn between the two attitudes but to be on the safe side he decided to imprison this agitator. To the Ḥanbalites, who wanted his head, this punishment fell too far short of the offence; to others it was too much.[5] Meanwhile the controversy continued to simmer and was to be thrown wide open after a lapse of nine years.[6]

As if this was not enough to diminish the credentials of the *wazīr* with his conservative supporters, he, of his own volition, decided to add to their suspicions. Without any apparent reason, he

[1] Ṣābī, *Wuzarā'*, p. 335.
[2] See above, p. 34.
[3] Ṣābī, *Wuzarā'*, p. 286.
[4] Miskawayh, vol. I, p. 245.
[5] Ṭabarī, III, p. 2289.
[6] See below, p. 152.

opened negotiations with the Qarāmiṭa of Baḥrayn who had been quietly busy with their own affairs for over seven years, and indeed were to continue to do so for another decade. When they asked for spades, the request was generously met and almost incidentally they were allowed to trade with Sīrāf across the Gulf.[1] The only possible explanation, and it is not quite convincing, is that he had the foresight to take precautions against the forthcoming Fāṭimid attacks on Egypt and thwart any concerted action by the Qarāmiṭa. To be sure, within a year the Fāṭimids had occupied Cyrenaica and in 915/302 attacked Alexandria. Mu'nis mobilized an army of more than 40,000 men and marched to Egypt where he was able to expel the attackers.[2] While the Qarāmiṭa made no hostile moves, the Ḥamdānids tried to take advantage of the situation to extract from the central government more territory and privileges in Jazīra. Having finished with the Fāṭimids, Mu'nis marched straight against the ambitious Ḥamdānids who quickly dispersed.[3]

All these military operations required money, and in order to balance his budget the *wazīr* had to tighten his control over expenditure. In his zeal he went over the tolerance limits of those affected by his austerity measures and began to feel their resistance. He tried to resign and was persuaded to carry on, but the pressures against him that had been building up, soon reached breaking point. After almost four years in office 301–4/913–17 the Jarrāḥ 'Alī b. 'Īsā was dismissed, and his team was replaced by a Furāt team.[4]

The new team was headed by the same Furāt *wazīr* who had held office in 908–12/296–9 but the circumstances this time were different. While Mu'nis and his men were satisfied with their pay arrangements, Muqtadir and his Mother were clamouring for the Palace expenses to be paid in full by the public treasury. Pledging to them a daily payment of 1500 dinārs in addition to all other expenses, Furāt resorted to a most extraordinary method of raising the necessary money. He knew that corruption was rampant among all government officials, and that it was no use trying to stop it or simply hiding one's head in the sand and pretending the trouble was not there. He also knew that there had been a long tradition, reputedly introduced by 'Umar in Madīna, that every government appointee should submit an account of his wealth upon dismissal and would be

[1] Ṣābī, *Wuzarā'*, pp. 292–3; 'Arīb, p. 59.
[2] Ṭabarī, III, pp. 229–30; 'Arīb, pp. 51–5.
[3] Miskawayh, vol. I, pp. 36–9.
[4] *Ibid.*, pp. 41–2.

heavily fined for any irregularities. However, as this had been left to the discretion of the ruler, it had not been always enforced. Accepting corruption as the order of the day, Furāt decided to standardize the practice of taxing it, and for this purpose he set up a Department of Bribes.[1] Ingenious as it was, this method by its very nature could not assure a regular flow of revenue. After being in office for eighteen months and being unable to meet his commitments, Furāt and his team were dismissed in 918/306.

To satisfy the needs of Mu'nis and the demands of the rulers a new team, that combined the efficiency of the Jarrāḥs with the wealth of the tax-farmers, was brought into office. It was headed by Ḥāmid b. ʿAbbās the biggest tax-farmer of his time, whose power and wealth were as excessive in Baghdād as in his home region of Wāsiṭ. Although a very genial and successful businessman he had had no past experience in government. His first assistant, who was appointed in charge of all departments, was the Jarrāḥ ʿAlī b. ʿĪsā, the "good vizier".[2] The essence was that while the *wazīr*, Ḥāmid, should concern himself with finding better means to collect more revenues, the assistant *wazīr*, ʿAlī, should devote all his efforts to devising measures to cut down the expenditure. As was to be expected tax-farming was applied wherever possible, and the distinction between the tax-official and the tax-farmer disappeared for they became one and the same. The *wazīr* contracted for himself the tax-farming of all the lands under the immediate jurisdiction of Baghdād for the total sum of 54 million dirhams. Then, at a handsome profit, he sub-contracted these to his own representatives in the areas concerned.[3] The tax-farming of Egypt and Syria was granted to the tax-official there, who had been a long-time associate of the assistant *wazīr*, for three million dinārs.[4]

The flow of revenues into the treasury did not offset the drawbacks of the system and it soon began to crumble. The *wazīr*, who had his own private army, ran the government as a private business.[5] The newly established Department of Tax-farming was under the efficient direction of Kalwadhānī, a man whose expertise must have been widely recognized. His presence in the administration for the following decade represented a rare element of stability and continuity which may explain the durability of the central government. However, the *wazīr*'s right-hand man was Ibn al-Ḥawwārī, whose

[1] *Ibid.*, p. 42; Athīr, vol. VIII, p. 73.
[2] Miskawayh, vol. I, pp. 58, 70–1.
[3] *Ibid.*, pp. 59–60, 154.
[4] *Ibid.*, p. 107.
[5] *Takmila*, pp. 20, 33.

appointment truly reflects the corruption of the time. This man, as his name indicates, was a flour merchant whose interests were fully involved with the interests of the *wazīr*, who was also a grain merchant. Having both official power and private means, this absolutely profit-orientated pair applied all their talents to making gains beyond their wildest dreams. The new corrupt practices they introduced in government were bad enough in themselves, but were less serious in their results than the monopolies set up to speculate in commodity prices. Inflated prices of flour and grain in particular brought about riots in Baghdād, not only by the civilian population but also by the military. Although these riots were contained, steps had to be taken to rectify the situation. After some struggle on the part of the *wazīr* to hold on to his powers, his tax-farming contract was cancelled and his Jarrāḥ assistant was given the responsibility of collecting the revenues. Tax-farming continued in operation with the strict proviso that government officials should be excluded from accepting such contracts. It is significant that while the assistant *wazīr* was given a free hand to dominate all departments, the *wazīr* himself was not dismissed and continued in office for at least three more years.[1] In other words the rulers realized that they could not, at that stage, alienate the powerful circles the *wazīr* represented.

This political manoeuvring to maintain a united front was inspired by developments in the eastern and western regions of the empire. To take the west first, another Fāṭimid expedition arrived in Egypt in 919/307 and successfully occupied bases in Alexandria, Giza and Fayyūm. It took Mu'nis almost two years and the help of the Tarsus navy to dislodge the enemy, a success for which he was rewarded by being given control over the affairs of Egypt and Syria.[2] In the eastern regions rapid developments had been taking place everywhere from Central Asia to Ādherbayjān. Disconnected as they may seem, these developments once more revolved around the northern trade. We have already explained the changes that had been taking place with regard to the routes of this trade. The Sāmānids, the main beneficiaries of these changes, were not at one in how to deal with the new situation. The prosperity of Khwārizm was at the expense of Ṭabaristān and both were parts of their domain. Any unrest in Ṭabaristān would echo in Khurāsān, particularly in Nīshāpūr, where the merchants of Ṭabaristān had had good relations since the

[1] Miskawayh, vol. I, pp. 56–100; Athīr, vol. VIII, pp. 82–6; *Takmila*, p. 91; 'Arīb, pp. 70–9.

[2] Miskawayh, vol. I, pp. 75–6; 'Arīb, pp. 79–86.

days of Ṭāhirid power.[1] This difference of opinion manifested itself in the defection of general Pārs and his troops to Baghdād in 907/295. Three years later the Sāmānids sent to Muqtadir an unusual present of furs, especially sable, which was in effect like sending samples to a prospective customer.[2] At the same time they began attempts to dominate Rayy, a vital link on the route from Ṭabaristān to the west. Although these attempts were officially disavowed by the Sāmānids they soon produced adverse results.[3]

In 914/301 a Shī'ite revolt broke out in Ṭabaristān and at the same time the Sāmānid ruler was assassinated. The Shī'ite revolt was that of the famous Ḥasanid Uṭrūsh who had been living among the Daylamites for thirteen years. The regime he set up had two interesting features; the imposition of an income-tax of 10%, and the undermining of the power of the big landowners.[4] He established his headquarters at Chālūs, a strong point that dominated a northern route from Ṭabaristān via Qazvīn.[5] This move brought about a chain reaction in Ādherbayjān. There the main interest in this trade was in dealing with the Khazars through the trans-Caucasian land-route. As this was in direct competition with the sea-route from Khazar country to Ṭabaristān, the interests of the latter were incompatible with those of Ādherbayjān.[6]

The assassination of the Sāmānid ruler allowed the opposing factions the opportunity to push foward their claims. This was vigorously expressed in two rebellions; one in trade-conscious Samarqand and the other in Ṭabaristān-orientated Nīshāpūr. Fortunately the Sāmānid regime had the inner strength to overcome such difficulties. The son of the assassinated ruler, a boy of eight years, was proclaimed successor to his father, but the real power fell to Jayhānī, the head of the administration and one of the most sagacious men of his time.[7] After attending to his internal problems and pacifying the Sāmānid domains, the external issues became his concern. There was every reason to encourage the prospering trade and since Baghdād was a main *entrepôt* for this trade, it was only sensible to reach an understanding with the interested parties there. The co-operation of the two capitals Bukhārā and Baghdād would

[1] See above, p. 67.
[2] 'Arīb, p. 35.
[3] Athīr, vol. VIII, p. 76; Miskawayh, vol. I, pp. 39, 45.
[4] Athīr, vol. VIII, pp. 61–2; Miskawayh, vol. I, p. 63.
[5] Ṭabarī, III, p. 2292; Iṣṭakhrī, p. 206.
[6] Miskawayh, vol. I, p. 45; Khurdādhbeh, p. 154, Iṣṭakhrī, p. 218; Ḥawqal, pp. 388, 394, 398.
[7] Ṭabarī, III, p. 2289; Athīr, vol. VIII, pp. 58–60, 86–8.

surely be enough to overwhelm the minor powers in the regions in between, be it in Ṭabaristān or Ādherbayjān. The authorities in Baghdād were of varying degrees of enthusiasm about the extent of such co-operation. The merchant *wazīr* Ḥāmid might be expected to encourage and indeed be involved in such commercial transactions. Naṣr, a real power in the capital, although a Khazar, understood all the implications of co-operating with the Sāmānids and threw his support behind it.[1] On the other hand Mu'nis, who had always shown a particular interest in the *thughūr* and Ādherbayjān, was watchful for the interests of these regions, and did not want to see them sacrificed for the interests of the East.[2] He was also aware that the Byzantines, who sent a trade mission to Baghdād in 918/305, with the ostensible reason of exchanging prisoners of war, were also interested in this trade, part of which passed through their hands.[3]

The culmination of all these schemes was a full-fledged trade mission that started from Baghdād on 21 June 921/11 Ṣafar 309 and arrived at the capital of the country of the Bulghār, up the middle Volga at its confluence with the River Kama, on 12 May 922/12 Muḥarram 310. Every aspect of this most unusual journey, its timing, starting point, route, destination and the identity of every person involved, helps to focus the attention on the concern of all parties with the northern trade. It also brings together all the threads needed to understand the relations between these complex events that involved peoples, not only from within, but also from outside the empire.

This mission was a response to a combined approach by Jayhānī and the chief of the Bulghār. A Muslim Khazar representing the latter accompanied by a man from Khwārizm as a messenger from Jayhānī, had journeyed to Baghdād not long before 921/309.[4] A fellow countryman from Khwārizm, Tigin, who as a blacksmith in his native land had been acquainted with the country of the Bulghār, had helped to introduce these messengers to his superior in the Palace.[5] The latter, in turn, had persuaded higher personages to listen to their persistent pleas.[6] At last, it had been decided to respond to this important message by sending a delegation representing Muqtadir to negotiate with the chief of the Bulghār. The members of this delegation were carefully chosen because of their special knowledge of and interest in these faraway lands. Leading

[1] 'Arīb, p. 51; Miskawayh, vol. 1, p. 52.
[2] Miskawayh, vol. 1, pp. 62–3.
[3] *Ibid.*, pp. 53–5; Ṣābī, *Rusūm*, pp. 11–14.
[4] Faḍlān, pp. 69, 77.
[5] *Ibid.*, pp. 80–1, 136.
[6] *Ibid.*, p. 81.

them was a high-ranking officer in the service of Muqtadir who was descended from the Russians of the Volga.[1] Second to him was general Pārs, who had earlier defected from the Sāmānid ranks and who also happened to be a Slav.[2] Third was, of course, the intermediary, Tigin of Khwārizm. Fourth was Ibn Faḍlān, to whose diligence we owe the fascinating description of their voyage. He pointedly related himself to Muḥammad b. Sulaymān, who had played a major role in bringing down the Ṭūlūnids, and who until 917/304 had been in charge of the fiscal affairs of Rayy. He was to act as the secretary for this important mission, and his interest is indicated by his association with Rayy.[3] Of course the emissary of the Bulghār accompanied the delegation back but the representative of Jayhānī was detained in Baghdād.[4]

Starting from the capital they advanced east on the main route to Rayy, where they anxiously waited for eleven days in expectation of some protection on their way further east.[5] This seems not to have been available, for they then joined the trade caravan and had to conceal their identities while passing through Ṭabaristān territory controlled by the Shī'ites of the region.[6] Arriving at the Sāmānid capital Bukhārā, they, in company with the defector Pārs, were cordially received by Jayhānī and were introduced to the boy ruler. Moreover, they were given all the help they needed for the following stages of their journey to Khwārizm and then around the Caspian to the Volga.[7] Apart from the usual hazards of travelling, their main difficulty was to secure permission to pass through the territories of the nomadic Turkish tribes of the Ghuzz and Pecheneg. Their escorts, credentials and familiarity with the area helped them to convince the reluctant nomads to permit such an unprecedented breach of their code of secrecy.[8] Finally reaching the Bulghār capital they saw for themselves the cause of the strength of these people and the justification of their own mission. The Bulghār had just begun to settle astride the crossroads of east–west and north–south trade; the former by land from Khwārizm to Kiev, and the latter from the Caspian up the Volga to the Baltic shores. They did not need to go anywhere for the trade because it all came to them, and they had no difficulty collecting their 10% tax.[9] However, as they were not politically united they were to some extent subject

[1] *Ibid.*, p. 69.
[2] See above, p. 136; Faḍlān, p. 69.
[3] Faḍlān, pp. 65, 69; Miskawayh, vol. 1, p. 51; see also above.
[4] Faḍlān, p. 77.
[5] *Ibid.*, p. 74.
[6] *Ibid.*, pp. 74–5.
[7] *Ibid.*, pp. 76–7.
[8] *Ibid.*, pp. 98, 103–4, 107.
[9] *Ibid.*, p. 145.

to the more powerful Khazars, their neighbours to the south-west who also controlled the estuary of the Volga. To keep the peace the Bulghār were obliged to pay to the Khazars a tax of one sable-fur per household.[1] Pressured from both the Khazars and the Turks, the Bulghār were looking for allies. The Sāmānids were just as eager to find allies who would help them bring in line the troublesome Turkish nomads and shake the Khazar domination off the Caspian. The presence of Muslims among the Bulghār and the willingness of more of them to be converted, helped to cement their alliance with the Sāmānids.[2] The subsequent prosperity of both was at the expense of the Khazar, whose power collapsed in 965/355, and of the Shī'ites of Ṭabaristān, who in a decade were reduced to insignificance.

The rulers of both Bukhārā and Baghdād must have been greatly surprised by the results of the economic demise of Ṭabaristān. Their hopes that between them they could overcome any resistance to their concerted policies from the region to the south and the south-west of the Caspian, were speedily dashed by the Daylamites. These people who had previously confined their energies to their own mountainous territory must have been hard hit by this economic decline. Hitherto, they were hard to find amidst the multitude of races in the various armies of the empire. Although Islam had long struck roots among them, there had not been much change in their socio-political organization. Their adherence to Shī'ism, in its Zaydī form, was due more to missionary activities than to any particular need for a vehicle of protest. The new economic situation now gave them reason for protest and forced them out of their isolation. First, every chief of a clan or a tribe, every leader of a village, a town or district, and every prince from the many ruling families in the region, supported by his men, rose up in arms to defend their interests and establish their control at every possible point on the secondary route from Rayy to Baghdād via Qazvīn, or on the main route via Hamadān. The people of Ādherbayjān, who were just as badly affected by the decline of their own trade, jumped into the ring to defend their territory against the encroachments of the Daylamites. The rulers of Bukhārā and Baghdād were extremely anxious to safeguard the link between their respective territories, and were willing to go to any length for this purpose. Their attempts merely complicated the situation and worked to the advantage of the Daylamites. The Sāmānids tried to exploit the internal differences of

[1] *Ibid.*, pp. 113, 145.

[2] *Ibid.*, pp. 67–8, 117–18, 120–2, 135.

the latter to use some of them against their fellow-countrymen. The result was a series of bewildering alliances in which the partners changed sides with surprising agility to the confusion of all concerned. The central government tried to intimidate some and placate others. When military expeditions failed, military–administrative *iqṭā'* was extended to include any leader, Daylamite or otherwise, who could establish his control over any area. Then outright land-grants, i.e. simple *iqṭā'*, were given to persuade some leaders even just to accept military–administrative *iqṭā'*. But the dike was breached and all efforts to contain the Daylamites failed. Three of their leaders were able to establish short-lived dynasties that were of no significance except for the fact that they were the precursors of the Būyids who, in due course, were to occupy Baghdād itself.[1]

Unable to cope with all these disturbances, the authority of the central government began to weaken and the reactionary Ḥanbalites of the capital were quick to take advantage of the situation to assert their own strength. To placate them the ineffectual *wazīr* Ḥāmid offered a scape-goat. The harmless mystic Ḥallāj, who had been languishing in prison for nine years, was brought out, put to an elaborate trial and finally executed in 922/309.[2] Perhaps there is nothing better to illustrate the atmosphere of Baghdād than the fact that when the great scholar Ṭabarī died there in 923/310, public demonstrations were allowed to be held against him and he was subsequently denied a decent burial simply because he had refused to recognize Ibn Ḥanbal as a jurist.[3] Nevertheless, these convulsions did not do the government any good because they were only attempts to sidetrack the main issue – lack of money. Revenues had decreased because of the turmoil caused by the Daylamites in the central regions, and expenditure had increased because of the military measures taken against them. When the assistant *wazīr*, 'Alī b. 'Īsā, tried to tighten his hand on expenditure, the military objected.[4] Accordingly the whole Jarrāḥ team headed by Ḥāmid was dismissed in 923/311 and replaced by the ever ready Furāt team.

Significantly our sources refer to this year as the Year of Ruination.[5] The events of the year themselves justify such an epithet, but there is also justification in the events of the preceding and following years; it was the beginning of the end. Four days after the change of

[1] Miskawayh, vol. I, pp. 117, 161–2, 213–4; Athīr, vol. VIII, pp. 128–9, 138–45, 157–9, 199; *Takmila*, pp. 38, 51–2; 'Arīb, pp. 137–8, 154, 161.
[2] Miskawayh, vol. I, pp. 76–82.
[3] Athīr, vol. VIII, p. 98; Miskawayh, vol. I, p. 84.
[4] Miskawayh, vol. I, pp. 85–8.
[5] 'Arīb, p. 110.

wazīrs, and as if it was timed to coincide with it, the Qarāmiṭa of Baḥrayn started a series of devastating and lightning attacks on towns and caravans. The first attack was on Baṣra, where a force of only 1700 men was able to occupy and loot the town for seventeen days.[1] Ten months later they attacked a pilgrimage caravan on its way back to Baghdād, plundered it and captured many distinguished pilgrims.[2] These two attacks were to typify all the others that occurred spasmodically over a period of almost half a century. For seventeen years these Qarāmiṭa had chosen to remain quiet and had contented themselves with receiving some spades and minor trade concessions from Baghdād. In 913/301 their first leader Ḥasan Jannābī had been assassinated and succeeded by his son Sa'īd. As the latter had not been able to assert his leadership, he had been replaced by his younger brother Sulaymān who started to give the movement a new life. Although in 923/311 he was only seventeen years old, he must have had considerable talent for leadership. The constant appearance of the figure 17 in his first moves suggests that he was trying to stress that the past quiet 17 years had been wasted, and that he was determined to celebrate his own seventeenth birthday with a bang. It is futile to try to establish whether or not his movement was related to that of the Fāṭimids in North Africa. Any reports or arguments to this effect are far-fetched and are always contradictory. Such reports might even have been encouraged and circulated by the parties concerned themselves. After all it does not hurt to let one's enemy think that one has support from other quarters. However, the fact remains that the activities of the Qarāmiṭa of Baḥrayn and the Fāṭimids were not co-ordinated, and that the first time they came into touch with each other they fought against each other.[3]

The designs of Sulaymān and his Qarāmiṭa were aimed at capturing a share in the profits of the trade of the Persian Gulf, the Syrian–'Irāqī desert and the Arabian desert. They had been granted trading rights in Sīrāf, but they had soon come to realize that this was literally a drop in the ocean.[4] Therefore, under the vigorous leadership of Sulaymān, they proceeded to occupy the ports of 'Umān and thus dominated all the Arabian coast of the Gulf. They next tried to establish points of control on the Persian side of the Gulf. Their attacks on Baṣra were enough to frighten the trade away from this

[1] Miskawayh, vol. 1, pp. 104–5; 'Arīb, pp. 110–11.
[2] Miskawayh, vol. 1, pp. 120–1.
[3] See below, p. 204.
[4] See above, p. 145.

flourishing port and divert it to their own ports where they imposed and collected their own taxes.[1] For the land routes they first turned to an easy target, the pilgrimage caravans, which were also important trade caravans. The sanctity of the occasion did not deter the Qarāmiṭa, though they were not against the pilgrimage in particular; they were against its use by the merchants to enhance their profits, in much the same way as many of us now are against the commercial exploitation of Christmas. Having thus announced their intention, the Qarāmiṭa turned to the north–south trade route skirting the Syrian–'Irāqī desert, and tried to attack and dominate the market-towns along this route. Their intention, which was eventually achieved, was to collect what they considered taxes and what their opponents preferred to call protection money.[2]

The rulers in Baghdād were naturally alarmed by this new threat to trade, the more so because of the ease with which the Qarāmiṭa won their military successes. It was not that the latter had formidable forces – the biggest number mentioned is 2700 men – and it was this very fact that daunted them.[3] It clearly indicated that the Qarāmiṭa were able to win their victories only because they had the sympathy of the local population of the areas in which they operated, especially in 'Irāq. Something was manifestly wrong with a government that lost the support of its subjects to that extent. If it were to continue to govern some radical changes had to take place, and fast. It is no wonder that our sources associate the Year of Ruination 923/311 with a military near take-over of control of government. That this did not happen at this point was due only to the fact that general Mu'nis, the only military leader who could accomplish it, at the time, did not want it.[4] Over the years he had acquired more strength, as men realized that the one way of ensuring their payments was to put themselves under his command.[5] He had arrived at a working arrangement with the administrators to guarantee the regularity of these payments, and in exchange had supported them as long as they had kept their end of the bargain. He was not against military–administrative *iqṭā' per se*, but he took care that it should not be applied in areas where the revenues had been allocated for the payment of his men, i.e. Syria and Egypt. Military leaders in other provinces believed that this type of *iqṭā'* was the only way to salva-

[1] Ḥawqal, p. 25; Mas'ūdī, *Tanbīh*, p. 393; Miskawayh, vol. 1, pp. 139, 284.
[2] Miskawayh, vol. 1, pp. 145–6, 173–82, 201; 'Arīb, pp. 118, 134; *Takmila*, p. 53; Ṣābī, *Qarāmiṭa*, p. 56; Mas'ūdī, *Tanbīh*, p. 390.
[3] Ṣābī, *Qarāmiṭa*, p. 49.
[4] Ṣābī, *Wuzarā'*, pp. 45–6.
[5] Miskawayh, vol. 1, p. 115.

tion, especially under the circumstances of the Daylamite torrent. The most important military commander in Baghdād, Naṣr, was convinced that a military take-over was inevitable and acted as if it had already happened.[1]

The civilian officials, whether in the capital or the provinces, were divided in their opinions about their own relationship to the military. While most of the Jarrāḥs and their associates were willing to continue to co-operate with the military, some of them had no compunction about being completely subservient to them. The Furāts remained adamant in their convinction that military leaders should be subjugated to the civilian authorities. For this the Furāt *wazīr* and his son had to pay with their lives, on the insistence of the military leaders, after their dismissal from office in 924/312.[2] The remaining eight years of Muqtadir's reign were dominated by the struggle between various factions of the military and civilians to establish a new order. The situation was not helped by the fact that Muqtadir, who had come of age, saw no reason why he should not exercise his prerogative and actually rule. In this period of extreme instability there were nine *wazīrs*, one of them staying in office no more than two months. In 929/317 Mu'nis, worried about the diminishing revenues and the effect on the payments of his men, organized a coup against Muqtadir. The meddlesome ruler was deposed and a more mature 'Abbāsid was installed in his place under the title Qāhir. However, the elite forces of Baghdād, whose functions were now mostly ceremonial, supported by some of the police force, were soon able to reverse the situation and reinstate Muqtadir.[3] Confident in his renewed strength, the latter audaciously proceeded to establish civilian supremacy over the military. For this purpose, Ḥusayn b. Qāsim, a descendant of a long line of *wazīrs*, was put in charge of the whole administration in 931/319.[4] To emphasize his responsibility and authority a glorified title was bestowed upon him, and it was decreed that his name should appear on the coinage along with that of the ruler.[5] To begin with, he took advantage of a developing tendency in some provincial areas to set his policy in motion. Some of the civilian administrators in the provinces had begun to recruit their own private amies from among the available Daylamites, and had used such forces to set up a semi-autonomous administration in their respective areas. Such officials offered an

[1] *Takmila*, p. 57.
[2] *Ibid.*, p. 137.
[3] *Ibid.*, pp. 187–200.
[4] See above, p. 118.
[5] 'Arīb, p. 165; Miskawayh, vol. 1, p. 223.

ideal opportunity to demonstrate the principle of civilian supremacy. They were therefore recognized and confirmed as appointees of the central government in charge of all affairs in their regions.[1] This was easy enough, but when the *wazīr* turned his attention to the military it proved a different matter. His attempts to divide and rule were too transparent to achieve the desired results and succeeded only in pushing Mu'nis against the wall. When the latter began to show definite signs of disagreement, the glorified *wazīr* was hastily dismissed after only seven months in office. But it was too late; Mu'nis marched on Baghdād and Muqtadir was killed in the ensuing fight in 932/320.[2]

Once more Qāhir, who had been Mu'nis's choice three years earlier, was proclaimed the new ruler. Mature he might have been; stupid he certainly was, for as soon as he came to power he got himself immersed in conspiracies to support one military faction against another.[3] In 933/321 he succeeded in having Mu'nis eliminated, but the murder of the old and respected general only helped to remove from the scene one more element of stability. As all this strife was taking place in Baghdād, the population there, with its Ḥanbalite and Shī'ite tendencies, was drawn into the conflict.[4] The conspiracies multiplied and finally the conspirators turned against Qāhir and had him deposed after a turbulent reign of only eighteen months, 932–4/320–2.

At this point the military commanders, realizing that none of them had enough strength to dominate the others, decided to give the politicians, so to speak, the opportunity to resolve their own dilemma. Towards this end they agreed on the succession of a son of Muqtadir, who was proclaimed as Rāḍī.[5] Though an inexperienced young man, at most in his mid-twenties, he made a valiant effort to meet the crisis. He appointed a *wazīr*, who included in his team a coalition of Jarrāḥs and Furāts, and gave him a free hand to do as he saw fit.[6] It was almost inevitable that, under such circumstances, the *wazīr* should find himself in conflict with one military leader or another. After a year of hard work trying to reconcile the interests of the government with those of the military leaders in Baghdād and the provinces, he had to take some stern measures against one particularly officious commander. As this action did not bring about

[1] Miskawayh, vol. I, pp. 147, 158–9, 166; Athīr, vol. VIII, p. 135; 'Arīb, p. 138.
[2] Miskawayh, vol. I, pp. 166–79.
[3] *Ibid.*, pp. 259–64.
[4] *Ibid.*, p. 322; Athīr, vol. VIII, p. 204.
[5] Miskawayh, vol. I, p. 290.
[6] *Ibid.*, pp. 292–5; Athīr, vol. VIII, p. 211.

any immediate reaction from the latter's supporters, the *wazīr* thought his position was secure enough for him to take matters into his own hands and put the military in their place. He then dismissed his coalition team and replaced them with his own son as a second *wazīr*.[1] Obviously he overestimated his power because in a few months the military had forced him out of office, and replaced him with their favourite Jarrāḥs.[2] In two months they too had to resign and were succeeded for another few months by another two *wazīrs*. The civilians had declared their bankruptcy, and Rāḍī had no alternative but to call in the military to take over all affairs of government.[3]

This year 936/324 marked the beginning of another decade of, if it were possible, even more turmoil. A new office was created, the holder of which was called *Amīr al-Umarā'*, supreme commander, and was invested with complete powers over all military forces as well as over all government departments. He was not only made the superior of the *wazīr* but also put in charge of all fiscal affairs in the capital and the provinces. This was all very well and might have worked if the central government had had anything left to give. The treasury in Baghdād could hardly claim to be a central treasury and in any event it was empty. The "provinces" had been reduced to the immediate vicinity of Baghdād. The Sāmānids were still in control of most of their domains in the East but were busy trying to stem the Daylamite tide. The Daylamites were roaming over the central Iranian Plateau fighting each other, and everybody else, to make room for themselves. Those who were squeezed out by their fellow Daylamites drifted to southern 'Irāq where they enlisted in the service of the Barīdīs, the former tax-officials who now controlled the region.[4] The Qarāmiṭa had mellowed a little but were still dominating east Arabia and making their presence felt in the rest of the Peninsula. Jazīra and the *thughūr* were in the hands of the Ḥamdānids, while Egypt and Syria were virtually autonomous under Ikhshīd.[5]

The installation of a strong man and the sacrifice of the long cherished principle of the separation of military and fiscal affairs, did not save the empire because there was no empire to be saved. These desperate measures had produced nothing but more chaos. In a period of ten years 936–45/324–34 five military commanders fought

[1] Miskawayh, vol. I, pp. 305–6, 318–23.
[2] *Ibid.*, p. 336.
[3] *Ibid.*, pp. 351–2.
[4] *Ibid.*, pp. 254–8, 301.
[5] *Ibid.*, pp. 366–7.

over and succeeded each other in the supreme office. At one point the men in the ranks demanded that an 'Abbāsid should be appointed to this office, but this was only an echo of things past.[1] Neither the Qarāmiṭa nor the Daylamites would take much cognizance of such a figurehead; the former were brought into the fight as allies of one of the contenders and the latter were recruited by all of them.[2] The main forces of the Daylamites under the effective leadership of the Būyids were closing in on 'Irāq from the east and the south-east.[3] Their objective was to capture Baghdād and, in the circumstances, this was a more realistic aim than saving it. They needed only to bide their time until the forces of the capital had exhausted themselves in futile fighting. When Rāḍī died in 940/329, he was succeeded by his brother Muttaqī who got himself too involved in the struggle; he was easily deposed and was blinded for his efforts in 944/333.[4] He in turn was succeeded by another brother Mustakfī who witnessed the end of this episode. It came soon after his succession when the office of the supreme commander fell to a civilian official, which in effect meant that the military had given up trying to save the central government of Baghdād.

[1] Ṣūlī, *Rāḍī*, p. 204.
[2] Miskawayh, vol. II, p. 24; Athīr, vol. VIII, p. 278.
[3] Miskawayh, vol. II, pp. 37, 55.
[4] *Ibid.*, pp. 67–72; Ṣūlī, *Rāḍī*, pp. 248–9.

8

THE BŪYID CONFEDERACY

The collapse of the central government and the emergence of the Daylamites mark the beginning of the division of the Islamic lands into two distinct spheres, the line of demarcation running along the western slopes of the Zagros mountains down the east coast of the Persian Gulf. To the east of this line the Iranian world, though by no means united, consistently regained its identity. To the west, the Arab world, also disunited, continued to survive almost on the same lines as we know it today. The Arab conquerors had succeeded in pushing the Buddhist wall as far back as the Chinese borders and thereafter the regions of Outer Iran had become an integral part of the Islamic domain. Yet these regions of what the Arabs had called the East, because of the circumstances of the conquest, had continued to have a rather special status within the empire.[1] On the other hand, western Iran, the seat of the Sāsānians, had been more affected by Arab penetration and subsequent control. From the point of view of the Arabs the areas extending eastwards into the Iranian central plateau had been considered their property. In the first two centuries of Islam, Ṭabasayn, to the north-east of the Dasht-i-Kavīr desert, had been the border point and the "door" to the East.[2] Under the Ṭāhirids, this point had been pushed westward to Rayy, and now it was the turn of the Daylamites to push it further west into 'Irāq. These people, mainly the highlanders of the Elburz mountains, who had remained virtually independent under both Sāsānians and Arabs, swept down through the central plateau and almost unintentionally revived the claims of the Iranians to their own territory. It would be incorrect to give the impression that this was a nationalist movement, because it was not. Indeed the first reaction of the Daylamite leaders, after settling down in their new domains, was to immerse themselves in Arab culture and adopt it as their own. All the same, they gave other Iranians, especially those of Fārs, the opportunity to reassert themselves over the more Arabicized population of 'Irāq. It is interesting to note that later non-Iranian

[1] Shaban, *The 'Abbāsid Revolution*, pp. 1–15.
[2] Bal., *Futūḥ*, p. 403.

peoples, the Saljūqs and the Mongols, moved further in this direction and thus helped to buttress the claims of the Iranians.

In their own territory the Daylamites were ruled by various princes, some of whom were of ancient lineage; or by local tribal chiefs and there were as many chiefs as there were hills in the Elburz range.[1] These simple but important facts were reflected in the three-pronged outburst of these people into neighbouring regions. One group led by the prestigious line of the Musāfirids, while maintaining their home base, branched out and established control over an enclave on the Caspian coast in Ādherbayjān. Their influence with their peers among the autonomous or independent rulers of the Caucasus region, helped them more than their military forces to preserve their interests for almost seventy years.[2] Other Daylamite leaders of less distinction but with more forces led their followers east where for a time they served in the Sāmānid armies. Eventually they were able to occupy the prosperous regions of Ṭabaristān and Gurgān where they set up the Ziyārid dynasty and upheld it for over a century until these regions were taken over by the Saljūqs in 1030/421. Significantly the Ziyārids made a point of staying on good terms with the Sāmānids and their successors the Ghaznavids, yet they had a protracted conflict with their fellow Daylamites, the most important of whom were the Būyids.

It is ironic that the Būyids first made their name in the service of the Ziyārids. Three brothers whose father's name was Būyeh commanded between them a few hundred men. Whether by design or by accident their energies were diverted southwards where they achieved some measure of success. This initial success and the opportunities it offered persuaded other leaders to join them with their men.[3] Under this kind of collective leadership the Būyid forces grew steadily and soon they found themselves in control of most of southern and western Iran. Their pressure against southern 'Irāq helped to speed the downfall of the central government and when this happened they entered Baghdād unopposed in 945/334. They did not think this feat had required special effort or meant a change of plan. The peculiar arrangement they had had, almost from the beginning of their successful adventure, continued in operation, as if acquiring this big metropolis was of no more importance than conquering a provincial town. Indeed this arrangement lasted, almost unchanged, throughout their hundred and ten years in power.

[1] Ḥawqal, pp. 376–7.
[2] *Ibid.*, pp. 348, 354.
[3] Miskawayh, vol. I, p. 353, vol. II, pp. 5, 122; Athīr, vol. VIII, p. 201.

It was a Būyid Confederacy under which the regions remained separate, each with its own forces and resources. Co-operation for a specific purpose was desirable, and it was given, but unification was out of the question. When it happened by force of circumstances in 978/367, it was only for five years and no effort was made to perpetuate it when it lapsed in 983/372. The corollary here is that the Būyid brothers must have been aware of the spirit of regionalism prevalent in these territories and it was decided therefore to allow every region to pursue its own interests with the least possible interference from others. They must have also been aware of the nature of their own position among their followers. Although other chiefs had placed themselves under Būyid leadership, their individuality and their recent jealously guarded independence in their own mountains would still have to be taken into consideration. Accepting the principle of their own equality under this system of collective leadership, the brothers were in effect setting an example to be followed in the regions, where each one of them would be no more than an equal among equals. Thus other chieftains would also have some measure of power in their new domains. Accordingly, one brother was set up in the northern sector of the plateau from Rayy to the Jibāl province. Another, the eldest, was in charge of the Fārs province. The youngest was given the southern coastal provinces of Kirmān and Khūzistān, whence he was able to march into southern 'Irāq and finally Baghdād. The fact that he was left in charge of all these regions has its economic and political significance. From an economic point of view these regions controlled almost all the inlets of the Indian Ocean trade in addition to Baghdād, the main *entrepôt*. Politically, the principle of equality as between the brothers was emphasized by leaving the youngest in charge of 'Irāq. On the other hand, this says a great deal about the contempt the Būyids felt for the seat of the defunct central government.

Having decided the general lines of their rule the Būyids had to turn to the infinitely more complicated question of how to apply them in detail to the existing circumstances in their territories. It has to be recognized that these rather unsophisticated people had thrust themselves upon a developed society. Their task was more difficult than that of the Arab conquerors. The latter had inherited functioning governments and their concern had only been to keep them operating. In contrast, the Būyids had inherited a brokendown system of government for which they now had to provide a substitute. Rescue came from the provincial oligarchy of the long subdued regions who saw in the advent of the Būyids a chance to press for their interests. It was from Fārs, the centre of the ancient Sāsānian civilization, and particularly from Shīrāz that most of the members of the Būyid bureaucracy were recruited. Generations of families serving in the same functions helped the Būyids to administer their three domains.[1] In this situation the office of *wazīr* acquired more power than it had ever had before. The 'Abbāsid rulers could have governed without *wazīrs* and had done so; the Būyids could not, for their experience was very limited.

It was fortunate for the Būyids that they had arrived at Baghdād via Fārs, because as soon as they entered the former they badly needed experienced advice. Their first problem was what to do with the 'Abbāsid *Amīr al-Mu'minīn* who was also the recognized *Imām* and *Khalīfa* of most of the community. Their first instinct was probably to get rid of such an unnecessary figurehead, but they were reminded that this would create more problems than it would solve. They could not be expected to stop to think about the finer points of the juridical differentiation between his various functions. They themselves were Shī'ites only because they had recently accepted Islam in this form. As they had been converted at the hands of Zaydīs they were supposed to belong to this sect. But at this stage they could not have had more than the most rudimentary knowledge of the development of Shī'ism. It is very possible that they did not know of the existence of other Shī'ite sects, let alone of the contending schools of orthodoxy, until they had left their native land. It is no wonder, then, that throughout their rule they tolerated all sects and schools and tried only to keep the balance between them. They did not consider the Qarāmiṭa extreme heretics, nor did they worry unduly about Ismā'īlī missionaries in their domains. They fought against and allied themselves with the Shī'ite Ḥamdānids but certainly not on religious grounds. They did not have as much difficulty with the Ḥanbalites of Baghdād as these themselves had with their orthodox Shāfi'ite fellows. However, despite their differences, all orthodox circles were agreed on the necessity of the continuation of the office of *Amīr al-Mu'minīn*. Over the years the 'Abbāsids had succeeded in hammering into the conscience of the community the fact that the administration of justice and the conduct of the religious life of the community must be the responsibility of the holder of this office. As this did not interfere with the Būyids' political objectives they were only too happy to oblige and

[1] Miskawayh, vol. II, pp. 120–1, 124, 147–8, 260, 269, 301; Iṣṭakhrī, pp. 147, 149.

to allow the office to continue, but only for these specific purposes.[1] All secular powers remained in their hands, a fact which was signalled by their bestowing on themselves an endless list of honorific titles.[2]

The question of the military forces of the fallen central government was another problem that confronted the Būyids in the provinces, and which became acute in Baghdād. They were keenly aware of their own shortcomings. They knew better than anyone that there were not many Daylamites left behind in their native mountains. If they were to control their vast domains they would have to supplement their forces from another source. They also knew that as mountaineers their fighting capability was only as infantry, and therefore in the southern and western plains they needed the protection of a cavalry force.[3] The forces of the fallen adversary offered a solution to both problems. In the provinces, as there were not many of them, they were quietly absorbed in the Būyid forces and treated on an equal footing with regard to pay. But this in itself represented another problem for there was not enough cash on hand to pay all concerned. The only assets available to the conquerors were the extensive land-holdings of the 'Abbāsid family and their associates. These were taken over by the Būyid administration and a new type of *iqṭā'* was introduced for the benefit of the men and their commanders for whose pay there was not enough ready cash. Such men were assigned the income from a specific land-holding in lieu of their fixed stipends or as a supplementation to them. This was meant to be a temporary arrangement which could be changed at the wish of these men or the administration, and the ownership of the land remained in the hands of the latter.

In Baghdād the situation was different because of many factors. First, the remnants of the armies of the capital, although divided among themselves, were still numerous enough to make them a force with which to contend. Second, of course there was no farm-land in the city, but there was much of it nearby and still much more to be taken over in other parts of 'Irāq. Third, there was more cash available than in the provinces. Fourth, while the new Būyid ruler would need his Daylamites, for obvious reasons, to remain in Baghdād, the old forces could be utilized to extend his rule in the rest of 'Irāq. As these forces outnumbered the Daylamites, there was

1 Miskawayh, vol. II, p. 86; Mas'ūdi, *Tanbīh*, pp. 399–400.

2 See the very interesting list included by Cl. Cahen, *Encyclopaedia of Islam* (New Edition), Leiden, 1954, s.v. "Buwayhids".

3 Athīr, vol. VIII, p. 473; Miskawayh, vol. II, pp. 77, 329.

no question of absorbing them into the latter and thus the former remained a separate force under their own commanders. To pay them the Būyid *iqṭāʿ* system was extended to ʿIrāq, to include not only the farm-lands there, but also inter-regional trade taxes.[1] Naturally this arrangement would help to establish the administration's authority over more territory and more revenues, and at the same time secure the pay of these forces. As for the Daylamites, it was determined, almost as a favour, to pay them directly from the treasury in Baghdād. Although the *Amīr al-Muʾminīn* himself was now paid an allowance from the same treasury after his properties had been taken over by the Būyid administration, the Daylamites were in a better position to demand what they wished.[2] They considered it an affront to give the defeated forces an assured pay while they had to rely on a possibly empty treasury. The Būyids had to give in and grant their leaders the same privilege in areas more accessible to Baghdād. These *ad hoc* arrangements, which were supposed to be temporary, continued throughout the Būyid domains until their downfall, despite attempts by the rulers and even demands from the beneficiaries themselves to revoke them. They created a two-tier system for the payment of the military forces and neither side was completely happy with its deal. Competition for more and better farm-land was intensified by demands for a change from one system to the other. In most cases the collateral security rights were passed from father to son and consolidated into outright ownership. Some of the holders of *iqṭāʿ* neglected the irrigation systems and when these were destroyed, they simply demanded to exchange the ruined lands for others still in production. Other holders used their *iqṭāʿ* as means to acquire more land, using their influence to intimidate both the tax-collectors and neighbouring landowners.[3] The land-tax collection continued under the tax-farming system and gradually the tax-farmers gave up the impossible task of collecting their dues from such influential land-holders.[4] The harmful effects of tax-farming were greatly increased by the instability of the *iqṭāʿ* system, to the utter detriment of the treasury. The attempts of some Būyid administrations to win the support of a particular army group did not help the cause of the treasury either. One of the most curious examples occurred in Baghdād in 958/347, where the ruler had never been happy with his Daylamites since they had exacted *iqṭāʿ* from him in 945/334. In order to win over the old troops completely

[1] Ṣābī, *Rasāʾil*, pp. 343, 358.
[2] Miskawayh, vol. II, p. 87.
[3] *Ibid.*, pp. 96–100.
[4] Ḥawqal, pp. 239–40.

and use them to restrain the Daylamites, the Būyid authorities devised an ingenious way of giving them a bonus. Those men whose pay was assigned to farm-land in southern 'Irāq were to travel there, one group after another in rotation, to collect their pay. This was not exactly necessary but to arrange for them to receive free hospitality *en route* in addition to a travel allowance of ten dirhams per day for every man with the rank of *ghulām* and twenty for the higher rank of *naqīb*, defies reason. As our source puts it, they found it both convenient and profitable to prolong their travels; the allowances gave them a comfortable income and accordingly they invested their salaries in all sorts of commercial enterprises.[1] Later when the authorities wanted to stop this mockery they were met by very stubborn resistance.[2]

The teething difficulties, even though some of them turned out to be chronic diseases, did not hinder the Būyids from looking outside their domains to examine their situation vis-a-vis their new neighbours. The interesting fact here is that their attention focussed simultaneously on all four corners. Of course their regional division helped them to cope with more than one front at a time, yet there was, as was to be expected, a good deal of co-ordination of effort especially at this early stage. Sitting astride the Iranian plateau and extending into 'Irāq, the Confederacy was in an advantageous position to dominate most of the east–west and north–south trade routes. Furthermore, its southern shores could be encouraged to attract a good deal of the Indian Ocean trade. Obviously the Būyids had good advice and also knew their own limitations, for they proceeded systematically to make the best of their situation with a minimum of military adventures, using peaceful means whenever possible. Therefore, they ruled out of court any conflict with either Byzantium or Egypt and throughout their rule refrained from interfering with these two powers even when the opportunity to do so offered itself.[3]

The activities of the Būyids in the Gulf are the best illustration of their methods and intentions. Soon after occupying Baghdād they set out to capture Baṣra, which had been in the hands of the tax-farmers, the Barīdīs, since the last years of the central government. This was an easy task; the important port was captured and the Barīdīs fled to the Qarāmiṭa in Baḥrayn. The Būyids then reimposed

[1] Miskawayh, vol. II, pp. 173–5.

[2] Ṣābī, *Tārīkh*, part 8, ed. H. F. Amedroz, and published as vol. IV in *Dhayl Tajārib al-Umam*, Cairo, 1916, pp. 374, 387.

[3] Qalānisī, p. 11.

the trade-taxes that had been abrogated by the Jarrāḥs over thirty years earlier. At the same time they reduced the land-tax that had been increased by the greedy tax-famers.[1] Having established themselves in Baṣra the Būyids proceeded to woo the Qarāmiṭa. The latter had reached the peak of their agitation under Sulaymān when in 930/317 they had committed the unforgivable sacrilege of looting the Ka'ba and carrying away the Black Stone. This act is not quite as bad as it sounds for they could also have destroyed the Ka'ba itself had they wanted to do so. They had nothing against the pilgrimage itself; their action was the clearest possible assertion of their objection to the use of this religious occasion for commercial purposes, from the benefits of which they had been excluded. Attacking the pilgrimage caravans had not always been possible and had not achieved the desired results. Until such time as arrangements were made with them the whole enterprise had better be stopped altogether. The best way to accomplish this was to take away the Black Stone which was, and still is, indispensable to the rituals of the pilgrimage.

Although the Qarāmiṭa seem to have been agreed on this act, they had had their differences with regard to their attempts to establish control over the Persian side of the Gulf. These differences had manifested themselves in a doctrinal and political struggle among them until the death of Sulaymān in 944/332. Therefore when the Būyids captured Baṣra four years later, the Qarāmiṭa were not averse to being wooed. The arrangements reached by the two sides made it possible for each to live at peace with the other. It is surprising to find that the Būyids allowed the Qarāmiṭa to have their own customs-house alongside theirs in Baṣra. It is almost certain that similar arrangements of mutual convenience to both sides were made for the all-important pilgrimage land-routes leading in and out of Baghdād, Kūfa and Baṣra. We are fortunate to have examples of the duties levied at some of these points; four dirhams a sheep in Baṣra; sixty dirhams a pilgrim for every camel-load, and fifty for a mule-load in Kūfa and Baghdād; in Baṣra one hundred dirhams for any load, and in all three places one hundred dirhams on any load of linen cloth.[2] The Būyids, who were willing to go to some lengths to win over the Qarāmiṭa, were also ready to discourage trading with the port of Sīrāf and divert all trade to Baṣra where both could share its benefits.[3] Soon all the East African Zanj, well-established in 'Umān, felt the

[1] Miskawayh, vol. II, pp. 25, 88, 112, 115, 127–9.

[2] Maqdisī, pp. 133–4.

[3] *Ibid.*, p. 426.

pressure of this competition and persuaded a faction of the Qarāmiṭa to co-operate with them in an attack on Baṣra. The Būyids overlooked the participation of the Qarāmiṭa and directed their rancour against the Zanj. In 965/354 an army from Baṣra and a navy from Sīrāf successfully occupied ʿUmān for a time. When this was not enough another expedition was dispatched there in 974/363 and put an end to the whole affair, while the Qarāmiṭa did not have to lift a finger.[1] Moreover, the Būyids took it upon themselves to police the waters of the Gulf and curtail the activities of the pirates who were operating from Qaṭar, next door to Baḥrayn.[2] On the other hand the Qarāmiṭa actively supported the Būyids in their fight against the Sāmānids to maintain their hold over Rayy.[3] It is worth noting that this is the only area where the Qarāmiṭa twice made the effort to help their partners in this uneven alliance. One can only conclude that they, the Qarāmiṭa, were interested in retaining their access to Rayy, an important link on the east–west trade-route. When it came to the repeated fighting between the Būyids and the Ḥamdānids to the north, the Qarāmiṭa remained absolutely neutral. Indeed they kept on very good terms with their former enemies the Ḥamdānids, who in appreciation of this stand were quick to send them a present of iron ore when it was requested.[4]

It was under these cordial circumstances that the Qarāmiṭa decided, of their own accord, in 951/339 to return the Black Stone to Makka after keeping it for 22 years.[5] Their newly acquired gains and respectability in addition to their good relations with the Būyids, who had their politics to worry about in Baghdād, convinced them that keeping the Stone did not serve any purpose. Any reports that they returned it on the orders of the Fāṭimids in North Africa have been invented to give credit where it was not deserved; and any arguments put forward by modern scholars to support these reports are without foundation.[6] Indeed the Ikhshīdids of Egypt and southern Syria were in a better position than the Fāṭimids to exert influence with the Qarāmiṭa to whom they paid the handsome amount of 300,000 dinārs a year.[7] This offering was not to encourage the religious principles of the Qarāmiṭa, neither was it a result of any common cause between the two sides. It was to secure the safety of

[1] Miskawayh, vol. II, pp. 46, 143–4, 196, 213–18.
[2] *Ibid.*, pp. 300–1; Ḥawqal, p. 48; Iṣṭakhrī, p. 33.
[3] Miskawayh, vol. II, pp. 117, 129.
[4] *Ibid.*, p. 203. [5] *Ibid.*, pp. 126–7.
[6] Bernard Lewis, *The Origins of Ismailism*, Cambridge, 1940, pp. 81–2.
[7] Athīr, vol. VIII, p. 452.

the caravans travelling on the land-routes from Egypt and Syria to Ḥijāz. As we shall see, when the Fāṭimids, upon their appearance in Syria 971/360, cut off this subsidy, they invoked the wrath of the Qarāmiṭa who did not hesitate to attack them.[1] Significantly, the Būyids remained in the background, almost unconcerned, satisfying themselves and their allies the Qarāmiṭa by supporting them with money and arms.[2] In the event the Qarāmiṭa were defeated, but in the process they went through a turmoil of organizational change. They installed their own model of collective leadership in the form of a council of six men presiding over a community with some remarkable progressive features. Communal property, no taxation and social security were the principles of this new regime.[3] Surprisingly, even the orthodox circles of Baghdād did not object to the constitution of such a dangerous precedent in an area so near. If anything the relationship between the two sides was strengthened. The Qarāmiṭa were given land-grants in southern 'Irāq, allowed a considerable presence in Kūfa and influential representation in Baghdād itself.[4] However, they were soon drawn into the internal affairs of the Confederacy and supported one side against another in a conflict over succession. The Būyids did not tolerate this unwarranted interference and inflicted a military defeat upon the intruders in 986/375.[5] For all practical reasons this was the end of the Qarāmiṭa who withdrew to Baḥrayn where they led a quiet life.

In southern 'Irāq the Būyids had a problem reminiscent of that which the central government had had with the Zanj a century earlier, and in the same area. This was in the Baṭīḥa, literally the marshland that covered the lower course of the Tigris and Euphrates between Wāsiṭ and Baṣra.[6] Swampy as it was, this area had considerable fertile lands of which the main produce was rice.[7] It also controlled the river traffic, between Baṣra and Baghdād, which had to pass through an intricate system of canals. During the years of the decline of the central government and almost immediately before the arrival of the Būyids on the scene, the natives of the Baṭīḥa had decided to take their destiny in their own hands.[8] The independent little republic they established there was able to defy the repeated attempts of the Būyids to subjugate it, and for over a century it

1 See below, p. 204.
2 Qalānisī, p. 1.
3 Athīr, vol. VIII, p. 506; Ḥawqal, pp. 25–7; Nāṣir-i-Khusraw, Safar-Nāme, ed. C. Schéfer, Paris, 1881, p. 82.
4 Abū Shujā', pp. 102, 109; Ṣābī, *Rasā'il*, pp. 360–83.
5 Abū Shujā', pp. 109–10; Athīr, vol. IX, pp. 27–9.
6 Mas'ūdī, *Tanbīh*, p. 40.
7 Maqdisī, p. 119.
8 Athīr, vol. VIII, p. 362.

survived and flourished under its own native rulers. It was able not only to impose its taxes on all the trade going up and down the river, but also to exact tolls from all travellers, including military personnel.[1] The ideological orientation of this republic seems to have suited all parties; while it maintained good relations with all Shī'ites, the conservative elements of Baghdād found refuge in it when they needed to escape Būyid intimidation.[2]

In the north-western corner of their domains the Būyids had a difficult problem, the troubled and troublesome Ḥamdānids. These Khārijites turned Shī'ites were as divided in their loyalties as they were amongst themselves. Their interests were more involved with the Byzantines than with their fellow Muslims. These native Arab chieftains had less support from their fellow Arabs than from the conglomeration of races in the region, including the Greeks. There were two Ḥamdānid power centres whose interests were incompatible, the line of division running north–south from Armenian Qālīqala (Erzurum) to Mawṣil. To the west of this line the Ḥamdānids of Ḥalab (Aleppo) were in competition with Tarsus, and for this matter, southern Syria, in the Byzantine trade. They were willing to fight their fellow Muslims as much as the imperial forces of Constantinople to achieve their ends. Yet they had more allies within the eastern Byzantine territories than they had in Syria or 'Irāq. As they had access to the desert land-route along the Euphrates they had very little to do with Baghdād. The rulers of the latter were quite happy with this relationship because they had no intention of getting involved in controversies with the Byzantines.

To the east of that line, the Ḥamdānids of Mawṣil were busy promoting their interests in Armenia and Ādherbayjān. They had no interest in fighting the Byzantines and were satisfied to trade with them through the Armenian intermediaries.[3] At the same time they were all intent on expanding their network into Ādherbayjān, reaching out north into the Caucasus regions, and east into the Jibāl province.[4] In their relationship with Baghdād they were torn between two factors. On the one hand, they appreciated the volume of their trade with the metropolis down the Tigris and were reassured by the strong support they had there.[5] On the other hand, they did not want to be subservient to the Būyids to the extent of paying them a

[1] Miskawayh, vol. II, pp. 130, 158.
[2] Athīr, vol. VIII, p. 473; Ṣābī, *Tārīkh*, part 8, p. 413.
[3] Ḥawqal, p. 225, Maqdisī, p. 126.
[4] Athīr, vol. VIII, p. 310.
[5] Miskawayh, vol. II, p. 108.

tribute, or indeed accepting the taxes on trade the latter levied at Takrīt to the north of Baghdād.[1] The tense relationship between these two parties contributed to the complexity of the situation in the neighbouring regions to the east.

During the last years of Muqtadir's reign and the following years of deterioration in Baghdād, the Byzantines stepped up the pressure against the *thughūr* and in the process captured Malaṭya.[2] It was mainly due to the Bulghār and Magyar attacks in the Balkans that this pressure was not sustained. It is interesting to learn that, in Constantinople, around that time, the emperor used to invite Muslim prisoners-of-war to a Christmas dinner where pork was specifically excluded from the menu, and actually gave them presents of cash and clothes.[3] With such a show of goodwill one begins to understand the frequent incidence of the changing of sides and religions as between Muslims and Christians on both sides of the Arab–Byzantine borders.[4] The toleration of one side was matched by the magnanimity of the other. It was not quite an entente between Christendom and Islam, but more in the nature of a decision to co-exist taken by two adversaries. The almost continual fighting on the borders was due more to the meddling interference of importunate groups on both sides, especially the Arabs of the *thughūr*, than to the deliberate policies of either power. They both realized the benefits that could accrue from trade and accordingly it was encouraged to flow. The problem was that neither side was in complete control of its own borders. Under the circumstances, lasting agreements and arrangements of mutual convenience could not be reached despite numerous embassies between Baghdād and Constantinople.

When the Būyids came to power the Ḥamdānids had been well established in Mawṣil and the surrounding regions of Jazīra for almost forty years. During this period the latter had been deeply involved in the politics of Baghdād. In 942/330 a Ḥamdānid had attained the office of *Amīr al-Umarā'* but, after realizing the hopelessness of the situation of the central government, had decided to withdraw to his safer seat in Mawṣil.[5] As heirs of Baghdād's domains the Būyids, after some difficulty, were able to assert their authority over the reluctant Ḥamdānids. The agreement they reached with

[1] *Ibid.*, pp. 115, 204–6, 285.
[2] Rāḍī, p. 251; Ḥawqal, p. 181.
[3] Rusteh, pp. 122, 123, 125.
[4] Ḥawqal, p. 211; Miskawayh, vol. II, p. 354; Athīr, vol. VIII, pp. 415, 447, 491.
[5] Miskawayh, vol. II, pp. 28, 44.

them provided for a tribute to be paid by the latter, but as it was not their intention to keep to its terms it was more often broken than not.[1] While this uneasy relationship continued with the Būyids, the Ḥamdānids earnestly applied themselves to the business of consolidating their position in their territories. Although they had control over all the *thughūr*, with the exception of Tarsus, the effect of the fall of Malaṭya to the Byzantines had been to drive the trade further south and east. This presented no problems to the Ḥamdānids and in fact helped them by diverting the trade to the more controllable towns of Aleppo, Naṣībīn and Mawṣil.[2] However the Byzantines had different ideas, and for the first time they put into effect a plan that would enable them to take full charge of the trade with all their eastern neighbours. Henceforth all this trade was confined to two ports of entry. One was Trebizond on the Black Sea coast where it was decreed that all the Muslim merchants should gather to enter Byzantine territory. The other was Anṭāliya on the Mediterranean coast to the west of Tarsus, and here it was that the sea-trade would be carried out.[3] This simple plan had far-reaching repercussions for all concerned. It enabled the Byzantine authorities to enforce the collection of the taxes due on all the incoming and outgoing trade, and while the Egyptian and Syrian ports could continue to trade with Anṭāliya, the role of the *thughūr* as trade centres was clearly ended. Furthermore, the prosperity of the Ḥamdānids of Aleppo and Naṣībīn was put in great peril. Those in Mawṣil were not particularly affected except in so far as their relationship with the Armenians to the north was concerned. Under these new arrangements the latter, with the full support of the Byzantines, acquired a sudden importance. Instead of being subservient to all their powerful neighbours, they became major partners in a highly desirable trade. Indeed their interests were now more involved with those of the Byzantines than they had been for centuries.[4]

As was to be expected, this change in the pattern of trade created a political upheaval of great magnitude. The first to react were those who were most threatened, the Ḥamdānids of Aleppo. Starting in 948/336, for twenty years they tried desperately to re-establish the position of the *thughūr* by incessant military campaigning, but to no avail.[5] It is significant that while the Ḥamdānids of Mawṣil sent

[1] *Ibid.*, pp. 108, 115, 204–6.

[2] Athīr, vol. VIII, p. 164; Ṣūlī, *Rāḍī*, p. 251; Ḥawqal, p. 214.

[3] Ḥawqal, pp. 176, 178, 197–8, 344; Istakhrī, p. 188.

[4] Athīr, vol. III, pp. 173, 377, 407, vol. IX, p. 67; Qudāma, *Kharāj*, p. 254.

[5] Athīr, vol. VIII, pp. 361, 365, 375, 381, 387, 388, 393, 396, 399–402.

presents of horses, wine and golden crosses to the emperor in Constantinople, those of Aleppo received presents of mules, clothes and golden trinkets from the Byzantines of the eastern territories.[1] This contradictory behaviour on the part of the latter can only mean that they approved of the Ḥamdānid attempts to re-establish the *thughūr*. Such consorting with an actively hostile enemy did not escape the eyes of the authorities of Constantinople, and could have been considered a factor contributing to the prolongation of this unnecessary war. In 969/358 a major Byzantine counter-offensive succeeded in capturing Antioch and Aleppo. As a result Antioch was permanently occupied while in Aleppo the Byzantines set up their own protectorate.[2] From this point on the Ḥamdānids of Aleppo ceased to be of any significance. They deteriorated into factions fighting each other for survival, only serving as pawns in the ensuing struggle between the Byzantines and the Fāṭimids over Syria.[3] It will be noticed that neither the Būyids nor indeed the Ḥamdānids of Mawṣil interfered to save their brethren of Aleppo from the fate that befell them.[4] Now that all the *thughūr* were in the hands of the Byzantines, curious developments began to take place on both sides of the borders. First, the clan of Ḥabīb, cousins of the Ḥamdānids and numbering as many as 12,000 men, defected to the enemy, were converted to Christianity and helped the Byzantines to capture more Arab strongholds.[5] Then, brewing discontent in the eastern Byzantine territories broke out in a rebellion led by two distinguished members of powerful families in the area, Bardas Phocas and Bardas Sclerus. It could have been a coincidence that the latter held Ḥiṣn Ziyād, one of the former Arab strongholds in the *thughūr*, but the fact that he allied himself and inter-married with the Ḥamdānids of Mawṣil throws a different light on the matter. However, as his in-laws failed to provide him with the support Bardas expected, Basil II, eventually and soon after his succession to the throne in 976, was able to subdue the rebellion with the help of the Russians. Bardas Sclerus fled to the Ḥamdānids only to end up in Baghdād taking refuge with the Būyids and seeking their help against his own compatriots in 980/370. The Būyids, who had never wanted to get involved with the Byzantines, had other more pressing problems and kept Bardas under guard for five years until it suited their

[1] Ṣābī, *Rasā'il*, pp. 132–3; Miskawayh, vol. II, p. 208.
[2] Miskawayh, vol. II, pp. 177, 180–1, 190–5, 210; Athīr, vol. VIII, pp. 404, 414–15, 423, 434, 444–5, 447; Anṭākī, p. 358; Ḥawqal, pp. 177–8.
[3] See below, p. 204.
[4] Athīr, vol. VIII, p. 455.
[5] Ḥawqal, pp. 211–12, 221.

purposes to send him back after some unsuccessful negotiations with the Byzantines.[1]

Within the Confederacy, another group, the Būyids of Jibāl, had its problems too. Their geographical location left them in control of the east–west trade-routes across the Iranian plateau and in a position where conflict was possible with those who had a special interest in this trade. As there was also trade coming down from the north through the Caucasus, other interests were involved, such as those of the Musāfirids. These were the branch of Daylamites who had managed to keep a foothold in their native lands while establishing another in Ādherbayjān on the Caspian coast. Their conflict with the Būyids was limited to fighting for ascendancy in their home territory and it was of no significance. On the other hand the Musāfirid enclave in Ādherbayjān was of considerable importance at least in its long-term effects. They managed to reach reasonable agreements with the local princes and leaders of the region according to which each group had an equitable share in the benefits of the trade; judging by the revenues from one point, where taxes were collected on the outgoing trade from Ādherbayjān to Rayy, which amounted to 100,000 dinārs a year, these benefits were considerable.[2] The Musāfirids also maintained good relations with the all important Armenians, but they did not reckon with the Kurds and that was a serious mistake. Perhaps it was also a justifiable one; for centuries nobody had bothered to take Kurdish interests into consideration. These people had been left alone to carry on their semi-nomadic way of life in their mountains without much outside interference. Sometimes they had taken part in minor uprisings in the Jibāl, but hitherto one can hardly see any traces of them outside their own territories. With the breakdown of the central government they had begun to show signs of defiance such as pillaging passing caravans.[3] The rise of the Daylamites and the fact that they were now surrounding the Kurds on all sides must have not only given the latter reason for alarm but also caused them to think about their own situation. It was not difficult for them to realize that they were not very different from the Daylamites, and if these people could assert themselves so strongly, there was all the more reason why the Kurds should control at least their own territories. With remarkable dexterity they set out gradually and under various leaders to establish

[1] Athīr, vol. VIII, pp. 491, 506–10, 517–18, vol. IX, pp. 12, 30–1; Abū Shujā', 38, 111–12; Baṭrīq, p. 82; Anṭākī, pp. 130, 166–7.

[2] Ḥawqal, p. 353.

[3] Athīr, vol. VIII, pp. 445–6, 518; Ṣūlī, *Rāḍī*, pp. 192–3.

their domain. They made a point of not antagonizing the Būyids too much while at the same time strengthening their ties with the Armenians and, accordingly, the Byzantines.[1] The Būyids on their part tolerated the Kurdish advances, especially as these were increasingly directed towards the north. Even when the Kurds set up their own trade centres and improved the roads leading to them, the Būyids did not take these actions as a direct threat to the prosperity of their own trade activities.[2] On the other hand the Musāfirids were greatly alarmed by the increasing Kurdish rivalry, particularly when it began to show its effects in Ādherbayjān.[3] This inevitable conflict ended with the disappearance of the Musāfirids from their enclave on the Caspian coast in 984/374, and the rise of more Kurdish powers in Ādherbayjān. Almost immediately the latter clashed with the Ḥamdānids of Mawṣil who were at that time under pressure from the Būyids and the 'Uqaylids. The result was the final collapse of the Ḥamdānids and the division of their Mawṣil domains between the Kurdish Marwānids who dominated the eastern half of Jazīra, and the Arab 'Uqaylids who occupied Mawṣil and the western half of Jazīra.[4] It is worth noting that these Arabs had been among the first to settle in the *thughūr* more than two centuries before.[5] The Byzantine drive had forced them out of their favourite haunts into the troubled domains of the Ḥamdānids. Although the 'Uqaylids were to survive in Mawṣil until after the Saljūq invasion, their presence and behaviour were responsible for many disorders in the intervening years.[6]

In the north-eastern corner of the Confederacy the most important issue was, in one word, Rayy. The Sāmānids desperately needed to control it, the Ziyārids of Ṭabaristān and Gurgān badly wanted it, and the Būyids captured it.[7] From this central position directly in the centre of the bottleneck between the Elburz chain and the desert, the Būyids were in an ideal situation to control the flow of almost all the east–west trade. The Sāmānids, who had just been able to attract the northern trade to their territories, came to be at the mercy of the Būyids and their whole trade policy was a shambles. It

[1] Athīr, vol. VIII, pp. 130, 289, 375–7, 519, vol. IX, p. 67; Miskawayh, vol. II, pp. 150–1.
[2] Abū Shujā', p. 290; Ṣābī, *Tārīkh*, part 8, pp. 453–4.
[3] Athīr, vol. VIII, pp. 289–91; Ḥawqal, p. 334.
[4] Ḥawqal, pp. 225–6; Abū Shujā', pp. 83–6, 144, 175–9; Athīr, vol. IX, pp. 25–6, 49–50, *idem*, vol. X, p. 11.
[5] See above, p. 52.
[6] See below, p. 204.
[7] Miskawayh, vol. II, pp. 100, 115, 119–20, 123, 129; Athīr, vol. VIII, pp. 333–4, 351, 365–8, 378–9, 460–1.

was no use having all the goods of Europe if they could not have an outlet for them. The Ziyārids, Daylamites as they were, found themselves in the odd position of being allied to the Sāmānids against their fellow-countrymen. However, as the magnitude of the difficulties of the Ziyārids was not as great as that of the Sāmānids, they managed to survive and live through the Ghaznavid domination and the Saljūq invasion. It was the Sāmānids, whose political structure could not take the strain of the economic crisis, that began to crumble. Admittedly, they had a very sophisticated government machinery but such things were not unusual at the time – even the unsophisticated Daylamites had been able to set up at least five governments. One can appreciate Barthold's pioneering preoccupation with the details of Sāmānid administration, but it has to be realized that he was looking at "Turkestan" from an insular point of view. These two factors put severe limitations on the validity of his interpretation of the broader issues. In the seventy-five years since his study was first published, none of his conclusions has ever been questioned. His disciples, perpetuating his narrow outlook, have simply taken them up and reiterated them in variant forms.

Although Barthold recognized some elements of the Sāmānid power-base, such as the Khwārizm-shāhs whose origin "goes right back into mythological times", and the Muḥtājids of Chaghāniyān who continued to rule their domain regardless of the rise or fall of the Sāmānids, he could not relate these people to the political structure of the Sāmānid regime.[1]

The Sāmānids, the heirs of the Ṭāhirids, were basically presiding over a federation of the ancient Principalities of Ṭukhāristān, the city-states of Soghdiana and the little Khurāsān of the Sāsānians, a fact that Ibn Ḥawqal understood and clearly stated.[2] The difference between the Ṭāhirids and their successors was a question of the emphasis on the interests of the various areas, and the ascendancy of one group over another. Nothing had happened since the Arab conquest to necessitate a change in the geo-political structure of these regions. Indeed the local leaders had continued to exercise their authority, albeit under Arab suzerainty, long after the 'Abbāsid revolution. Afshīn is but one example of such rulers, and the rise of the Ṭāhirids is a confirmation that families of old lineage had gained even greater power under the 'Abbāsids; just as the Muḥtājids of Chaghāniyān had done, the Farīghūnids of Gūzgān held their own

[1] Barthold, *Turkestan*, pp. 233–4.
[2] Shaban, *The 'Abbāsid Revolution*, pp. 3–15; Ḥawqal, p. 430.

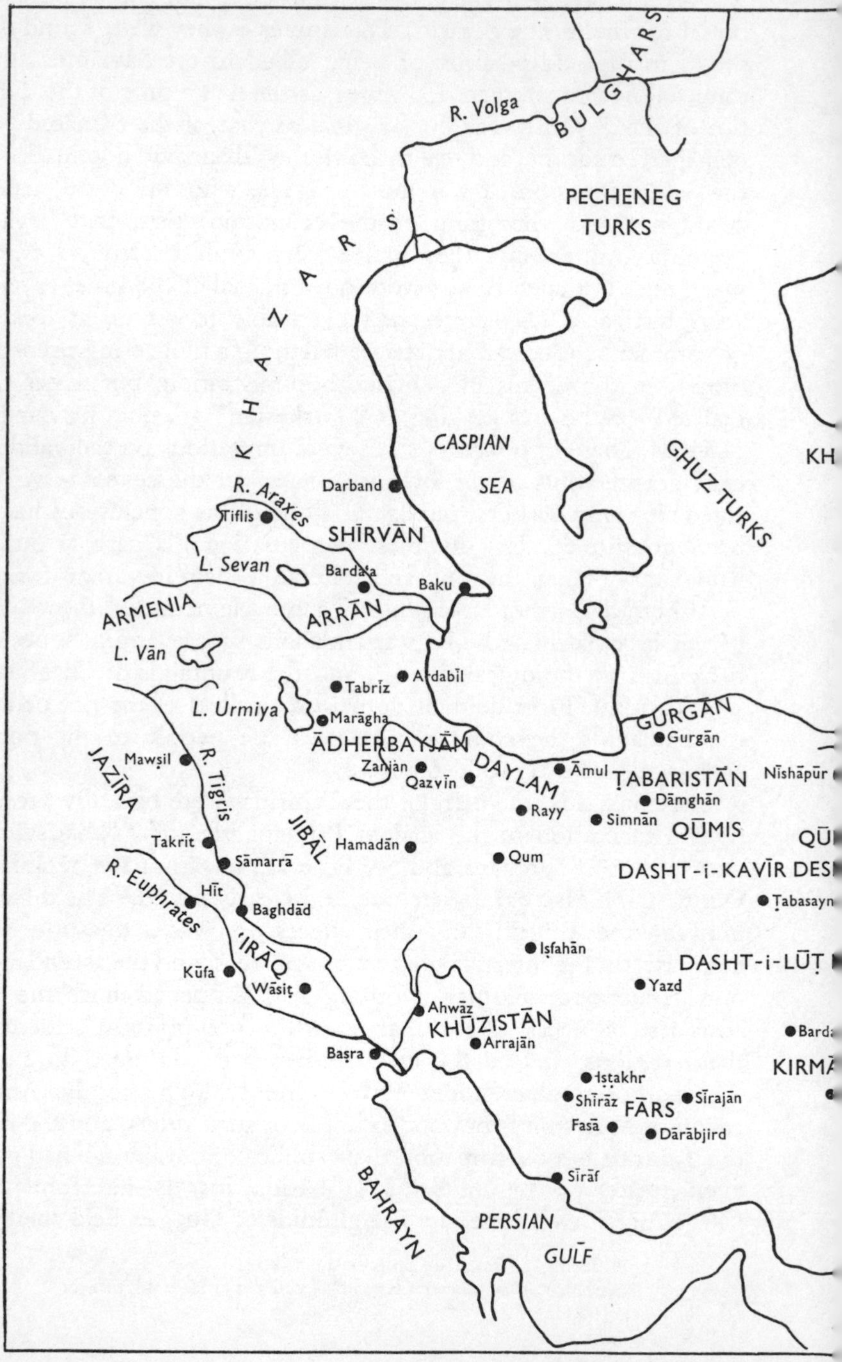

3 Iran and the East

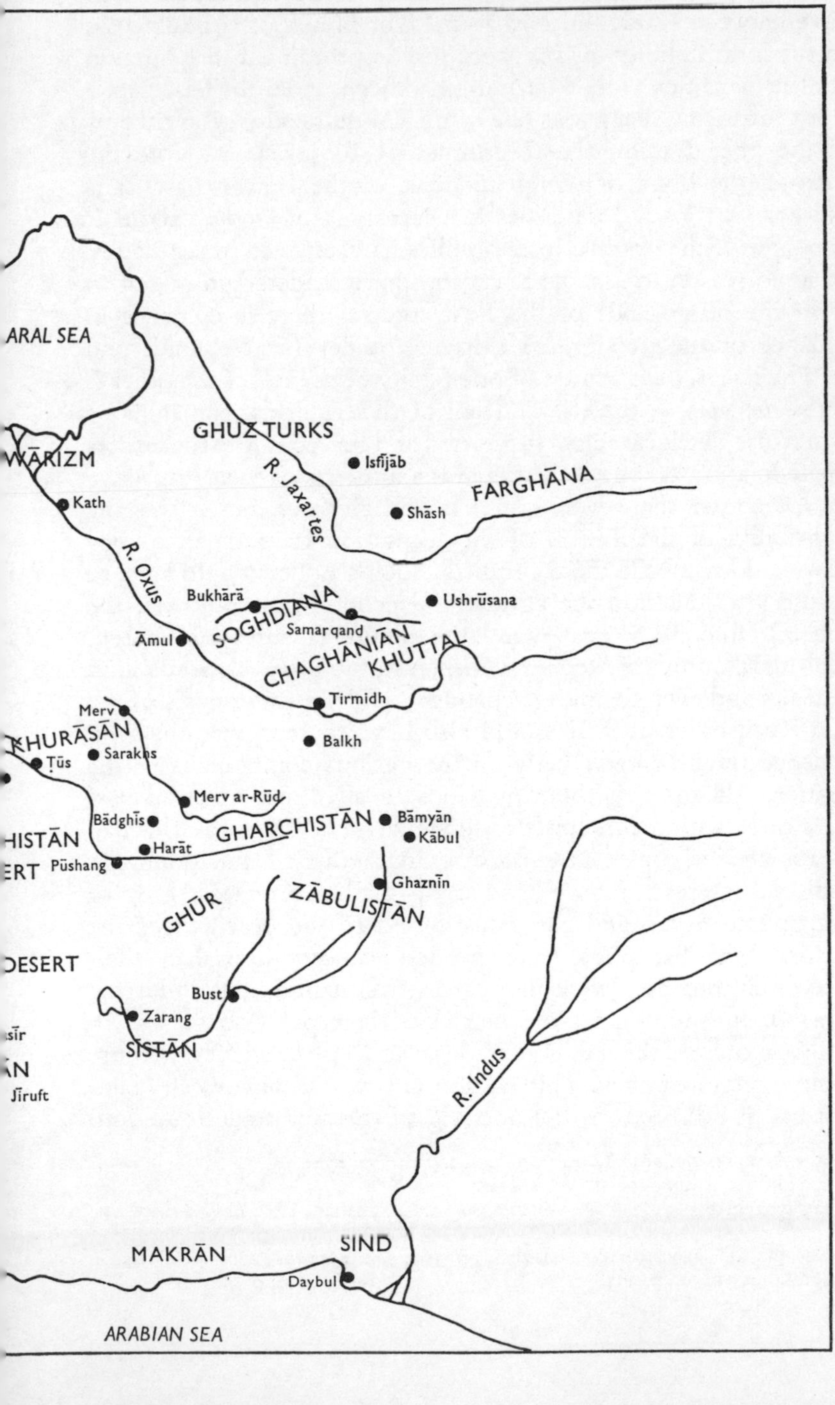

ARAL SEA
GHUZ TURKS
R. Jaxartes
Isfījāb
FARGHĀNA
WĀRIZM
Kath
Shāsh
R. Oxus
Bukhārā
SOGHDIANA
Samarqand
Ushrūsana
Āmul
CHAGHĀNIĀN
KHUTTAL
Tirmidh
Merv
KHURĀSĀN
Balkh
Ṭūs
Sarakhs
Merv ar-Rūd
Bādghīs
GHARCHISTĀN
Bāmyān
Kābul
HISTĀN
Harāt
ERT
Pūshang
Ghaznīn
GHŪR
ZĀBULISTĀN
DESERT
Bust
Zarang
SISTĀN
Jīruft
R. Indus
SIND
MAKRĀN
Daybul
ARABIAN SEA

under the Sāmānids, and for long after that.[1] The Sīmjūrids had their enclave between Harāt and Nīshāpūr.[2] The family of 'Abdulrazzāq from the local nobility of Ṭūs were just as prominent in Khurāsān under the Sāmānids as the Kanārang had been under the Sāsānians.[3] It is not surprising that it was one of the 'Abdulrazzāqs who encouraged the poet Daqīqī, the forerunner of Firdawsī, to write the *Shāhnāmeh*, the Book of Kings and epic of the Iranian past. It is significant that Daqīqī describes his patron as of *dihqān* origin. If such people of the original local nobility had survived in Khurāsān, there is no reason to assume that other local leaders had ceased to exist in the other lands of the East. Indeed there is evidence in abundance of their continued existence under the Sāmānids and after. The rise in the fortunes of one family or the fall of the other is in the same vein as the rise and fall of the Ṭāhirids, Sāmānids or Ghaznavids. The local rulers supported and served under the leaders of the federation as long as it served the interests of their respective areas. Of course there were conflicts and rivalries, but it was the responsibility of the leaders of the federation to pursue a policy which would reconcile these conflicts. Such a policy would have to take into consideration the agricultural economy of Bukhārā, the commercial interests of Samarqand, the mineral resources of Khuttal, the industrial output of Merv and Nīshāpūr, the livestock production of Gūzgān and even the meagre produce of the semi-nomads of the Hindū-Kush mountains. It would also have to recognize the long established trade contacts between the various components of the federation and the neighbouring lands in all directions, and harmonize these with the interests of the federation.[4] The Ṭāhirids had tried to steer a conservative course in favour of the dominant agricultural interests. As we have seen, this had aroused the ire of the people of Sīstān and had contributed to the downfall of the Ṭāhirids.[5] The Sāmānids were no less conservative than their predecessors, but they were in a different situation. The industrial expansion, in addition to the fact that their power-base was in Soghdiana, obliged them to give trade an equal place with agriculture in their economic policy. This equilibrium would have been maintained had it not been for the opening of the new trade-route into

[1] Athīr, vol. IX, pp. 69, 103; Maqdisī, p. 337; Iṣṭakhrī, p. 272.
[2] Athīr, vol. VIII, p. 292, vol. IX, pp. 18, 69.
[3] Miskawayh, vol. II, p. 117; Athīr, vol. VIII, pp. 353–4; Shaban, *The 'Abbāsid Revolution*, p. 5.
[4] Ḥawqal, pp. 432, 449, 450, 477; Iṣṭakhrī, pp. 166, 244, 255, 265, 280, 281; Maqdisī, p. 469; Athīr, vol. IX, p. 305.
[5] See above, p. 96.

Europe. The vast profits that this generated created a new economic situation. Faced with this change the Sāmānid Naṣr b. Aḥmad was forced, before his death in 943/331, to deviate from the orthodoxy of his ancestors to the extent of being accused of Ismā'īlism.[1] We do not know exactly what he did to deserve such an extravagant indictment, but perhaps a clue can be found in the developments in nearby Rayy and Ṭabaristān. There, about the same time, the flexible Shī'ite Daylamites, who had just captured the region, had introduced a novel tax of one dinār per head. Our source explains that this tax was imposed specifically to balance the burden of taxes between the merchants and the landowners who, hitherto, had had to carry the load alone.[2] It is possible that Naṣr had in mind such a reform.

However, the economic decline that soon set in in the Sāmānid domains as a result of the Būyid blockade at Rayy, could not be remedied by a simple tax reform. It required an urgent solution; a political one on which all members of the federation would agree. The disagreement that followed only hastened the disintegration of the federation. Every constituent in every corner became increasingly concerned with its immediate interests. Every leader had his own approach to a solution that favoured his area. The 'Abdulrazzāqs of Khurāsān did not see why they should jeopardise the interests of Nīshāpūr and fight the Būyids simply to protect the commercial interests of Samarqand. Such an attitude in an area so close to Rayy would certainly encourage the ambitions of the Būyids. Other leaders did not take kindly to this negation of responsibility and proposed to dislodge the delinquent 'Abdulrazzāqs.[3] Others still supported the view that it was easier to find another opening for the trade via the southern route through Sīstān and Kirmān, than to fight the intrepid Būyids.[4] All these differences represented themselves in a fruitless internal struggle within the federation. The frequent change of the commander-in-chief of the Sāmānid army only indicates that a particular group had temporarily won the upper hand in this endless struggle.[5] The resulting economic plight forced the government to exact more taxes from its subjects.[6] As it worsened as many as 20,000 men were persuaded to leave their homes and seek

1 Ibn al-Nadīm, *Al-Fihrist*, Cairo, A.H. 1348, p. 266.
2 Mas'ūdī, *Murūj*, vol. IX, p. 14.
3 Miskawayh, vol. II, pp. 117–19; Athīr, vol. VIII, pp. 353, 378–81.
4 Athīr, vol. VIII, p. 482.
5 Miskawayh, vol. II, pp. 101–3, 154–6, 177, 191–2; Abū Shujā', p. 27; Athīr, vol. VIII, pp. 292, 344–8, 359, 370, 396, 404, vol. IX, pp. 7, 18–20, 69, 102.
6 Maqdisī, p. 340.

their fortunes elsewhere in the more prosperous west.[1] The Būyids were ready to offer generous peace terms and to conclude a truce for ten years, but they would not give up Rayy.[2] By 961/350 any hope of saving the federation had vanished and what followed was a scramble for the remnants. Any leader who could muster some tangible military strength tried to lay his hands on as much territory as possible.[3] Out of this situation the militaristic regime of the Ghaznavids was born in the remote region of Ghaznīn, 7280 feet up the slopes of the Hindū-Kush mountains.

The rise of the Ghaznavids has been explained as the fulfilment of a sudden urge of a slave to carve himself an empire.[4] This ludicrous interpretation of history completely ignores the circumstance in which these developments took place. Furthermore, Sebüktigin, the man responsible for this episode, had never been a slave. Reports to the contrary are almost certainly fictitious, and indeed come only in a source of more than three centuries later.[5] The reliability of this particular source has never been established and has actually been doubted by one scholar who put it under close scrutiny.[6] According to this source Sebüktigin was kidnapped as a boy alone in his home in Central Asia, whence he was brought and sold in Sāmānid territory. Yet, it is rather striking to learn from a more reliable source that much later in his life he had with him a brother and a sister who apparently had not gone through the process of slavery.[7] Of course it can be argued that as he acquired power he brought them to share his glory, but under the circumstances this was hardly likely. In fact we are told by the same contemporary source that Ghaznīn was the nest of the clan and relatives of Sebüktigin.[8] Furthermore when he died his body was transported for burial to Ghaznīn in the same tradition that required the body of a Muḥtājid to be transported for burial to his home in Chaghāniyān.[9] It is now clear that Sebüktigin was a native leader of the region of Ghaznīn who came to fame during the period of the disintegration of the Sāmānid federation. Like many other local leaders, he was looking

[1] Miskawayh, vol. II, pp. 222–9.
[2] *Ibid.*, p. 100.
[3] Athīr, vol. VIII, p. 398.
[4] Barthold, p. 81; C. E. Bosworth, *The Ghaznawids*, Edinburgh, 1963, p. 40.
[5] Shabankārī, *Majma' al-Ansāb fī al-Tawārīkh*, Istanbul manuscript, Yeni Cami 909, ff. 164A–6A.
[6] Bosworth, pp. 11, 39–40; M. Nazim, "The Pand-Nāmah of Subüktigin", *Journal of the Royal Asiatic Society*, London, 1933, pp. 569–622.
[7] Al-'Utbī, *al-Tarīkh al-Yamīnī*, Cairo, A.H. 1286, vol. I, pp. 236, 255.
[8] *Ibid.*, p. 274.
[9] *Ibid.*, p. 256; Athīr, vol. VIII, p. 384.

for a solution for the economic dilemma within the framework of the interests of his own region. Being on the periphery of the Sāmānid domains and on the trade-route into India, Ghaznīn must have suffered considerably from the general economic decline. On the other hand its location on the very borders of the pagan subcontinent offered an easy way out of the problem. Taking matters in his own hands, Sebüktigin started and continued over the twenty years 977–97/366–87, a long campaign of plundering and looting the plains of India. His success attracted more men to join his campaigns and more men brought back more wealth. Eventually his son, Maḥmūd, 998–1030/388–421, was to invade India and establish an empire that extended from the Oxus to the Ganges. But it was an empire that fizzled out almost as soon as it was established. It had a highly organized army that congregated from all directions, including Arabs who came out of the blue.[1] Any claims that these were slave armies are based on the wrong interpretation of the terms *'abīd* (sing. *'abd*) and *mamālīk* (sing. *mamlūk*). Although these words originally mean slaves, over the years they have acquired different connotations. We have already seen *'abd* used to denote a loyal subject of the highest rank in the service of the ruler.[2] Indeed, the great Maḥmūd himself and the powerful Būyid leaders, whose many honorific titles are too long to repeat here, were proud to adopt the title of *'abd Amīr al-Mu'minīn*, in spite of the fact that the impotent *Amīr al-Mu'minīn* was more of their *'abd* than anything else.[3] In an age when empty and lengthy titles were handed out to everybody in sight, the words were debased and came to mean very little. The Būyids and the Ghaznavids considered themselves *'abīd par excellence*, and it was only appropriate to apply this term to the loyal members of the army in relation to their leaders.[4] Therefore the term *'abīd* was used to signify the members of the standing army in Spain, North Africa, Egypt, Syria, 'Irāq, Jazīra, Iran and Central Asia. It has to be remembered that all these *'abīd* were well paid and their demands for regular pay always represented major problems for every regime.

As well as an organized army, the Ghaznavids also had an efficient administration fashioned after the Sāmānid pattern which has been admirably described by Bosworth. However, this was not enough

[1] *Ibid.*, p. 387.
[2] See above, p. 65.
[3] Ṣābī, *Tārīkh*, part 8, p. 343; *Idem*, *Rasā'il*, p. 119; *idem*, *Rusum*, p. 109; Athīr, vol. VIII, p. 480.
[4] Abū Shujā', p. 50; Rāḍī, p. 153.

to maintain an empire that did not have the allegiance of its subjects. On the Indian side the Ghaznavids represented plunder. Whatever has been said about their service to the cause of Islam by spreading it into India ignores the fact that they introduced to the Indians the worst facet of Islam. It was much in the same vein as the unattractive image the Ottomans presented to the Europeans. It is instructive to compare the relatively strong position that Islam has in Malaya and Indonesia where it spread by peaceful means and its position in India where the Ghaznavids left a long trail of blood.

On the Central Asian side, the Sāmānids were fast crumbling, and it did not take the Ghaznavids under Maḥmūd much effort to advance to the Oxus but no further. For here they were checked by another power marching from the north from the steppes of Central Asia. These were the semi-nomadic Turks who had been living outside the Sāmānid borders and amongst whom Islam had quietly spread. Taking advantage of the collapse of their neighbour's power they easily occupied Soghdiana and established a dynasty there known to us as the Qarakhānids. Their only contribution to Islamic history is that in their internal quarrels they enlisted the help of yet another branch of Muslim Turkish nomads, the Ghuzz, and these in turn paved the way for the Saljūq invasion. Replacing the Sāmānids in the lands to the south of the Oxus, the militaristic regime of the Ghaznavids failed to win the loyalty of the population who had no interest whatever in invading India. On their part, the Ghaznavids behaved as an occupying power in an area which had had a long tradition of autonomy.[1] Furthermore, in 1025/416, Maḥmūd allowed the Saljūq nomads to cross the Oxus and roam around the plains of Khurāsān. Letting such a force loose in a densely populated urban region was bound to create disorders. When Maḥmūd tried to quell these disturbances he succeeded only in driving them west into the central plateau. In 1035/428 after Maḥmūd's death, the main bulk o the Saljūq forces crossed the river and wrought havoc in Khurāsān. The helpless population of Merv and Nīshāpūr had no option but to make the best of a bad situation. Recognizing the suzerainty of the invaders the Khurāsānian oligarchy placed themselves in their service and used them to drive out the hated Ghaznavids in 1040/431. In Cl. Cahen's words, and there is no better way of putting it, the Ghaznavids "fled to India. Khurāsān was lost, and the Iranian plateau was wide open. The evolution of the Iranian and Turkish worlds had led the former to admit the Turks into its own bosom.

[1] Athīr, vol. IX, p. 247; Ḥawqal, p. 450.

Like that of the German empire, the conquest by the Turks, from then on, was accomplished from inside".[1]

The struggle to save the Sāmānid federation created some ripples in Sīstān and Kirmān. The Būyids, who also had a foothold in Kirmān, were not unduly perturbed. Taking the necessary precautions they decided to wait for their adversaries to exhaust themselves.[2] But it was a different matter when Sebüktigin attained power in Ghaznīn, especially as he immediately occupied Bust in 977/367.[3] The rise of an aggressive military power in an area where complete disintegration had been expected alarmed the Būyids who reacted almost instantly. The Confederacy had had its share of internal problems, whether as a result of fights over succession, or from the demands of refractory armies. However, these problems did not necessitate a change in the basic structure of the body politic. But as soon as the spectre of the Ghaznavid menace appeared on the horizon, there was an immediate effort to muster all the military and financial resources of the Confederacy. The Būyids were not to know that Sebüktigin was going to concentrate his attacks in a completely new direction, and his advance on Bust must have convinced them of an imminent attack on their own territory. The most threatened Būyid ruler, Fanā-Khusraw, who also happened to have held power in Fārs for twenty-nine years, took it upon himself to impose his authority over all Būyid domains. It was a temporary policy that lasted only for five and a half years 978–83/367–72, and was never attempted again in the remaining seventy years of the life of the Confederacy.

Fanā-Khusraw's objectives were to stamp out any nagging problems which any one region had been unable to handle by itself, and rectify the anomalies which were bound to exist under such a system, especially with regard to the ruinous arrangements for military pay. In short he wanted stability and he set out to establish it. Baghdād was a hot-bed of sedition, and obviously the Būyid in charge had not been able to control the riotous Ḥanbalites, Shāfi'ites, and Shī'ites, let alone his own army which had got itself involved in their almost daily squabbles.[4] Therefore it was occupied, and law and order were swiftly imposed. The Ḥamdānids of Mawṣil were more of a threat than the Byzantines. Indeed, when Fanā-Khusraw

1 Cl. Cahen, "The Turkish Invasion: The Selchükids", *A History of the Crusades*, ed. K. M. Setton, London, 1958, pp. 135–76, the quotation is from p. 142.

2 Miskawayh, vol. II, p. 249; Athīr, vol. VIII, pp. 416–17, 431, 462–3; Maqdisī, p. 472.

3 Athīr, vol. VIII, p. 504.

4 *Ibid.*, pp. 455–6, 462–4, 466–9; Miskawayh, vol. II, pp. 323–52.

attacked them they sought the help of the Byzantines and the Fāṭimids, but none came to their rescue. They were driven out of Mawṣil and lost all their citadels in the region which had contained a fabulous amount of wealth.[1] The Kurds had just lost one of their strongest leaders, so they were in no position to resist the Būyid strong man.[2] Although both Kurds and Ḥamdānids were to make a come-back they presented no problem for a time. The Arabs close to the desert borders of ʿIrāq were brought into line and so were some isolated Kurdish groups in Jibāl.[3] The independent republic of Baṭīḥa offered strong resistance when it was attacked, and Fanā-Khusraw pragmatically arranged peace terms with its ruler.[4] In the Gulf strict surveillance was organized to drive away the pirates, secure control over ʿUmān, and ensure the friendship of the Qarāmiṭa in Baḥrayn. Kirmān was fortified and Fanā-Khusraw sent his own son to reside there.[5]

The most interesting moves made in this hectic period were in the fiscal field. Fanā-Khusraw tried, not without success, to cut down to a minimum the *iqṭāʿ* system for paying the military. He had to be careful not to interfere too much with the interests of some powerful leaders of the Daylamites.[6] For those men who were paid directly from the treasury, measures were taken in order that they should receive their stipends on time. On the other hand, it was decided that no pay increases should be allowed except as a reward for military victory.[7] While tax-farming was allowed to continue in operation it was brought under the close supervision of the regional governments.[8] Under the long rule of Fanā-Khusraw in Fārs, it seems that he allowed his officials to experiment with some radical tax innovations. There is no doubt whatever that the purpose of these radical measures was to make the urban population pay its proper share of taxes. These officials must have resorted to their remote Iranian past to devise means for new taxes, and it is more than likely that some of these measures were echoes of ancient Sāsānian practices. It was certainly un-Islamic to impose taxes on brothels, and it was against all the rules of Islamic law to exact water rates.[9] The hold of the tax-collector over the towns was considerably tightened, to the extent that anyone leaving town was required to have a

[1] Miskawayh, vol. II, pp. 382–93.
[2] Athīr, vol. VIII, pp. 519–21.
[3] *Ibid.*, p. 522; *idem*, vol. IX, p. 5; Miskawayh, vol. II, pp. 398–9, 414–15.
[4] Miskawayh, vol. II, p. 412.
[5] Abū Shujāʿ, p. 28.
[6] *Ibid.*, p. 47.
[7] *Ibid.*, p. 43.
[8] *Ibid.*, p. 171.
[9] Maqdisī, p. 441; Ḥawqal, p. 302; Iṣṭakhrī, p. 157.

passport.[1] On every load of goods entering town a tax of thirty dirhams was collected.[2] Inside the town the authorities set up market places, shops and arcades and rented them for double the usual rate.[3] Brokers' houses were also built where important commercial transactions were to take place, and we are told that the government's revenue from one of these houses was 10,000 dirhams a day.[4] The government also monopolized a wide range of industrial activities, such as the making of ice and the production of raw silk, and in every town it had its own clothes factory. All grain mills and rose-water factories were taken over by the authorities. New taxes were imposed on the sale of all kinds of cattle in the markets.[5] For the import and export trade old rates were increased, and hitherto untaxed items brought under taxation.[6] The one conspicuously absent measure, which was fashionable with other Shī'ites, was the imposition of an income tax. Perhaps all those urban tax increases were supposed to compensate for this default; or perhaps it was because the Būyids did not have a recognized Shī'ite *Imām* in whose name the fifth or the tenth was collected as income tax. Or was it the other way around? That is to say, was it that they did not want to recognize such an *Imām* because they did not want to impose the tax? It is probably for this reason that they took the easy way out and recognized the 'Abbāsids and unmistakably declared their intentions of safeguarding the vested interests of the wealthy.

As for the rural communities, measures were taken to enforce the strict collection of taxes. The nomads were required to pay taxes on their herds, and for this purpose an elaborate system of regrouping them under appointed chiefs was instituted and registered. In return these unruly people, whose numbers were over 2,000,000, were drawn into the system and were made to serve the purposes of the government. They were given the responsibility of guiding and protecting the trade caravans, and naturally these services were not free of charge.[7] For the land-tax, an infinitely more complicated three-tier system was introduced. The complication arose because the system was designed to exact maximum amounts while taking existing conditions into consideration. Accordingly the assessments were made by way of a fixed proportion of the produce, by a fixed sum, or by measurement of the land. Nevertheless, the amount of

[1] Maqdisī, p. 429.
[2] *Ibid.*, p. 400.
[3] *Ibid.*, pp. 413, 429; Iṣṭakhrī, p. 158.
[4] Maqdisī, p. 434.
[5] *Ibid.*, pp. 413, 431; Iṣṭakhrī, p. 158; Abu Shuja', p. 71.
[6] Athīr, vol. IX, p. 16.
[7] Ḥawqal, pp. 265, 269; Iṣṭakhrī, pp. 99, 113, 115.

taxes due differed from one district to another even when assessed on the same basis.[1] On the other hand, the government did not shrink from the responsibility of maintaining and indeed improving all irrigation systems. Astonishing engineering skills were utilized and great sums of money were spent to build dams and dig new canals to help agriculture.[2] With regard to minerals, the tax of one fifth continued in operation except for pissasphalt which became a state monopoly.[3]

When Fanā-Khusraw extended his authority to include Baghdād and 'Irāq, most of these fiscal measures were put into effect as soon as possible. While expenditure was not spared to improve irrigation, a general 10% land-tax increase was decreed. Monopolies were set up and a grand plan to rebuild Baghdād was initiated. Any house owner who wanted to renovate his property was offered a free loan from the treasury.[4] One can imagine that the hospitals built at that time were of a better standard than the lunatic asylums of previous days.

It is almost sad to have to stop writing about this unexpectedly imaginative and promising period, but like all good things it had to come to an end. It is even sadder that the end came so abruptly and that these reforms, belated as they were, were not given an opportunity to take root. The death of Fanā-Khusraw in 983/372 was followed by a reversion to conditions as they had been before his energetic last five and a half years. It was not because of the absence of a strong man that this happened; it was because of the absence of the threat that had given the impulse to those urgent measures. The Ghaznavid danger proved to be a false alarm and it was to be half a century before it materialized in the form of an attack on Rayy which the Ghaznavids occupied in 1029/420, only to give it up soon after to the Saljūqs. During this half century the Būyid Confederacy continued willy-nilly its struggle for survival. The increasing demands of the military and the accumulative bad effects of the *iqṭā'* system had had less harmful consequences on its prosperity than the disastrous drying up of trade. It was in this period that the Pecheneg Turks started to attack the Volga basin from their territory to the north of the Caspian. These attacks coincided with the emergence of the Russians whose good relations with the Byzantines helped to

[1] Ḥawqal, pp. 302–3; Iṣṭakhrī, pp. 157–8; Maqdisī, pp. 448, 451–2.
[2] Abū Shujā', p. 69; Maqdisī, pp. 404, 419, 444.
[3] Ḥawqal, p. 302; Iṣṭakhrī, pp. 154–5.
[4] Miskawayh, vol. II, pp. 405–6; Abū Shujā', pp. 45, 71; Athīr, vol. IX, p. 16.

divert the whole northern trade to Kiev and Constantinople. The Italian merchant states at the same time began to attract a good deal of this business and to export goods across the Mediterranean. Central Asia and the Caucasus region lost completely in this race, and subsequently Iran, east and west, the main duct for this trade, began to suffer severe economic decline. In fact, the hitherto all-important Rayy suddenly became of no importance and its loss to the Būyids in the last decades of their existence did not make much difference to their fortunes. As if the loss of the northern trade was not enough, the Būyids also lost all their southern trade. Thanks to the Fāṭimids who managed to attract all the Indian Ocean trade, the Būyid Confederacy was practically bankrupt when it fell to the Saljūqs in 1055/447. Significantly the new conquerors did not have much of a trade policy.[1]

[1] Athīr, vol. x, pp. 51, 105, 111.

9
THE FĀṬIMIDS

It is surprising to realize that more research has been done on the Fāṭimids than on any other aspect of Islamic history. Conveniently M. Canard has summed up the results of all this research, including his own, in an article of thirteen large and crowded pages in the new edition of the *Encyclopaedia of Islam* to which he and others have also contributed numerous other relevant articles. Therefore, the basic facts of Fāṭimid history have been well established. Bernard Lewis, who started working on the subject almost forty years ago, has recently given us his interpretation of Fāṭimid history.[1] All these researches have in common one principal weakness; they do not take into consideration earlier developments nor all of the important circumstances in the areas the Fāṭimids controlled. They are also unbalanced in that more has been said about the birth certificate of the first Fāṭimid ruler than about economic conditions in his domains. His genealogy, interesting as it may be, is unimportant because enough people believed in his cause to make possible his rise to power. They also believed his claim to be a descendant of the Prophet through his daughter Fāṭima, a claim which was an easy target for the attacks of his opponents. It has to be realized that, at the time, there were hundreds if not thousands of such descendants and it was well nigh impossible to prove or refute their claims. The important thing is that this particular leader put forward an Ismāʿīlī Shīʿite ideology of radical revolutionary dimensions.

We cannot comprehend the history of the Fāṭimids without understanding the full implications of their wide-ranging economic policies about which little has been said. Although Lewis had long recognized that the trade activities of the Fāṭimids reached as far as India, they were judged to be blind to the African trade in their own backyard.[2] Their taxation system, a cornerstone in their success and failure, has not been discussed and has gone as unnoticed, as if they

[1] Bernard Lewis, "An Interpretation of Fāṭimid History", *Colloque International sur L'Histoire du Caire 27 Mars–5 Avril 1969*, Cairo, n.d. pp. 287–95.

[2] *Idem*, "The Fāṭimids and the Route to India", *Revue de la Faculté de Sciences Economiques de l'Université d'Istanbul*, 11 année. No. 1–4, Istanbul 1953, pp. 1–5.

had none. From scholars like Canard and Lewis, this woeful neglect is surprising. Furthermore, it is indefensible for Lewis to compare the rise of the ʻAbbāsids in Khurāsān with that of the Fāṭimids in Tunisia.[1] Any accidental similarities are superficial and should be treated with the greatest caution because there were major differences between the two movements in the nature of their support, their institutions and organizations, and their purposes and ideologies.

The Fāṭimids first established themselves in Tunisia and sixty years later they took a most extraordinary step, which has been looked on as if it were an everyday occurrence. They moved literally lock, stock and barrel to Egypt, never to glance back again. While in Egypt their relationship with their former subjects was of little importance to the Fāṭimids, and indeed within a few decades these subjects became independent and even hostile to them. This transplantation of the Fāṭimids has been explained as part of their grand plan to overthrow and supersede the ʻAbbāsids. If that was the case then the Fāṭimids went about it in the strangest possible way, spending more effort on controlling northern Syria than in achieving their primary objective. They might have dreamt about a universal empire that would envelop all Islamic domains, but their efforts in this respect never went beyond sending missionaries to Baghdād as well as to India and Central Asia. Any such ambitions they may have entertained remained in the realm of ultimate objectives rather than practical policies, and had no effect whatever on the situation at the time. Indeed, it is inaccurate to speak about a vast Fāṭimid empire of which the "centre was Egypt; its provinces at its peak included North Africa, Sicily, Palestine, Syria, the Red Sea coast of Africa, the Yemen, and, of special importance, the Ḥijāz, possession of which conferred great prestige on a Muslim ruler and enabled him to use the potent weapon of the pilgrimage to his advantage."[2] At no point did such an empire exist. For soon after the Fāṭimids left Tunisia, their western borders retracted to a point hardly west of Alexandria and their interest in Sicily had evaporated before they could even establish a foothold in Syria. Palestine was more often than not out of their control and they never *possessed* Ḥijāz. To say that Yaman was part of the Fāṭimid empire requires a long stretch of the imagination; thus describing a relationship by correspondence as an actual marriage. It is more realistic to say that after leaving Tunisia, the Fāṭimids dominated Egypt but despite

[1] *Idem, Interpretation*, p. 288.
[2] *Ibid.*, p. 289.

desperate attempts failed to establish more than a foothold on the Palestinian coast. Considering the chaos that prevailed in Syria and Palestine at the time this was a conspicuous failure.

In 893/280 an Ismā'īlī missionary, Abū 'Abdillah, arrived in Little Kabylia in present-day Algeria, in the company of pilgrims from the Berber tribe of Kutāma whom he had met in Makka. It is significant that such an astute man should have chosen to go straight to North Africa to propagate his cause and by-pass Egypt altogether. It indicates that the Ismā'īlīs, who saw possibilities for success in the central province of 'Irāq, did not believe that such possibilities existed in Egypt. They knew that outside Fusṭāṭ and Alexandria the Egyptian population was overwhelmingly Coptic, and they reckoned that they would have better chances of converting Muslims to their cause than converting of Copts to Islam. North Africa was perfectly suited to the purposes of the Ismā'īlīs, because most of the population there had long been Islamized. Furthermore, heterodoxy was not new to the area; if anything it was the norm. The Shī'ite Idrīsids and the Khārijite Rustamids had successfully maintained their regimes for over a century and were still very stable. The only instability emanated from Tunisia where the Aghlabids had had one trouble after another. From the very beginning their regime had been based on military control. However, as their forces were constituted of Khurāsāniyya, Berbers and Arabs, there had been a great deal of disharmony and quarrelling amongst them. The problems of the Aghlabids had been aggravated by their complete dependence on an agricultural economy while their neighbours, east and west, had been busy reviving and capturing the ancient trade across the Sahara. This situation had forced upon the Aghlabids an unhealthy isolation for which they had had to find a solution. Hence the long and expensive military campaigns to occupy Sicily 827–902/212–91. To meet these expenses it had been decreed that the land-taxes should be paid in cash and not in kind, and significantly this was revoked only when the Fāṭimid threat became imminent.[1] Meanwhile, the Aghlabids had begun, at last, to try to attract some of the trade by encouraging the use of an east–west route through their territories.[2] Nevertheless, this attempt had not been particularly successful, as sailing along the coast was a less expensive and easier means of communication. Towards the end of the rule of the Aghlabids, the Byzantines, who had lost Sicily to them, made some

1 'Idhārī, vol. I, pp. 95, 131; Athīr, vol. VI, p. 231.
2 Maqrīzī, *Khiṭaṭ*, vol. I, p. 174.

overtures to establish trade relations with them through the island, but by then it was too late.[1]

The task of the missionary Abū 'Abdillah was not a difficult one. It was easy to incite and organize the Kutāma Berbers of Algeria against the Aghlabids with whom they had no particular affinity. Sensing that the enterprise was about to bear fruit the Ismā'īlī *Imām*, 'Ubaydullah, in whose name it was launched, began cautiously to journey from his base in Syria to North Africa in 902/289. His surreptitious route led him to Sijilmāsa where he was ignominiously imprisoned. After bringing down the Aghlabids in 909/296 Abū 'Abdillah dutifully marched on Sijilmāsa, freed his leader and brought him to the conquered capital of the Aghlabids, Raqqāda, in 910/297. There, the *Imām* was installed as the legitimate Shī'ite *Amīr al-Mu'minīn* and proclaimed himself the *Mahdī*, the long awaited leader who would initiate an era of divinely guided rule. Almost immediately, differences of opinion on the course of action to be pursued began to appear among the victors. Abū 'Abdillah disagreed with his own brother, a senior advisor to the new regime. The latter wanted to take extreme measures against the intellectuals who had supported the fallen adversaries.[2] Then Abū 'Abdillah himself fell out with the ruler over the question of taxation. The former advocated a return to the most elementary form of taxation in Islam, that is tithes in kind on some agricultural produce and cattle.[3] Realizing that this would be impractical and might in fact raise problems with many Berbers who were not accustomed to paying taxes on their live-stock, the *Mahdī* introduced a different system of taxation. A fixed sum in cash was levied on acreage, and no measures were taken to tax cattle. Although this was in effect a return to the system which the Aghlabids had abandoned before their downfall, some adjustments were made to alleviate its worst effects.[4] Perhaps these differences could have been reconciled if another major discordant note had not been struck. It is possible to discern that Abū 'Abdillah, who was obviously less ambitious than his master, was convinced that the best course of action after victory was to turn quietly to the west and consolidate Fāṭimid power as much as possible at the expense of the Rustamids and the Idrīsids.[5] Furthermore, having spent almost twenty years among the Berbers, he had become familiar with their problems and interests to

[1] 'Idhārī, vol. 1, p. 144.
[2] *Ibid.*, pp. 150–1.
[3] *Ibid.*, pp. 141–2.
[4] *Ibid.*, p. 173; Maqrīzī, *Khiṭaṭ*, vol. 1, p. 352.
[5] Maqrīzī, *Khiṭaṭ*, vol. 1, p. 351.

the point of identification with them. On the other hand the *Mahdī*, a relative newcomer to the area, was free from such attachment. Moreover, as the leader of a sectarian movement which was putting forward claims to universality, he could not support a policy that would effectively make his regime no more than a successor to the pronouncedly Berber sectarianism of the Rustamids and the Idrīsids. To him turning towards the east was the logical solution to the dilemma. Therefore, Abū 'Abdillah and his brother had to be sacrificed for the loftier objectives of the movement, and when some Berbers rebelled they were swiftly subdued. It is significant that the *Mahdī*, and his successors, practically ignored the existence of the Umayyads in Spain. The latter had extensive trade interests over all of North Africa as is evident from many emporiums on the North African coast, and the presence of commercial colonies as far east as Alexandria and the Island of Crete.[1] To interfere with these vested interests was not only inviting the wrath of a powerful enemy, but also stirring up a hornets' nest. Therefore the Fāṭimids, the claimants to all Shī'ite heritage, chose of all things to leave alone an Umayyad *Amīr al-Mu'minīn* in nearby Spain and tolerate the challenge to their universal claims.

At this stage it is difficult to see how far east the Fāṭimids contemplated extending their domains. Their well-known long term and detailed planning did not come into play at this time. Knowing that their military forces were still narrowly based and limited only to the Kutāma, themselves a minority among the Berbers, the Fāṭimids sensibly confined their objectives to the possible. As heirs to the Aghlabids they captured, though with some difficulty, Sicily and Tripolitania. Once these were secured an aggressive policy developed simultaneously on two fronts, one at sea and the other on land. For the first an impressive ship-yard with at least two dry-docks was constructed in the newly built capital of Mahdiyya, and in no time it had 900 warships. This powerful fleet was soon engaged in wide-ranging and far-reaching attacks against Italian ports as far afield as Genoa, and against the islands of the western Mediterranean.[2] Of course such attacks could be expected to yield a certain amount of booty, but this could not have been expected to compensate for the immense expenses involved in maintaining such a large fleet. It is noteworthy that the Fāṭimid fleet did not clash much

[1] 'Idhārī, vol. I, pp. 116, 136, 169, 175, vol. II, pp. 242–3; Athīr, vol. VI, pp. 281–2, vol. VIII, p. 459; Ḥawqal, pp. 74, 104.

[2] 'Idhārī, vol. I, pp. 174, 187–94, 209; Athīr, vol. VIII, pp. 116–17, 212, 232.

with the equally powerful fleet of Muslim Spain. It is also remarkable that while the Italians did not take any counter measures against these attacks, the Arabs of Sicily strongly objected, to the extent of attacking the naval base in Tunisia.[1] This strange quadrangular entanglement suggests that Sicily with its mixed population and its position as a trade intermediary between the Italian and the Spanish ports, was the loser in this situation. In other words, in announcing their presence the Fāṭimids were trying to reach out directly to the Italian market at the expense of Sicily and without causing unnecessary conflict with Spain.

On the land front the Fāṭimids' objective was just as prudently planned. There was no question of conquering Egypt or confronting the 'Abbāsids, the Fāṭimids knew very well that they did not have the military power to embark on such adventures which were obviously beyond their resources. What they aimed for was the domination of the coast as well as the desert between their holdings in Tripolitania and the Nile Valley. The expeditions of 913–15/301–2, 919–21/307–9, 935/323 were not meant to occupy Egypt, they were intended to drive Egyptian influence out of Cyrenaica, and as far as possible to limit it to the Valley itself. In these expeditions Fāṭimid forces came as close as possible to the city of Alexandria and then proceeded through the desert to a point opposite Fusṭāṭ. From there they continued to advance through the desert to the Fayyūm Oasis and then to the rest of the Egyptian Oases before returning home.[2] The clear conclusion is that the Fāṭimids were striving to gain control of the African trade flowing through the north–south routes across the Libyan–Egyptian desert to the flourishing ports on the coast.[3] Achieving this end in addition to having access to the European market would have put the Fāṭimids in a commanding position as a major trading power in the Mediterranean basin. One can see the necessity of a powerful navy for such an enterprise. There is no doubt that trade was the most important motive in almost every action taken by the Fāṭimids throughout their history.

Contrary to their expectations the frantic activities of the Fāṭimids produced just the opposite results. The long-established equilibrium in the rest of North Africa was radically upset. The fall of the Rustamids in 909/296 put an end to the prosperity of their commercial centre in Tāhart and all its trans-Saharan trade was driven

[1] 'Idhārī, vol. I, pp. 168–74.

[2] Athīr, vol. VIII, pp. 50, 230; Maqrīzī, *Khiṭaṭ*, vol. I, p. 174, vol. II, p. 27; 'Idhārī, vol. I, pp. 188–9.

[3] Ḥawqal, pp. 67, 69, 103–4.

much further west. The result was a series of Berber revolts that were encouraged by the Umayyads of Spain. The more the Fāṭimids tried to contain these revolts the further they themselves got involved and to no avail. At one point a revolt became so serious that it threatened the very existence of the Fāṭimids in Tunisia.[1] On their eastern flank the first expedition of 913–15/301–2 gave the Fāṭimids a foothold in Cyrenaica, but it also created such a panic there that much of the population moved to Alexandria and its vicinity.[2] Those who remained in Cyrenaica took part in the revolts that occurred in Tripolitania against the Fāṭimids. Under these circumstances the trade which had found its way back to the Oases gradually reverted to Nubia. It is interesting to note that the king of Nubia, who had been worried about the drying-up of trade through his territory, found it necessary to attack the Oases in 950/339.[3] This action could not have helped the cause of the Fāṭimids and indeed induced them to change their plans. On the coast neither Tripolitania nor Cyrenaica was content with the outcome of the Fāṭimid adventures. However, the unrest in Cyrenaica and its close contacts with Alexandria drew the attention of the Fāṭimids to the possibilities in this direction. On the other hand Fāṭimid attempts in the western Mediterranean only helped to bring the Byzantines and the Umayyads of Spain closer together. In 945/334 and 949/338 the emissaries of Constantinople arrived at Cordova seeking its friendship.[4] The rising star of the Umayyads persuaded the emperor Otto the Great to send his own embassy to Cordova in 953/342.[5] In spite of their many allies in North Africa the Umayyads thought it prudent to occupy Ceuta and establish a stronghold on the African coast.[6] Perhaps it was this move, more than anything else, that convinced the Fāṭimids that their plans had rebounded upon them. The *Mahdī* and his two successors had persevered with their efforts to push for the success of these plans for over forty years. The new ruler Mu'izz who came to power in 953/341, had different ideas which he gradually put into effect. He began to widen the military base of the regime. It is no coincidence that it is in his reign we find a noticeable element of Sicilians and probably also Italians in his army. When this army arrived in Egypt it had two separate contingents of "Rūm".[7] He also brought Berbers from tribes other than the Kutāma into his

[1] Athīr, vol. VIII, pp. 315–22; 'Idhārī, vol. I, p. 191.
[2] Maqrīzī, *Khiṭaṭ*, vol. I, p. 174; Kindī, *Wulāt*, p. 274.
[3] Anṭākī, p. 112; Maqrīzī, *Khiṭaṭ*, vol. I, p. 236.
[4] 'Idhārī, vol. II, pp. 213, 215.
[5] *Ibid.*, p. 218.
[6] 'Idhārī, vol. I, pp. 203–4.
[7] Maqrīzī, *Khiṭaṭ*, vol. II, p. 8.

forces, such as the Zuwayla of Tripolitania.[1] But his major achievement in this respect was to win over the powerful tribe of Ṣanhāja by giving them a share in the power structure of the regime. In 958/347 an apparently unnecessary expedition was organized under the command of the redoubtable Sicilian general Jawhar and with the full participation of the Ṣanhāja, to pacify the regions of central North Africa.[2] Militarily this expedition did not accomplish much; it even failed to recapture Ceuta from the Umayyads. Yet politically it was an unqualified success for it involved the Ṣanhāja in the defence of these regions. Mu'izz now became free to pursue his plans elsewhere, plans that took ten years of preparations.

The fall of the Tūlūnids in 905/292 was followed by thirty years of direct control of Egypt from Baghdād. The remnants of the Tūlūnid forces were transferred to Syria and instead a strong contingent from Baghdād under a succession of military governors was stationed in Egypt to hold the province. The real power, however, remained in the hands of the fiscal administrators both in Egypt and in Syria. As has already been explained the revenues of these two provinces were allocated for the needs of general Mu'nis's armies. In case of emergency these armies were quick to come to the rescue, as happened when the Fāṭimids attacked Egypt.[3] The downfall of Mu'nis, the breakdown of the central government and the rise of the the Ḥamdānids made necessary a new arrangement for southern Syria and Egypt. It was felt that the continued threat of Fāṭimid attacks demanded a strong military presence in Egypt. Ironically the only available troops were the remnants of the Ṭūlūnid forces which were consolidated in Syria under the leadership of Muḥammad b. Tughj, better known as Ikhshīd, himself a former associate of the Ṭūlūnids. As it happened he was also a descendant of a long line of loyal 'Abbāsid generals that had been recruited from Central Asia over a hundred years earlier in the heyday of Sāmarrā. These qualifications and his knowledge of Egypt and its problems offered the desired solution. In 935/323 Ikhshīd was appointed governor of Egypt in addition to his governorship of Damascus. As he was granted these territories as a military–administrative *iqṭā'*, this appointment was in effect a return to the Ṭūlūnid system by which Ikhshīd had full control over the military and fiscal affairs of his domains. Arriving in Egypt with his army and navy, he was soon able to establish his rule and integrate whatever forces had been

[1] *Ibid.*, p. 4.
[2] Maqrīzī, *Khiṭaṭ*, vol. 1, p. 352.
[3] See above, p. 145; Kindī, *Wulāt*, pp. 278–86.

there into his army.[1] During his eleven years in power 935–46/323–34, he managed to hold his own against the encroachments of the Ḥamdānids and maintain the integrity of southern Syria, including Damascus, in a period when the central government was in utter disarray. He also kept the Qarāmiṭa at bay by paying them 300,000 dinārs a year.[2]

Although Ikhshīd was supposed to have started a dynasty and indeed was succeeded by three of his descendants, yet the real power throughout the years of his dynasty was firmly in the hands of Kāfūr. He is supposed to have been a black slave, a eunuch, with a pierced lower lip and flat-footed to boot. He is reported to have been brought to Egypt and sold as a slave when he was ten years old. It is also reported that at that point he expressed the hope that one day he would rule Egypt. According to these reports Ikhshīd had bought him at the bargain price of eighteen dinārs which could have happened only after the arrival of the former in Egypt in 935/323. Yet in ten years' time we find Kāfūr as a general of Ikhshīd's army in Syria and subsequently as the virtual ruler until his death in 966/355.[3] It is important here to point out that Kāfūr was unfortunate enough to encounter one of the greatest Arab poets of all times. Apart from his poetical gift, this man was extremely vitriolic as well as a great liar, as is evident from the name by which he was known, Mutanabbī, he who claims false prophethood. When he eulogized Kāfūr he made him the greatest of the great, and when Kāfūr did not pay him his price the poet satirized him as the scum of the earth. Although one finds echoes of the praise in the sources, the colourful terms of the satires reverberated far more and were soon taken as facts. Naturally such facts would come to be embellished with the appropriate stories, and it is left to the researcher to apply his common sense.

Kāfūr recruited *sūdān* in his army, a fact that would make it more than probable that he was of the same origin.[4] These new recruits were needed primarily to hold Syria and strengthen Egyptian defences in the west. However, Kāfūr had to cope with a new front which hitherto had been very peaceful. In 955/344 the Nubians attacked Aswān and accordingly an army had to be sent to protect the southern borders.[5] The sudden anger of the Nubians which had

1 Maqrīzī, *Khiṭaṭ*, vol. I, pp. 328–9; Kindī, *Wulāt*, p. 287.
2 Athīr, vol. VIII, p. 452.
3 *Ibid.*, p. 343; Maqrīzī, *Khiṭaṭ*, vol. I, p. 329, vol. II, p. 26.
4 Maqrīzī, *Khiṭaṭ*, vol. I, p. 94.
5 *Ibid.*, p. 198; Anṭākī, p. 112.

provoked this attack must be related to their attack on the Oases only six years earlier. After making the considerable effort of cutting the important links of the trade-routes at the Oases, they attacked Aswān in order to put pressure on the authorities in Egypt to take Nubian interests into consideration. The dilemma of these authorities was that if they were to co-operate with the Nubians to restore the trade to Nubia, they would add to the pressures in Cyrenaica which were having serious effects on the stability of Alexandria. Besides, there was always the Ḥamdānid weight on Syria to worry about. These increasing dangers demanded more forces, and if the *sūdān* were to shoulder this responsibility they would have had to have a major say in the affairs of the country. Hence the accession to power of Kāfūr who must have been the most prominent leader of the *sūdān* in the army.[1] His task was not only to defend Egypt and Syria against outside attacks, but also to keep the balance between the various groups within these territories, the Copts, the Arabs of Alexandria and the Berbers of Cyrenaica who moved in with them, the *sūdān*, the rest of the army, the population of Damascus and the Syrian ports, and the increasingly troublesome Arabs of Palestine who were just beginning to constitute a force of their own. There is all the evidence that both the Ḥamdanids and the Fāṭimids were using all possible means to stir up discord within Kāfūr's domains. Yet with remarkable political acumen he contrived to preserve the integrity of his sway until his death in 966/355.[2] Within three years of this the Fāṭimids had occupied Egypt.

Arriving at Alexandria in 969/358 the Fāṭimid army met with no resistance and probably had not expected any. Its commander general Jawhar declared an amnesty and assured the people of the safety of their lives and property. Of greater importance and more significance is the fact that he also assured them that they would be allowed freedom of religion.[3] This was not the rash promise of a victorious general, it was in accordance with a general line of policy that had already been declared by Mu'izz. The latter must have realized that after many decades of proselytizing, Ismā'īlism had not really taken root in North Africa, though that was a favourable *milieu*. Egypt with a great majority of Christians divided into at least three sects, and a minority of Muslims following three schools of orthodoxy, would not be fertile ground for conversion. In fact Mu'izz had decided to curtail the preaching of the esoteric teachings of Ismā'īlism

[1] Maqrīzī, *Khiṭaṭ*, vol. I, p. 329. [2] *Ibid.*, p. 431; *idem*, vol. II, p. 430.
[3] *Idem*, *Itti'āẓ*, vol. I, pp. 151–2.

and limit that only to the initiated.[1] The writings of his chief theoretician Qaḍī Nu'mān, which are extant, do not differ much from orthodox writings except on the question of the position of the *imām*, and some other very subtle points which will be presently explained. This rather neutral religious policy was maintained in effect, with very few exceptions, throughout the rule of the Fāṭimids. This pragmatic attitude from a missionary and proselytizing sect allowed them to employ in their service not only Muslims of all shades of opinion, but also many Christians and Jews. On the other hand, as they did not penetrate to the roots of society, no trace of Ismā'īlism whatsoever remained in Egypt after two centuries of Fāṭimid rule.

Although building new capitals was a universal practice of this age, the fact that almost as soon as Jawhar arrived at Fusṭāṭ he proceeded to build Cairo in 970/359, confirms the determination of the Fāṭimids to have the least possible interference with the existing state of affairs. Everything had been planned in advance to the extent of laying the foundations of the Azhar, the intellectual centre of Ismā'īlism in Egypt. Although space was provided within the walls of the new city for reasonable future expansion it was designed to be strictly the administrative and military capital of the regime. Fusṭāṭ, which came to be known as Old Cairo, flourished and expanded as the commercial capital of Egypt.[2] When Mu'izz arrived from Tunisia in 973/362 everything was ready for him to put into effect his well conceived and detailed plans.

These plans were the culmination of Shī'ite experience during the previous three centuries. The continuity and unity of this experience were emphasized by the shining prominence given to the sixth *Imām* Ja'far al-Ṣādiq in all Ismā'īlī traditions. The Fāṭimids were determined to benefit from the history of the past Shī'ite movements and to avoid their mistakes. They put forward a clear ideology and an elaborate theology which continued to develop by virtue of the presence of a divinely guided leader. Being also the ruler, this leader would ensure justice for all. Although they knew only too well that they were a minority sect, they behaved as if their universal acceptance was an accomplished fact. They operated from one region and certainly pushed hard for its interests, yet their vast international relations enhanced their universal image. They were keenly aware of rural disaffection and the privileged situation of the urban communities, and they tried to plan for a more just society. There is no

[1] Athīr, vol. VIII, p. 389.

[2] Maqdisī, p. 199.

doubt that Egypt was the field chosen for this unique experiment in Islam. Indeed the rule of the Fāṭimids in Tunisia was on a completely different basis, and when they moved to Egypt they simply did not care what happened thereafter in the west. Tunisia was left to the care of the Ṣanhāja Berbers, their recently cultivated allies. The only stipulation was that Mu'izz reserved for himself the right to appoint judges and tax-administrators, but there is no trace that this condition was observed by the Zīrids, the leaders of the Ṣanhāja.[1] Sicily was entrusted to the Kalbids who had kept it under control, and Tripolitania was given to members of the Kutāma Berbers, the original supporters of the Fāṭimids, while Cyrenaica remained in the hands of the latter.[2] Theoretically all these territories remained under the suzerainty of the Fāṭimids, but in practice it was certainly a tenuous relationship. In 975/365 the Zīrids sent the Fāṭimids badly needed financial help; in 983/373 it was only a present that arrived at Cairo; in 987/377 the Zīrids annexed Tripolitania, and in 1012/403 the Fāṭimids conceded Cyrenaica to them.[3] In 1015/406 the Zīrids expunged any traces of Ismā'īlism that there might have been in their domains, and in 1041/433 they dropped all pretence and became actively hostile to the Fāṭimids.[4] In the meanwhile the Zīrids had been busy promoting their own interests and competing directly with the Fāṭimids for a greater share in the African trade. It is interesting to note that elephants and the giraffes which used to adorn Fāṭimid ceremonial processions in Cairo began to appear in the Zīrid court in 1032/423 as presents from the king of the *sūdān*.[5]

In Egypt the Fāṭimids started their rule by setting up the most centralized and hierarchical administration ever known in Islam. The architect of this elaborate plan was Ya'qūb b. Killis, a converted Jew who had originated in Baghdād, moved to Egypt, served Kāfūr in Palestine, fled to Tunisia and had come back with Mu'izz. Naturally the focal point of the whole system was the *Imām* who was unequivocally acknowledged as God's representative on earth. From him all authority emanated and to him all duties were due. The management of the affairs of the country was divided between three discernible branches, administrative, judiciary and missionary; the last two terms do not denote the exact function of the respective branches. The judiciary was the charge of a Chief Justice whose job

[1] Maqrīzī, *Khiṭaṭ*, vol. I, p. 353.
[2] Athīr, vol. VIII, p. 456.
[3] 'Idhārī, vol. I, p. 230; Maqrīzī, *Khiṭaṭ*, vol. II, p. 258; Athīr, vol. IX, pp. 25, 37–8.
[4] 'Idharī, vol. I, p. 275; Athīr, vol. IX, pp. 180, 366–7.
[5] 'Idhārī, vol. I, pp. 246, 247, 249, 275; Maqrīzī, *Khiṭaṭ*, vol. I, pp. 451, 461.

was not only the administration of justice but also included such things as supervising the mint.[1] On a par with him was the Chief Missionary who had his representatives in every district of the Fāṭimid domains, as well as in all parts of the Islamic world. His functions were at two levels. Internally, he was in charge of education, and surprisingly his agents were given the responsibility of collecting certain taxes which were more like membership dues of the Ismā'ilī sect.[2] Externally, he headed what was very similar to the Congregation of the Propaganda of the Catholic Church in charge of foreign missions. As such he was very much involved in the external relations of the Fāṭimids which most certainly included trade. It was possible for one person to hold at one and the same time the offices of Chief Justice and Chief Missionary. The administrative branch comprised various departments, each under its own head, and all under the direction of one person. This particular official was called *wāsiṭa*, i.e. intermediary between the *Imām* and the rest of the administration. On two occasions when this high official was given the responsibility of overseeing the military forces, he was given the rank of *wazīr*.[3] Normally the military were under the direct command of the ruler and sometimes there was a commander-in-chief, but the constitution of the army did not often allow this to happen. It was also possible for the *wazīr* or the *wāsiṭa* to be Chief Justice and Chief Missionary at the same time but this was only in times of crisis.[4]

Having established their administration they turned to the economy with much the same zeal for planning in an effort to exploit the resources of Egypt to the best advantage. On his arrival in Egypt general Jawhar, needing money for his immediate expenses, had simply doubled the land tax from 3½ dinārs per acre to seven.[5] But this had been a temporary measure and it was now time to think about a more permanent system. Here again the position of the *Imām* dictated the solution. As God's representative on earth he owned all the lands in his domains. He could give land-grants to whomsoever he wished and his fortunate favourites would own such lands. As for the rest of the people who had been in possession of land, they lost their titles to their properties but were allowed to continue to cultivate them. No one was forced off his land and it was passed from father to son, but as was well put by some astute observer at the time, such a person was no more than *qinn*, a heredi-

[1] Maqrīzī, *Khiṭaṭ*, vol. I, p. 404.
[2] *Ibid.*, p. 391.
[3] Māwardī, *Aḥkām*, pp. 41–3; Maqrīzī, *Khiṭaṭ*, vol. II, p. 5.
[4] Maqrīzī, *Khiṭaṭ*, vol. I, p. 464.
[5] Ḥawqal, p. 163.

tary slave or serf. The land-tax these serfs paid was aptly called *kirā'*, rent.[1] For the purpose of this tax a survey was made and the rates were reassessed.[2] Judging from the figures we have of the total revenues collected these rates do not seem to have been excessive.[3] Land-tax collecting continued on the basis of *qabāla*, i.e. contracting to pay a fixed sum for a given district. But there were crucial differences from the original system introduced by Ma'mūn a century and a half earlier. First, these contracts were auctioned and given to the highest bidder to the detriment of the tax-payer.[4] Second, the contractor was not required to be a member of the tax-community concerned. Indeed government officials and, more seriously, army commanders were allowed to undertake such contracts.[5] In most cases these contracts took the character of tax-farming. In due course a powerful contractor was able to pass his contract to his descendants and the district concerned became virtually an *iqṭā'*, land-grant. The third difference produced catastrophic results. Under the original system the contractor had had to undertake the responsibility for maintaining and repairing any damage to the intricate network of canals and dikes without which the irrigation system would collapse absolutely, and allowances had been made for the expenses involved.[6] Whether out of ignorance or on principle the Fāṭimids overlooked this vital factor in Egyptian agriculture. No provisions were made at all for the maintenance of the irrigation system, and for the first time in millennia of Egyptian history this task was left to the individual peasants. The only precaution the Fāṭimids took was against floods. The major dikes were divided into stretches, for the maintenance of which a levy of ten dinārs per stretch was imposed, and the government itself undertook to do the necessary work.[7] Needless to say, no work was done and the treasury found other urgent needs for spending the money.[8] In a few decades the inevitable and rapid deterioration of agriculture came about and the result was not only famines year after year, but also a drastic fall in taxes.[9] Maqrīzī never ceased to lament this situation, repeatedly reminding us that from time immemorial one fourth if not one third of the revenues of Egypt had always been

[1] Maqrīzī, *Khiṭaṭ*, vol. I, p. 85; Maqdisī, pp. 64–5 and the variant reading in the footnotes, also p. 212.
[2] Ḥawqal, p. 143; Maqrīzī, *Khiṭaṭ*, vol. I, p. 405.
[3] Maqrīzī, *Khiṭaṭ*, vol. I, p. 82.
[4] *Idem*, vol. II, pp. 5–6.
[5] *Idem*, vol. I, p. 85.
[6] See above, p. 60.
[7] Maqrīzī, *Khiṭaṭ*, vol. I, p. 110.
[8] *Ibid.*, p. 101.
[9] *Ibid.*, pp. 249–50.

allocated to the care and upkeep of the irrigation system.[1] He also pointed out that after the coming of the Fāṭimids the northern half of the Nile Delta was lost to agriculture and became waste land.[2]

As for trade the Fāṭimids had two objectives. One was to use it as a means to tax urban communities and thus introduce a more equitable tax system in their domains. As a consequence of their usual methodical approach not a single product, trade or profession escaped taxation. Taxes were imposed on all items entering any town and collected at gates, road-blocks, quays, market places, ports and custom-houses. Pottery makers, home spinners, trinket producers, leather tanners, vinegar distillers, bakers, oil pressers, beer makers and prostitutes all had to pay their taxes. Fish were taxed at the sea-side and when they were preserved. Cattle were taxed on grazing grounds, in transport and at the slaughter house.[3] A value-added tax was imposed on the all important textile industry at every stage of production from raw material to final product.[4] And of course custom duties were collected on imports and exports.[5] Also, broking houses were established wherever goods in large quantities changed hands and government agents collected stipulated commissions in addition to excise tax.[6] All these taxes were paid by Muslims and non-Muslims alike. However as the latter had to pay a poll-tax, the former were required to pay their *zakāt*. We have no information about the rate of this Muslim tax and it seems that it was difficult to enforce.[7] All the same, members of the Ismā'īlī sect had to pay what was called *najwā*, collection, and in fact it was not much different from a Sunday church collection. Living in a Christian environment the Fāṭimids seem to have learnt a great deal from their subjects. All Ismā'īlī believers were required to attend exclusive meetings held twice a week on Mondays and Thursdays, and under the guidance of a representative of the chief missionary they read the lesson. At every meeting this representative collected the *najwā* which varied from three and a third dirhams to 33 and a third dinārs according to the wealth of the believer.[8] One can imagine that such faithful members would receive special treatment from the state in much the same way as nowadays card-carrying members would expect special treatment in a one-party regime.

[1] *Ibid.*, pp. 61, 76, 100.
[2] *Ibid.*, p. 171.
[3] *Ibid.*, pp. 104–5.
[4] Maqdisī, p. 213.
[5] Maqrīzī, *Khiṭaṭ*, vol. 1, pp. 109, 111.
[6] *Ibid.*, p. 89.
[7] *Ibid.*, p. 368.
[8] *Ibid.*, p. 391.

The Fāṭimids' other objective with regard to trade was to capture a major share of international trade. Geographically Egypt was in an ideal location for this purpose, and it had access to African produce. The Fāṭimids went all the way and, unabashed, used all possible means to attract the Indian Ocean trade from the Persian Gulf to the Red Sea. They had long had missionaries in Yaman who had not yet achieved much result. Now, with increased efforts the Ismāʿīlī missionaries in India were more successful, not particularly in converting the Indians to Ismāʿīlism, but more as a kind of consular service. Gradually the Yamanīs began to realize the advantages of giving a sympathetic ear to the Ismāʿīlīs, but it took some time before an Ismāʿīlī regime was established in Yaman in 1048/439 under the Ṣulayḥids. As suggested before this did not mean that Yaman became part of a Fāṭimid empire. Indeed by this time the Fāṭimids had already begun to decline and the Ṣulayḥids were of no help to them. On the other hand Ḥijāz, which was dependent on Egypt for its grain, was more amenable to co-operating with the Fāṭimids, although Ismāʿīlism never gained a foothold there. The fact remains that it was of no vital importance for the Fāṭimids to dominate the east coast of the Red Sea, because the ports of the west coast were more than enough to handle all the available trade from the Indian Ocean. The co-operation of the Nubians was more important not only because it gave them access to the African trade, but also for the safety of the route from ʿAydhāb to Aswān.[1]

Securing the sources of trade was comparatively easy, but securing markets was a different matter. In their long term planning the Fāṭimids had justifiably counted on controlling Syria, but in the event these calculations proved costly. Their arrival in Egypt coincided with the devastating attack of the Byzantines in 969/358 and their domination of northern Syria. The outcome of this dubious victory was that while they were able to advance their borders well to the south of the Taurus Mountains, they had to sustain inordinate efforts to exercise any control over their conquests. The chaotic conditions that had existed in the relatively isolated *thughūr* in the north were simply transferred to Syria, where they were impossible to contain. In this densely populated province every town, city and district rose up in arms to defend its own interests. The Arabs of the Syrian–ʿIrāqī desert and those driven back from the *thughūr* roamed around establishing themselves wherever possible. They fought amongst themselves, sometimes in support of the Byzantines and at

[1] Ḥawqal, p. 150.

other times against them. The appearance of the Fāṭimids on the scene added to the confusion. The people of Damascus hired 400 defectors from the Būyids to fight for them against the Fāṭimids.[1] They were even willing to accept the suzerainty of the Byzantines over Damascus if they could only establish themselves there. Taking advantage of this situation the Qarāmiṭa of Baḥrayn attacked the Fāṭimids in Syria and advanced into Egypt but were repelled in 971/361. Two years later they attacked Cairo itself but were again defeated. It does not serve any purpose to recount the details of this endless fighting or even to mention the names of the various Arab petty dynasties that fell almost as soon as they came to power. The important thing here is to realize that while the Būyids stayed out of this situation, neither the Byzantines nor the Fāṭimids were able to establish any dominant presence in Syria.

The difficulties that the Fāṭimids encountered in Syria obliged them to try to strengthen their army. As there were no more Berbers available they tried to entice defectors from the armies of the Būyids and the Ḥamdānids, and soon Daylamites, Arabs and many others were serving in the Fāṭimid army.[2] When these were not enough the *sūdān* provided another source of new recruits. Members of this heterogeneous army spent more effort fighting amongst themselves than against the enemy. In the army there were no less than thirty groups; each group was known by a certain name, and of course they were all considered *'abīd*, slaves of the *Imām*.[3] However, there was another group who really were of slave origin who were known as *tarābī*, i.e. those who are fostered. As Maqrīzī explained it, they were young captives put into the charge of palace officials who would teach them writing and archery, and eventually some of them became commanders of the special guards of the ruler.[4] This is the first example of actual slaves in the army, and interestingly enough they were not even called *'abīd*.

The unsettled situation in Syria and the confrontation there between the Byzantines and the Fāṭimids did not stop the two powers from trading with each other. The Syrian ports continued to trade with Constantinople through Cyprus and Byzantine merchant ships brought goods to and carried them from Old Cairo.[5] Indeed the emperor Basil II 976/1025 sent 'Azīz 975–996/365–386 the magnificent gift of 28 enamelled trays inlaid with gold, each one valued at

[1] Maqrīzī, *Khiṭaṭ*, vol. II, p. 8.
[2] *Ibid.*, p. 12.
[3] *Ibid.*, p. 21.
[4] *Ibid.*, p. 194.
[5] Maqdisī, p. 194; Ḥawqal, p. 176; Athīr, vol. VIII, p. 388.

3000 dinārs.[1] On the other hand the Italian city states were quick to send their agents to Alexandria and Cairo to establish their commercial interests. This alternative venue for trade encouraged ʿAzīz to press for a military advantage in Syria even against the advice of his experienced *wazīr* Yaʿqūb b. Killis.[2] For this purpose ʿAzīz started the practice of recruiting men from the eastern regions, although his Berber troops were very much opposed to such a move which represented a threat to their own position within the regime.[3] This antipathy between the westerners, the Berbers, and the easterners eventually developed into open hostility which was in turn aggravated by the appearance of more *sūdān* in the Fāṭimid armies after the death of ʿAzīz.

To encourage trade the ingenuity of the theoretician Qāḍī Nuʿmān was utilized to find a solution to legitimise the practice of usury. We know that although Islam strictly forbids usury, it had long been practised in Baghdād, though it had continued to be a controversial issue.[4] In North Africa some obscure Shīʿite group had also found it necessary to practice usury to stimulate their trade, and had argued that it was not different from any other business transaction.[5] The ingenious Fāṭimid theoretician was more subtle, offering his own definition of usury. He argued that it was certainly illegal to make a loan in gold dīnārs and pay it back with interest in gold dinārs. But if a loan of 1000 silver dirhams and one gold dinār was repaid with 2000 silver dirhams then that was not usury, and the same applied to any transaction that involved any goods, as long as the repayment was made in different kind from the loan.[6] In his own way ʿAzīz was no less subtle than his advisers, and this shows very clearly in his manipulation of the Christians of Egypt. The majority of the peasants of Egypt were Monophysite as against the Greek Orthodoxy of the Byzantine Church.[7] In Cairo and particularly Alexandria, however, there were Melkites who recognized the supremacy of the Patriarch of Constantinople. ʿAzīz, who had a Christian wife, had her brother Orestes appointed as the Melkite Patriarch of Jerusalem and another brother Arsenius as the Metropolitan of Cairo in 986/375.[8] This intriguingly close association of a Muslim ruler with his Christian subjects is a good illustration of the nature of Fāṭimid rule

[1] Maqrīzī, *Khiṭaṭ*, vol. I, p. 415.
[2] Athīr, vol. IX, p. 54.
[3] Maqrīzī, *Khiṭaṭ*, vol. I, p. 451, vol. II, p. 12.
[4] Athīr, vol. X, p. 153; Māwardī, *Aḥkām*, p. 423.
[5] Bakrī, p. 161.
[6] Al-Qāḍi al-Nuʿmān, *Kitāb al-Iqtiṣār*, ed. M. W. Mirza, Damascus, 1957, p. 84; *idem*, *Daʿā'im al-Islām*, ed. A. Fayzi, Cairo, 1960, vol. II, pp. 37, 40.
[7] Maqrīzī, *Khiṭaṭ*, vol. II, p. 501.
[8] Anṭākī, pp. 164–5.

in Egypt. It also indicates that 'Azīz was encouraging the Melkites in order to build new bridges between his domains and Byzantium. Such links would help the cause of trade.[1] The existence in Egypt of a colony of Takrūr, *sūdān* from Mali where they had their own quay in Cairo, signifies that Aziz was not oblivious to the interests of the suppliers of the merchandise.[2]

When 'Azīz died he was succeeded by his son Ḥākim, 996–1021/386–411, one of the most controversial figures in Islamic history. He has been accused of schizophrenia, melancholia, mental and emotional instability and cruelty, among other things. On the other hand he has been credited with idealism, generosity, benevolence and even genius. Yet the best description of him is by a good historian who lived about two centuries later. He said that Ḥākim was trying to emulate Ma'mūn.[3] We know the difficult situation Ma'mūn had faced and how supple he had had to be to survive.[4] Ḥākim was no different, he had problems and tried to cope with them to the best of his ability. The difference was, perhaps, that he came to power at the age of eleven. The Berbers of Kutāma thought that they had an opportunity to purge the army of the easterners. The Christian *wāsiṭa* of 'Azīz was murdered and replaced by Ḥasan b. 'Ammar, a prestigious Berber leader. Nevertheless they seem to have overestimated their strength because within a year they were dislodged by the easterners who then installed Barjawān as the new *wāsiṭa*. Here again we have another white *khaṣiyy* who was significantly described as "physically perfect", i.e. definitely not castrated.[5] For four years Barjawān, with the help of a Christian administrator, was the real ruler of Egypt. He banished the Kutāma to Syria and continued to press for military advantage there. His last act however, was to respond to an approach by Basil II, made through Orestes the Patriarch of Jerusalem, to conclude a peace treaty for ten years beginning 1001/391.[6] Having reached the age of sixteen Ḥākim decided that it was high time for him to exercise his rights and accordingly he arranged for the assassination of Barjawān.

The first important action of Ḥākim in 1000/390 was to promote his uncle Arsenius the Metropolitan of Cairo to the office of Patriarch of Alexandria.[7] This was an auspicious sign that he intended to follow his father's policy, but soon things began to go wrong. In 1005/395

[1] Taghrībardī, vol. IV, pp. 151–2.
[2] Maqrīzī, *Khiṭaṭ*, vol. II, p. 326.
[3] *Idem*, *Itti'āẓ al-Hunafā'*, ed. M. Ḥilmī Aḥmad, Cairo, 1971, vol. II, p. 117.
[4] See above, p. 55.
[5] Maqrīzī, *Khiṭaṭ*, vol. II, p. 3.
[6] Anṭākī, p. 184.
[7] *Ibid.*, p. 185.

a revolt broke out in Cyrenaica which must have had an economic recession as a result of the loss of its trade through the Egyptian Oases. The Arabs in the vicinity of Alexandria also supported this revolt which was led by a descendant of the Umayyads. It took over a year to suppress this revolt. The unfortunate leader fled and ended up in Nubia where he was arrested. Dutifully the Nubian king delivered his worthwhile captive to Cairo. However, as Cyrenaica continued to be unsettled it was written off and conceded to the Zīrids of Tunisia.[1]

The agricultural policy of the Fāṭimids that had left the maintenance of the irrigation system to the public had begun to show its disastrous effects. After thirty years of neglect the canals gradually clogged up, and the inevitable result was not only a drop in the harvest but also the shrinking of the area of arable land. This was the worst crisis of the Fāṭimids and it was the major concern of Ḥākim. The measures he introduced and for which he has been accused of madness will all make sense when seen in this light. His target was to increase necessary food supplies, especially for the Cairo metropolis, and to stimulate the declining agricultural production as much as possible. His measures included the prohibition of beer and wine, the destruction of vines around Cairo, the prohibition of eating lupine, water-cress, *mulūkhiyya* and fish without scales and the killing of all dogs except hounds.[2] In a country where grain was in short supply and where bread was the basic diet, it was certainly absurd to use the grain for making beer which only the rich could afford. By the same token it was advisable to use the available land particularly around Cairo to grow grain rather than vines. Lupine is until this day an appetiser associated with drink in Egypt. Every Egyptian and every visitor to Egypt knows how popular *mulūkhiyya* is in the country: at one point the Egyptian Cultural Office in Washington D.C. turned its garden into a field for it. It is a mucilaginous vegetable, *Corchorus olitorius*, with the common name Jew's Mallow, and is essentially a weed. In the country it grows everywhere, but near the cities, because of the demand for it, it is cultivated like any other vegetable. Water-cress is almost in the same category as *mulūkhiyya*, and Ḥākim's reason for prohibiting the eating of both was the conservation of land for more essential foods. As for the fish without scales, the reference must have been to the barbel, the only kind of this species which is abundant in every

[1] *Ibid.*, pp. 188–91; 'Idhārī, vol. I, pp. 257–8; Maqrīzī, *Khiṭaṭ*, vol. II, p. 286.

[2] Anṭākī, p. 188; Maqrīzī, *Khiṭaṭ*, vol. II, pp. 286, 287 288, 342.

stretch of water in the country. It is a mud-fish which burrows into the mud and survives on the sediments at the bottom. Therefore it actually performs the environmental function of clearing up the waterways. This service is still recognized in Egypt in the fact that there is a self-imposed prohibition against fishing it out of the wells of water-wheels which are impossible to dredge. Ḥākim extended this prohibition to all canals to protect this useful species and allow it to do what the people did not do. It is interesting to know that this fish is known today as *qarmūṭ*, a clear reference to the Qarāmiṭa As masters of the art of propaganda, the Fāṭimids introduced this association to make this fish unpopular, and the term stuck in much the same way as the name 'Umar – the Devil incarnate from the Fāṭimid point of view – is still used as a term of abuse, particularly in the old parts of Cairo. The killing of all dogs, with the exception of hounds, is not as abhorrent as it may seem. In the first place there are millions of stray dogs in Egypt and many of them are infected with rabies. In the second place, stray or not, these animals are just as starved as the rest of the human population. They are not given tinned dog food and there are no scraps to be had; they eat bread. In the time of Ḥākim the dog situation must have been worse than it is now, and bread was scarce. There could not have been many hounds in Egypt at the time for there has never been much to hunt. However these hounds were spared for the meagre amount of game they might have helped to run down. Another measure Ḥākim introduced was to prohibit bakers from using their feet in kneading the dough, and this proves his sanity beyond any doubt.[1] He was not a genius but he certainly was doing his best in a difficult situation.

Turning to the political arena Ḥākim took a number of steps that were designed to curtail the influence of the Melkite Church in his domains. He confiscated the properties of his Melkite mother and in the process annulled many of the religious endowments of the Church.[2] A year later in 1010/400, he arranged for the assassination of his uncle Arsenius, the Melkite Patriarch of Alexandria.[3] Almost at the same time he ordered the destruction of the church of the Holy Sepulchre in Jerusalem where his other uncle Orestes had been the Melkite Patriarch a few years earlier. It will be remembered that it was this uncle who had arranged for the treaty with Byzantium. Of course the Byzantines were disturbed by this needless act of destruction and the more so because it amounted to a declaration

[1] Maqrīzī, *Khiṭaṭ*, vol. II, p. 341.
[2] Anṭākī, pp. 195, 196, 197.
[3] *Ibid.*, p. 197.

that their treaty with the Fāṭimids was at an end and was not going to be renegotiated. None of these moves was meant to eradicate the Melkite Church, their purpose was to appeal to the Coptic majority in Egypt and rally its support. These Copts were the peasantry of the country whose enthusiasm was a decisive factor in fighting the agricultural decline.[1] It was also for this purpose that certain taxes were abolished, although the frequency of Ḥākim's orders for the abolition and re-imposition of these taxes was rather a result of the economic malaise. We do not know exactly what these taxes were, but we know that land-tax was not involved in these orders. Yet, the fact remains that some of the Christians were satisfied with the abolition of some of the taxes.[2]

It was almost inevitable that Ḥākim's turn against the Melkites should adversely affect Fāṭimid trade with the Byzantines. However, the first reaction came from the Arabs of the Ṭayy in Palestine. They mounted a considerable revolt and in 1012/403 brought an obscure 'Alawid, who was ruling Makka, and proclaimed him their *Amīr al-Mu'minīn*.[3] Although this attempt came to nothing the Fāṭimids lost control of most of Palestine, and were only able to hold on to part of the Syrian coast. In 1015/406 Basil II severed all commercial relations with the Fāṭimids and confined all trading to Aleppo which was under Byzantine domination.[4] This marked the beginning of the decline of Fāṭimid trade with Europe and Africa. The Zīrids in Tunisia who controlled practically all the Mediterranean African coast were in a better position to trade with the Italian city states. Furthermore they succeeded in attracting all the African trade to their territories, and maintained good relations with the *sūdān*. It was as an advertisement of their commercial success that the Zīrids sent Ḥākim in 1014/405 a present of sables, of all things.[5]

Ḥākim's preoccupation with his Christian subjects did not preclude his concern for the Muslims. Although the latter were in the minority they provided the power base of the regime. Realizing that the Ismā'īlīs were themselves a minority among the rest of the Muslims, and trying to increase the popularity of his regime, he started in 1008/399 a new policy of toleration towards non-Ismā'īlīs by relaxing some of the restriction on certain ritual practices.[6] This deviation from strict Ismā'īlism angered the Old Guard of the move-

[1] *Ibid.*, p. 193.
[2] *Ibid.*, pp. 205–6.
[3] Athīr, vol. IX, p. 86; Maqrīzī, *Khiṭaṭ*, vol. I, pp. 185, 211.
[4] Anṭākī, p. 214.
[5] 'Idhārī, vol. I, pp. 260–1.
[6] Maqrīzī, *Khiṭaṭ*, vol. II, pp. 340, 343.

ment almost to the point of open revolt. Undaunted, Ḥākim persevered with his policy and, to intimidate the opposition, he went to the extent of executing, in 1011/401, two of the most illustrious leaders of the time – the son of general Jawhar and the son of the founding theoretician Qāḍī Nu'mān who had both inherited their fathers' positions.[1] In 1012/403 Ḥākim made a most astounding declaration, which was in effect a repudiation of the primary axiom of Ismā'īlism. Henceforth, he wanted to be considered only as the *Amīr al-Mu'minīn* and no more, i.e. he ceased to be the *Imām*. To emphasize his new position he declared that he should be addressed only by this title in the simplest possible form, and that none of his subjects should consider himself as '*abd*, slave of the ruler.[2] In the following year he departed further from Ismā'īlī dogma which strictly stipulated primogeniture, by appointing a cousin as his heir apparent.[3] These radical shifts confused some of the Ismā'īlīs to the extent that some believed that Ḥākim had transcended the human confine and had become the incarnation of the Divinity. Out of this confusion rose the movement, in 1017/408, of the Druze who still exist in various parts of Syria. However, the Fāṭimid establishment was further upset when Ḥākim abolished the twice-weekly lesson and collection.[4] Accordingly he was assassinated, almost certainly with the connivance of his sister, in 1021/411.

At this point there was a return to orthodox Ismā'īlism, yet the role of the *Imām* became less prominent, especially as many of the later Fāṭimid rulers came to power as children. Ḥākim was succeeded by his son Ẓāhir who was sixteen years old. For the first five years of his reign his aunt was the effective ruler and after her death he continued to rule on the same lines until he died in 1036/427. He in turn was succeeded by his seven year old son Mustanṣir 1036–94/427–87. The affairs of state were run by a succession of *wāsiṭas* whose main efforts were to try to maintain the *status quo*. But this was an impossible task. The annals of this period are simply repeated accounts of continuous chaos in Syria, endless fighting between the various groups within the Fāṭimid army, and constant deterioration in the economic conditions of Egypt. Although a new treaty was concluded with the Byzantines in 1038/429 and renewed in 1048/439, it had no effect either on the stability of Syria or as a stimulant to Fāṭimid trade.[5] The agricultural output declined so rapidly that in

[1] *Ibid.*, p. 15.
[2] *Ibid.*, pp. 285, 288.
[3] *Ibid.*, pp. 288, 289.
[4] *Idem*, vol. I, p. 391.
[5] Athīr, vol. IX, pp. 326, 380.

1054/446 the food crisis forced the Fāṭimids to beg the Byzantines for grain.[1] This "Greatest Crisis" continued unabated until 1074/466, when the Fāṭimids had no option but to allow a military take-over to save themselves and the country from total disintegration.[2] Ironically it was an Armenian mercenary, who happened to have been in control of Acre during the prevailing anarchy in Syria, whom the Fāṭimids invited to perform this rescue operation.

It was under these circumstances that the so-called "high water mark of Fāṭimid expansion came in the years 1057–9/448–51, when a Turkish general in 'Irāq called Arslān al-Basāsīrī went over to the Fāṭimid side and proclaimed the Fāṭimid Caliph first in Mawṣil and then, for a year, in Baghdād itself. Despite the efforts of the Chief Missionary, however, the Fāṭimid government was unable to provide effective support, and the strongly Sunnī Saljūqs drove al-Basāsīrī out of Baghdād."[3] The general in question had been a member of those crumbling Būyid forces who had fled in all directions when the Saljūqs had first entered Baghdād in 1055/448. Taking advantage of a temporary absence of the Saljūq forces from the city he entered it with no more than 400 bedraggled followers.[4] As soon as the Saljūqs returned in 1060/451, he fled for his life but was ignominiously captured and executed. If that was the "high water mark of Fāṭimid expansion" one wonders what would be considered the low water mark. The fact of the matter is that the high water mark of the Fāṭimids, as well as that of the Būyids, had long since passed, and Basāsīrī had had no choice of side open to him. The 'Abbāsids had no power, the Būyids had disappeared and the Fāṭimids were in total decline. After 1055/448 there was only one side, the Saljūqs.

[1] Maqrīzī, *Khiṭaṭ*, vol. I, p. 335.
[2] *Ibid.*, p. 337.
[3] Lewis, *Interpretation*, p. 292.
[4] Athīr, vol. IX, p. 441.

WORKS CITED

SOURCES

ibn al-Abbār, *I'tāb al-Kuttāb*, ed. S. al-Ashtar, Damascus, 1961.

'Arīb b. Sa'd, *Ṣilat Tārīkh al-Ṭabarī*, ed. M. J. de Goeje, Leiden, 1897.

ibn A'tham al-Kūfī, *Kitāb al-Futūḥ*, Istanbul manuscript, Library Ahmet III, no. 2956.

ibn al-Athīr, 'Izz al-Dīn, *al Kāmil fī al-Tārīkh*, ed. C. J. Tornberg, Leiden, 1866–71.

al-Azdī, Yazīd b. Muḥammad, *Tārīkh al-Mawṣil*, ed. 'A. Ḥabība, Cairo, 1967.

al-Bakrī, Abū 'Ubayd, *al-Mughrib . . .*, ed. De Slane, Paris, 1911.

al-Balādhurī, Aḥmad b. Yaḥyā, *Futūḥ al-Buldān*, ed. M. J. de Goeje, Leiden, 1866.

ibn al-Baṭrīq, Sa'īd, *Naẓm al-Jawāhir*, ed. L. Cheikho, Paris, 1909.

ibn Faḍlān, *Risāla*, ed. S. Dahhān, Damascus, 1959.

al-Hamdānī, Muḥammad b. 'Abdilmalik, *Takmilat Tārīkh al-Ṭabarī*, ed. A. Y. Kan'ān, Beirut, 1961.

Ḥamdullah Mustawfī, *Nuzhat al-Qulūb*, ed. G. le Strange, London, 1915.

ibn Ḥanbal, *Musnad*, ed. al-Sā'ātī, Cairo, A.H. 1357.

ibn Ḥawqal, *Ṣūrat al-Arḍ*, ed. J. H. Kramers, Leiden, 1938–9.

ibn Ḥazm, 'Alī b. Muḥammad, *Jamharat Ansāb al-'Arab*, ed. A. Hārūn, Cairo, 1962.

ibn 'Idhārī, Aḥmad b. Muḥammad, *al-Bayān al-Mughrib*, ed. G. S. Colin and E. Lévi-Provençal, Leiden, 1948–51.

al-Iṣfahānī, Abū al-Faraj, *Maqātil al-Ṭālibiyyīn*, ed. S. S. Ṣaqr, Cairo, 1949.

al-Iṣṭakhrī, Abū Isḥāq Ibrāhīm, *Kitāb al-Masālik wa al-Mamālik*, ed. M. J. de Goeje, Leiden, 1870.

al-Jahshiyārī, Muḥammad b. 'Abdūs, *Kitāb al-Wuzarā'*, ed. M. al-Saqqā et al., Cairo, 1938.

ibn Khaldūn, 'Abdulraḥmān, *al-Muqaddima*, Beirut, 1961.

ibn Khallikān, *Wafayāt al-A'yān*, ed. Iḥsān 'Abbās, Beirut, 1972.

ibn Khurdādhbeh, *Kitāb al-Masālik wa al-Mamālik*, ed. M. J. de Goeje, Leiden, 1889.

al-Kindī, Muḥammad b. Yūsuf, *Kitāb al-Wulāt*, ed. R. Guest, Gibb Memorial Series, vol. XIX, London, 1912.

al-Maghribī, 'Alī, b. Mūsā, *Kitāb al-Jughrāfiyā*, ed. Ismā'īl al-'Arabī, Beirut, 1970.
ibn Manẓūr, *Lisān al-'Arab*, Bulaq, 1891.
al-Maqdisī, Shams al-Dīn, *Aḥsan al-Taqāsīm* . . ., ed. M. J. de Goeje, Leiden, 1877.
Maqrīzī, Aḥmad b. 'Alī, *al-Khiṭaṭ*, Cairo, A.H. 1249.
Itti'āẓ al-Ḥunafā', vol. I, ed. J. Shayyāl, Cairo, 1948; vol. II, ed. M. Ḥilmī Aḥmad, Cairo, 1971.
al-Nuqūd al-Islāmiyya, ed. M. S. A. Baḥr al-Ulūm, Najaf, 1967.
al-Marvazī, Ṭāhir, *On China, The Turks and India*, Arabic text, ed. V. Minorsky, London, 1942.
al-Mas'ūdī, 'Alī b. al-Ḥusayn, *al-Tanbīh wa al-Ishrāf*, ed. M. J. de Goeje, Leiden, 1893.
Murūj al-Dhahab, ed. C. Barbier de Meynard and P. de Courteille, Paris, 1861–77.
al-Māwardī, *al-Aḥkām al-Sulṭāniyya*, ed. R. Enger, Bonn, 1853.
Miskawayh, Aḥmad b. Muḥammad, *Tajārib al-Umam*, ed. H. F. Amedroz, Oxford, 1920–1.
Nāṣir-i-Khusraw, *Safar-Nāme*, ed. C. Schéfer, Paris, 1881.
ibn al-Qalānisī, *Dhayl Tārīkh Dimashq*, ed. H. F. Amedroz, London, 1908.
Qudāma b. Ja'far, *Kitāb al-Kharāj*, part seven, published as part of A. Ben Shemesh, *Taxation in Islam*, vol. II, Leiden, 1965.
al-Qummī, Ash'arī, *Kitāb al-Maqālāt wa al-Firaq*, ed. M. J. Mashkūr, Teheran, 1963.
Rasā'il al Bulaghā', ed. M. Kurd 'Alī, Cairo, 1946.
ibn Rusteh, *al-A'lāq al-Nafīsa*, ed. M. J. de Goeje, London, 1892.
al-Ṣābī, Hilāl, *Kitāb al-Wuzarā'*, ed. H. F. Amedroz, Leiden, 1904.
Rusūm Dār al-Khilāfa, ed. Mikhā'īl 'Awād, Baghdād, 1964.
Tārīkh, part 8, ed. H. F. Amedroz, and published as vol. IV in *Dhayl Tajārib al-Umam*, Cairo, 1916.
al-Ṣābī, Thābit, *Tārīkh Akhbār al-Qarāmiṭa*, ed. Z. Bakkār, Damascus, 1970.
ibn Sallām, Abū 'Ubayd al-Qāsim, *Kitāb al-Amwāl*, ed. M. H. al-Fiqī, Cairo, A.H. 1353.
al-Sam'ānī, 'Abdulkarīm, *al-Ansāb*, ed. D. S. Margoliouth, Leiden, 1912.
al-Shabankārī, *Majma' al-Ansāb Fī al-Tawārīkh*, Istanbul manuscript, Yeni Cami, 909.
abū Shujā', *Dhayl* . . ., ed. H. F. Amedroz, Cairo, 1916.
al-Ṣūlī, Abū Bakr, *Akhbār al-Rāḍī* . . ., ed. J. H. Dunne, London, 1953

al-Ṭabarī, Muḥammad b. Jarīr, *Tārīkh al-Rusul wa al-Mulūk*, ed. M. J. de Goeje et al., Leiden, 1879–1901.
ibn Taghrībardī, *al-Nujūm al-Zāhira*, Cairo, 1963–72.
Ṭayfūr, Aḥmad b. Abī Ṭāhir, *Kitāb Baghdād*, ed. H. Keller, Leipzig, 1908.
al-'Utbī, *al-Tārīkh al-Yamīnī*, Cairo, A.H. 1286.
Yaḥyā b. Ādam, *Kitāb al-Kharāj*, ed. A. M. Shākir, Cairo, A.H. 1347.
al-Ya'qūbī, Aḥmad b. Abī Yaq'ub, *Tārīkh*, Beirut, 1970.
Kitāb al-Buldān, ed. M. J. de Goeje, Leiden, 1892.
Yāqūt, Shihāb al-Dīn, *Mu'jam al-Buldān*, Beirut, 1957.
abū Yūsuf, Ya'qūb, *Kitāb al-Kharāj*, Cairo, A.H. 1302.

BOOKS AND ARTICLES

Ayyūb, M. S., *Jirma*, Tripoli, 1969.
Barthold, W., *Turkestān Down to the Mongol Invasion*, London, 1928.
Bosworth, C. E., *Sīstān Under the Arabs*, Rome, 1968.
The Ghaznavids, Edinburgh, 1963.
Cahen, Cl., "L'évolution de l'*iqṭā'* du IXe au XIIIe siècle. Contribution à une histoire comparée des sociétés médiévales", *Annales: Économie, sociétés, civilisations*, VIII (1953).
"The Turkish Invasion: the Selchūkids", *A History of the Crusades*, ed. K. M. Setton, London, 1958.
de Goeje, M. J., *Mémoire sur les Carmathes du Bahrain et les Fatimides*, Leiden, 1886.
Lambton, A. K. S., *Landlord and Peasant in Persia*, Oxford, 1953.
"Reflections on the IQṬĀ'" in George Maqdisi, ed., *Arabic and Islamic Studies in Honor of Hamilton A.* R. *Gibb*, Leiden, 1965.
Lane, E. W., *An Arabic–English Lexicon*, reprinted, Beirut, 1968.
Lewis, Bernard, *The Origins of Ismā'īlism*, Cambridge, 1940.
"The Fāṭimids and the Route to India", *Revue de la Faculté de Sciences Economiques de l'Université d'Istanbul*, 11 année, no. 1–4, Istanbul, 1953.
"An Interpretation of Fāṭimid History", *Colloque International sur l'Histoire du Caire 27 Mars–5 Avril 1969*, Cairo, n.d.
Nazim, M., "The Pand-Nameh of Subüktigin", *Journal of the Royal Asiatic Society*, London, 1933.
Nöldeke, Th., *Sketches from Eastern History*, tr. by J. S. Black, Edinburgh, 1892.
Rekaya, M., "Mise au point sur Théophobe et l'alliance de Babek avec Théophile", *Byzantion*, t. XLIV, Bruxelles, 1974.

Shaban, M. A., *The 'Abbāsid Revolution*, Cambridge, 1970.
Islamic History A.D. 600–750 (A.H. 132), A New Interpretation, Cambridge, 1971.
Sourdel, D., *Le Vizirat Abbaside*, Damas, 1959–60.
Yule, Colonel Henry, *The Book of Ser Marco Polo, The Venetian*, London, 1875.

INDEX